Data Management Strategy at Microsoft

Best practices from a tech giant's decade-long data transformation journey

Aleksejs Plotnikovs

Data Management Strategy at Microsoft

Associate Group Product Manager: Niranjan Naikwadi

Associate Publishing Product Manager: Sanjana Gupta

Book Project Manager: Hemangi Lotlikar

Senior Editor: Tiksha Lad

Technical Editor: Kavyashree K S

Copy Editor: Safis Editing

Proofreader: Tiksha Lad

Indexer: Tejal Daruwale Soni

Production Designer: Shankar Kalbhor

Senior DevRel Marketing Coordinator: Vinishka Kalra

First published: June 2024

Production reference: 1110624

Published by Packt Publishing Ltd.

Grosvenor House

11 St Paul's Square

Birmingham

B3 1RB, UK.

ISBN 978-1-83546-918-7

www.packtpub.com

To my beloved son, Sasha, and my wife, Tatiana, for inspiring me to write my first book, and for the amazing support and care they provided while writing it, fueling it with fun, laughter, and success, and surrounding me with love.

– Aleksejs Plotnikovs

Contributors

About the author

Aleksejs Plotnikovs has been leading global data delivery at Microsoft for more than 15 years, navigating from the early stages of the establishment of data management practices up to the modern data platform strategy. He led diverse data office teams and helped to build market-leading products fueled by data and AI capabilities, emphasizing data value and data monetization, while always emphasizing the enormous potential of data to address emerging business opportunities. A passionate data professional and an active ambassador of data culture, he actively contributes to the broader data community by coaching, consulting, running data master classes, and inspiring fellow professionals on LinkedIn.

I want to sincerely thank all our team members who have been close to me and supported me on this book-writing journey! Special and massive thanks to Karthik Ravindran for his exceptional contribution and leadership, and to Wilhelm Klepsch, Chang Wee Loh, Antonina Steshenko, and Justin Tomboulian who tremendously helped with initial content, critical reviews, and motivation!

About the reviewer

Chang Wee Loh's career in IT spans 27 years across IBM, SAP, and Microsoft, where he has worked on various aspects of data as a discipline, from analysis and services to governance. He is based in Singapore.

Table of Contents

Preface   xiii

Part 1: Thinking Local, Acting Global

1

Where's My Data and Who's in Charge?   3

The journey begins   4   Summary and key takeaways   12
Forging collaboration   5   Takeaway 1 – becoming the change agent   12
                                                 Takeaway 2 – discovering the killer feature   13
Unveiling the ownership   6   Takeaway 3 – building the power of a virtual
The birth of MAL   8   team   13
Development overview of MAL   10

2

We Make Data Business Ready   15

The power of one sentence   15   Summary and key takeaways   31
Locally inspired, globally connected   19   Takeaway #1 – crafting an inspiring motto
Introducing a global request-tracking tool   21   for transformation   31
Moving ahead   24   Takeaway #2 – scaling from local to global
                                                 with trust   31
The rise of Data Management   Takeaway #3 – the formula for a centralized
Organization   25   data team   32
My personal story – Data Management
Organization announcement   29

3

Thousands to One – from Locally Siloed to Globally Centralized Processes 33

The opening story   34
Five inventory perspectives   35
One-stop shop   37
Aligning with role experiences   37
Corporate applications and tools   38
Shadow IT   39
Background work   40
The next steps   40

Consolidation paths   41
Getting started – streamlining from over
1,000 data services to 72   41
The first path – data enhancement through
applications   42
The second path – no-code solutions   44

The third path – data platform solutions   45
The fourth path – handling exceptions   47

Enabling globally but with
a local twist   48
Technology – the cornerstone of global data
management   49
Processes – the core of data management   50
People – the pillars of success   51

Summary and key takeaways   52
Takeaway 1 – approaching the inventory from
five diverse perspectives   52
Takeaway 2 – paths to consolidate effectively   52
Takeaway 3 – people, processes, and
technology   53

4

"Reactive! Proactive? Predictive" 55

Addressing urgency   56
Let's get proactive   60
Path to predictive data management   66
Summary and key takeaways   71
Takeaway #1 – addressing urgency and data
demand, with quick and impactful actions, to
win the time for the next steps   71

Takeaway #2 – add proactive capabilities,
converging from an initial and reactive
approach to a solid set of data services   72
Takeaway #3 – path to predictive data
maintenance – as your maturity grows, you
will be ready to tap into the next
evolutionary step   72

Part 2: Build Insights to Global Capabilities

5

Mastering Your Data Domains and Business Ownership   75

The path toward domain thinking	75
Defining data and business domains	77
Ownership – business teams versus the data team	83
The shift-left principle	85
Summary and key takeaways	**88**

Takeaway #1 – integration of data and business domains	88
Takeaway #2 – empowering business ownership with data	89
Takeaway #3 – evolving operational principles with shift left	89

6

Navigating the Strategic Data Dilemma   91

Setting up a global outsourced data operation	**92**
Attempt #2	92
Count to three	94
Where to start?	94
Taking the driver's seat	95
Our wins – embracing outsourcing as a key enabler	**97**
Building trust and partnership	98
Educational foundations	98
Documentation and pilot projects – essential tools	98
Fostering quality, upskilling, and collaboration	99
Choosing your approach	100
Contracts and KPIs – the triple-A approach	100
Navigating challenges and pitfalls	100
Evolution of outsourcing and insourcing	**101**
Outsourcing data engineering and beyond	103

Embracing outsourced education and data literacy	103
Data science – a selective outsourcing strategy	103
Outsourcing innovation and incubations	104
Achieving maximum performance – nearshore versus offshore	104
Insourcing – a strategic counterbalance	104
Shadowing and knowledge transition	104
Talent management	105
The integral roles of data engineering, data science, and data analytics – life learnings	**105**
Our real-life learnings	106
Summary and key takeaways	**108**
Takeaway #1 – a dynamic and collaborative journey	108
Takeaway #2 – a balanced ecosystem of outsourcing and insourcing	109
Takeaway #3 – a fair approach to technology and business	109

7

Unique Data IP Is Your Magic   111

Defining data IP   112
Documentation   115
Outsourcing   116
Community   116
Technology   117
Processes   118
People   118

Evolving, scaling, modernizing, and governing your data IP   119
Embracing interactive and in-depth feedback   119
Comprehensive tracking and celebration of each step forward   120
Fostering community participation   120

Seeking external inspiration   121
Creating a team that loves to learn and share   121

Protecting and navigating when managing change   122
Federate and share knowledge   122
Rely on the steady parts   122
Show how data helps the business   123

Summary and key takeaways   123
Takeaway #1 – define your IP, with six dimensions in mind   123
Takeaway #2 – evolve, modernize, and govern   124
Takeaway #3 – protect your company   124

8

The Pareto Principle in Action   125

Solid at the core, flexible at the edge   125
Data management is a team sport with a focus on people   127
The discipline of change management is key for landing the value of data   128
Any and all feedback is a learning opportunity   128
Listening to your partners and customers is critical to drive incremental value   129
DQ by design, must be implemented to instantly align with strategic and connected data work at the enterprise   129
Prioritize the demand and run an agile service portfolio   130
Get solid at the core first, before becoming flexible at the edge   130
What to avoid – personal experience   131

Addressing top enterprise data issues   133

Case study – the creation of the Unified Support service   136
The first idea   137
Unexpected turn   140
And off we go   141
We did it – what did we learn?   144

Summary and key takeaways   148
Takeaway #1 – using the Pareto principle as your compass   148
Takeaway #2 – practical application of the Pareto principle   149
Takeaway #3 – case study – building a multi-billion-dollar business   149

Part 3: Intelligent Future

9

Data Mastering and MDM   153

Setting the stage	154	Dos and don'ts	167
The legacy of Microsoft Organizations	154	Summary and key takeaways	169
		Takeaway #1 – start small, with high relevance	169
The rise and fall of Microsoft Individuals and Organizations	156	Takeaway #2 – business stakeholders are part of the solution	169
Hello Mr. Jarvis	158	Takeaway #3 – be a Chief Orchestration Officer	169
A meme? No, a MOM (aka Microsoft Org Master)!	163		

10

Data Mesh and Data Governance   171

Taking a look at a typical enterprise—"Data Mess"	172	Summary and key takeaways	187
From "Data Mess" to Data Mesh – how?	174	Takeaway #1 – digital transformation is the ultimate driver of change	187
Data Governance = Data Excellence	180	Takeaway #2 – Data Excellence that everybody loves	187
Where is our data? Again…	185	Takeaway #3 – if you don't have Data Governance, these three Fs will help	188

11

Data Assets or Data Products?   189

The challenge we face today with data	189	Summary and key takeaways	203
		Takeaway #1 – need for a modern data estate	203
The magnificent shine of data products	192	Takeaway #2 – several sources of inspiration for data products	203
Raw data deserves appreciation too	199	Takeaway #3 – the naked truth of data assets	204

12

Data Value, Literacy, and Culture   205

Introduction to three pivotal disciplines	**205**
Data Economics	206
Data Literacy	206
Data Culture	206
Unveiling the true worth of enterprise data	**206**
Data Literacy has no end state	**210**

Data culture for everyone	**215**
Summary and key takeaways	**219**
Takeaway #1 – data value is coming out of the shadows	220
Takeaway #2 – embark on the data literacy journey	220
Takeaway #3 – data culture is what we need	220

13

Getting Ready for GenAI   223

From pre-AI times to today's aspirations	**223**
The strategic role of data in AI	**226**
AI for Data	**229**
AI governance and ethics	230
AI-powered data governance – revolutionizing data management	231
AI over Data	**234**
Custom LLMs and orchestrators – the future of AI	234

Small versus large models	235
Custom and private models versus public LLMs	235
The role of RAG and orchestrators in AI	235
Human-reinforced input for AI success	236
Summary and key takeaways	**239**
Takeaway #1 – AI governance and AI ethics	240
Takeaway #2 – AI for Data	240
Takeaway 3 – AI over Data	240

Index   241

Other Books You May Enjoy   248

Preface

Microsoft pioneered data innovation and investments into the state of data ahead of many in the industry, leading to a distinctive and noteworthy advancement in data maturity. The book comprehensively explores every crucial facet of this journey and emphasizes that the wellspring of data-driven innovation is most often found with the data's business owners—the individuals who depend on data daily for their operational needs. Empowering these professionals with clean, easily discoverable, and business-ready data marks a significant breakthrough in how data is perceived and utilized throughout an enterprise.

This book unveils the comprehensive journey of successful end-to-end data enablement—beyond mere technology, it encompasses change management, alignment with business needs, enhancing data value, and fostering a data-driven culture. The book guides you along the path of maturity and offers insights into where to channel efforts most effectively. It also establishes a connection with your organization's own data enablement narrative. While many believe they face unique challenges, the reality is that data challenges tend to be strikingly similar across businesses. This enables the direct application of existing best practices. Such insights prove invaluable for business and data leaders, aiding them in advocating for essential data investments and competitive data and AI strategies.

This book adopts a storytelling approach to ensure a seamless reading journey, with essential insights summarized at the close of each chapter.

Moreover, the book is written by a data leader and practitioner with over 15 years of data experience at Microsoft, who has seen the company through numerous transformations and the reinvention of business and data processes to support ever-evolving organizational needs. This book covers how to foster the team spirit and *one company* approach that's needed to drive data and business outcomes, emphasizing the power of having a data-driven culture.

Who this book is for

This book is aimed at all data leaders, data practitioners, data engineers, data scientists, and data enthusiasts, along with modern business leaders who are interested in the power of data. From data stewards and data management experts to data governance professionals, it will be equally relevant to top leaders looking to capitalize on the rise of data and AI and enable digital transformation. This book reflects Microsoft's journey in transitioning into a data-driven enterprise and ultimately becoming a leader in the data and AI space. Unveiling an untold real-life, decade-long journey, this book takes a storytelling approach for a seamless reading experience and, unlike other tech-heavy books, is equally positioned for both experienced and inexperienced readers.

What this book covers

Chapter 1, Where's My Data and Who's in Charge?, addresses a common challenge for any enterprise: gaining clarity about its own data, how it is managed and stored, who is responsible for it, and how to make data discoverable.

Chapter 2, We Make Data Business Ready, is where we look at creating a data office, which involves appointing a dedicated data team to take care of enterprise data, make it highly qualitative and business-ready, and enable the core functions of data management.

Chapter 3, Thousands to One – From Locally Siloed to Globally Centralized, looks at how to simplify and streamline data usage and discoverability across an enterprise by executing an end-to-end inventory of data domains and connecting previously disparate data with respective business processes.

Chapter 4, Reactive! Proactive? Predictive, explores the maturity curve for various data services and data management operations – from the reactive and immediate approach for business issues to having a proactive catalog of services and predictive in-flight data corrections.

Chapter 5, Mastering Your Data Domains and Business Ownership, helps you to understand the various data domains across an enterprise and how they could be effectively combined and interrelated, as well as properly owned and responsibly consumed by both data and business teams.

Chapter 6, Navigating the Strategic Data Dilemma, navigates the golden balance between the scalability and cost efficiency of outsourcing work with the natural flexibility of working with in-house data teams, covering the various pitfalls and benefits.

Chapter 7, Unique Data IP Is Your Magic, explores how to develop and advance your company's data know-how and how data supports the business processes, which is often referred to as the data's **Intellectual Potential (IP)**. We look at effective ways to protect your data IP and use it for continuous business success.

Chapter 8, The Pareto Principle in Action, covers the famous 80/20 principle, also known as the Pareto principle. It can inspire highly effective frameworks and methodologies and was used to advance the state of data at Microsoft, helping to build innovative, multi-billion-dollar-revenue data products.

Chapter 9, Data Mastering and MDM, covers **Master Data Management (MDM)**. MDM is undoubtedly the cornerstone of modern data management and data governance, but ultimate success with it depends on the underlying business cases and implementation strategy. We will learn about this in this chapter.

Chapter 10, Data Mesh and Data Governance, looks at the Data Mesh approach, which was a much-needed innovation in the recent data architecture space, enabling a federated, de-centralized approach to data governance, ownership, and management. A significant part of this impressive win is attributed to business enablement through change management.

Chapter 11, Data Assets or Data Products?, looks at having a data-product-focused strategy, which is another great example of non-stop innovation with data. To truly unleash the power of product thinking, the relationship between raw data assets and data products must be understood. This chapter helps with that.

Chapter 12, Data Value, Literacy, and Culture, answers questions such as, *What makes data distinctively valuable? How can we monetize data and drive immense revenue increases and business growth using existing data?* These questions are tackled through the lens of data literacy and data-driven culture.

Chapter 13, Getting Ready for GenAI, talks about how data is everything in AI, as it plays a critical strategic role in any successful AI deployment. Unpacking this notion leads us to identify specific prerequisites for succeeding in a business transformation with data and AI.

Download the example code files

A referral link to Github has been included for any updates or erratas in future `https://github.com/PacktPublishing/Data-Management-Strategy-at-Microsoft`. If there's an update to the code, it will be updated in the GitHub repository.

We also have other code bundles from our rich catalog of books and videos available at `https://github.com/PacktPublishing/`. Check them out!

Conventions used

> Tips or important notes
> Appear like this.

Get in touch

Feedback from our readers is always welcome.

General feedback: If you have questions about any aspect of this book, email us at `customercare@packtpub.com` and mention the book title in the subject of your message.

Errata: Although we have taken every care to ensure the accuracy of our content, mistakes do happen. If you have found a mistake in this book, we would be grateful if you would report this to us. Please visit `www.packtpub.com/support/errata` and fill in the form.

Piracy: If you come across any illegal copies of our works in any form on the internet, we would be grateful if you would provide us with the location address or website name. Please contact us at `copyright@packt.com` with a link to the material.

If you are interested in becoming an author: If there is a topic that you have expertise in and you are interested in either writing or contributing to a book, please visit `authors.packtpub.com`.

Share Your Thoughts

Once you've read *Data Management Strategy at Microsoft*, we'd love to hear your thoughts! Scan the QR code below to go straight to the Amazon review page for this book and share your feedback.

https://packt.link/r/1835469183

Your review is important to us and the tech community and will help us make sure we're delivering excellent quality content.

Download a free PDF copy of this book

Thanks for purchasing this book!

Do you like to read on the go but are unable to carry your print books everywhere?

Is your eBook purchase not compatible with the device of your choice?

Don't worry, now with every Packt book you get a DRM-free PDF version of that book at no cost.

Read anywhere, any place, on any device. Search, copy, and paste code from your favorite technical books directly into your application.

The perks don't stop there, you can get exclusive access to discounts, newsletters, and great free content in your inbox daily

Follow these simple steps to get the benefits:

1. Scan the QR code or visit the link below

https://packt.link/free-ebook/9781835469187

2. Submit your proof of purchase
3. That's it! We'll send your free PDF and other benefits to your email directly

Part 1:
Thinking Local,
Acting Global

This part takes us through the foundational aspects of **data delivery** – from setting up a data team and data office to finding an immediate fit for emerging business needs with data while completing a comprehensive inventory of existing business and data processes. A set of highly useful, universal data services available in a well-defined catalog completes the picture of addressing the most urgent demand for data.

This part includes the following chapters:

- *Chapter 1, Where's My Data and Who's in Charge?*
- *Chapter 2, We Make Data Business Ready*
- *Chapter 3, Thousands to One – From Locally Siloed to Globally Centralized*
- *Chapter 4, Reactive! Proactive? Predictive*

1

Where's My Data and Who's in Charge?

This first chapter delves into common business challenges stemming from the necessity of maintaining data quality and effective data management within a company. Often, there is either a complete absence of these practices or, at the very least, a partial implementation. This challenge typically impacts the end users of data the most, including sales, marketing, pre-sales, go-to-market, and finance teams. Meanwhile, the IT team tends to lag behind and might not even fully comprehend the issue until they are confronted with urgent user concerns.

This was notably the case for Microsoft in its early years of data enablement. The IT division had limited exposure to data-related problems as its focus was primarily on engineering and developing long-term solutions within a specific ecosystem. Consequently, there was no single global team responsible for overseeing data, ensuring data quality, and managing data across key Tier 1 **Line of Business (LOB)** applications.

On the flip side, the sales, marketing, and other teams grappling with data quality challenges had to implement rapid fixes and day-to-day strategies to navigate these issues, striving to achieve success in their core responsibilities.

In this chapter, we're going to cover the following main topics, addressing the most popular and simple questions from the users of data. You will learn how to position data challenges alongside easy-to-implement investments that immediately will help to improve the "state of data".

- Where's my data? – a common question from users of any enterprise
- Who's in charge of owning the data and fixing issues?
- How do we fix the data quickly and efficiently?

The journey begins

As I settled into my seat on the plane bound for Prague, Czech Republic, I couldn't contain my excitement. This journey was unlike any other; it was the first time I would meet the individuals who represented the virtual data organization within our company face to face. Previously, our interactions had been limited to countless email exchanges and phone calls.

These individuals came from diverse backgrounds and hailed from various countries in Central and Eastern Europe. We were all part of something in its infancy, something that held the promise of significant transformation. The prospect of meeting them in person and learning from their experiences filled me with a lot of anticipation!

At the same time, I found myself wondering what we could offer them to enhance their daily work and address the unique challenges they faced. Our shared mission was clear: to improve data quality within the company. However, our path to achieving this goal was far from straightforward.

The team members brought with them a wealth of local data practices, each shaped by their specific regions. These practices often stood in contrast to the global standards we aimed to establish. Despite our business systems being classified as Tier 1 applications (the most critical) and operating on a global scale, there was a noticeable disconnect. It became evident that the technical data flow between systems was far from seamless, and the absence of consistent data quality standards posed a significant challenge.

The *lead-to-order* process, which appeared simple on the surface, harbored hidden complexities. There was a lack of clarity about how data flowed through this process, what triggered specific data creation events, and, most importantly, who owned the data. There were hundreds of individual users who relied heavily on this data for their daily tasks, yet they often found themselves asking a seemingly simple but critical question: *"Where's my data?"*

In their minds, an abstract corporate-level service was responsible for ensuring data accuracy and reliability. It was a common misconception that data maintenance was someone else's responsibility. This misalignment of expectations, combined with interruptions in data flow between key systems, led to a steep learning curve for our business partners.

I was determined to address this challenge head-on.

My role as the **Central and Eastern Europe** (CEE) area data lead, which I had assumed in the summer of 2008, was to bridge the gap between the business teams (predominantly in sales and marketing) and help establish a consistent approach to tackling data-related issues. Despite having no direct reports and limited influence over local business leaders in this vast and relatively undeveloped region, I drew on my extensive experience of navigating complex global data challenges at Microsoft.

In this new role, I was known to many of my colleagues, having previously been part of the consultancy team that worked on various data-related work aspects. The most common question I encountered from employees across the company was seemingly straightforward but carried profound implications: *"Where's my data?"*

In reality, we were all in the same boat. Many had not yet grasped the fundamental concept that data was an asset they needed to take ownership of. They believed that an abstract corporate entity would perpetually ensure that data remained up to date and in perfect condition.

As I delved deeper into this challenge, I soon realized that my region faced a more significant hurdle than others. While my peers in Western Europe, the Middle East, and Asia had already developed practices that suited their regions, CEE grappled with the lowest data quality standards and a less structured approach to data management.

Nevertheless, this presented an opportunity.

Starting from the bottom allowed us to develop modern data practices tailored to our unique needs, with each improvement meticulously noted. Although we were the last to embark on this journey, we benefited immensely from established data foundations, the learning curve, and the ability to test and refine our approaches, ultimately achieving comprehensive data management practices relevant to any other part of the company. So, how did we do this, and where to start?

Forging collaboration

In my quest to tackle the data challenges we faced, I initiated a close collaboration with my colleagues in sales and marketing.

Our first step was to understand the exact nature of their challenges and identify potential solutions. We quickly realized that some issues could be addressed with straightforward guidance and better education. By fostering a deeper understanding of the overall data flow and demonstrating how improved data handling could benefit each team, we made significant progress. Here's how we did this:

- One striking example of collaboration was the collaboration between the marketing and sales teams. The marketing team aimed to generate leads quickly from various internal and external sources, with minimal restrictions. They were focused on the quantity of data. On the other hand, the sales team required well-qualified leads, as they relied on accurate segmentation to identify sales potential and create profit opportunities.

  Bridging this gap required more than just a shared business language; it demanded a discussion in the language of data. We used real-world examples of good and bad data and illustrated how improvements in data handling by the marketing team could significantly benefit the sales team. We also made it clear that unqualified, low-quality data only goes to waste in the end, reducing the clarity of sales and marketing activities while it is present in the CRM system. Both teams immediately realized that they were sharing the pain of having bad data and urged for better cross-team collaboration.

  This practice was highly successful, combining elements of change management and stakeholder management. It hinged on the idea that using data as the common language could drive efficient collaboration and emphasize the benefits of getting it right the first time.

- Our second practice involved identifying the most critical business challenge that organizations faced. It didn't take long to pinpoint a recurring issue: managing top customer accounts in a structured and consistent way. These accounts were vital for revenue generation, yet they often had inaccurate revenue figures and faced challenges with segmentation.   The complexity arose when dealing with larger enterprises, which often had multiple branches and distinct company names under a single legal entity. In our case, this challenge, now known as **Master Data Management** (**MDM**), was limited to resolving the flow of revenue generated by these enterprises. It was vital to map this revenue back to existing accounts and maintain consistency to ensure effective forecasting and account management. Our proposed solution was the creation of a **Managed Accounts List** (**MAL**), which aimed to unify account definitions in **Customer Relationship Management** (**CRM**) and revenue collection flows, along with additional details from licensing, billing, and incentive compensation systems. It was a game-changer for us. It not only addressed a significant challenge but also demonstrated the value of data management and global data consolidation. The solution visualized one of the most critical data sets for business usage in one place, seamlessly connected and integrated into operational routines.

Before MAL, similar attempts were made at the country or subsidiary level but lacked a centralized, company-wide data standard. Our approach was to provide a global solution that could be adapted to local rules while offering global capabilities. This new, dedicated data management platform, separate from CRM systems and data warehouses, was operated by a virtual data team (more on this later). While creating the platform's foundation wasn't overly complex, the key takeaway was that when faced with a pressing business problem, we had to take action. The platform was designed to be global and reusable but not overengineered, focusing on delivering critical business capabilities immediately. In today's cloud-native environments, creating such a platform is simple, but back then, it required a bold approach driven by business needs, courage, and a network of data professionals worldwide.

Speaking further of our virtual team, another common question arose after the well-known "*Where is my data?*" – the question of "*Who is in charge of fixing the issues?*"

Unveiling the ownership

The question of who was in charge became increasingly pressing as businesses encountered persistent data quality issues hindering their operations. Business leaders were eager to pinpoint responsibility for particular systems, processes, and data-related problems. Dealing with Tier 1 systems and applications as such posed no challenge; corporate engineering teams owned and managed them, and handled developments, change requests, and fixes. However, when delving into the intricacies of data collection and processing, things got complicated.

One issue was the lack of data education among business units. A disconnect existed between various teams, each focused on its immediate needs. However, data was the common thread that connected them all.

It became evident that educating stakeholders about data issues, their root causes, and potential solutions was crucial. We aimed to instill a sense of data ownership within these business stewards, clarifying what could be fixed and what couldn't. Data examples were used to illustrate desired outcomes and encourage businesses to take greater responsibility for their data assets.

The second challenge was related to the corporate ownership of systems. In large enterprises such as Microsoft, the central IT department typically owned most Tier 1 business applications and their content, including data and business rules. However, in our case, corporate ownership wasn't so effective and well-defined due to the complexity of local rules, diverse languages, and varying data capture practices worldwide. It was unrealistic to expect corporate engineering to address data quality challenges comprehensively because they lacked the necessary context and knowledge of local intricacies and policies.

To bridge this gap, we needed to foster efficient connections between the global and local sides of the organization. Corporate system owners were instrumental in resolving technological and application issues but couldn't address data quality challenges effectively. On the other hand, local data professionals were hired by sales, marketing, and operations teams focused on improving data quality and reporting. However, they often operated in isolation, mirroring the segmented approach of business groups.

This scattered but dedicated community of data professionals presented a unique opportunity. My goal, as the area data lead, was to transform them from individual contributors into a virtual data team. This team wouldn't report to me but would act as a collective entity, sharing knowledge and supporting one another across geographical boundaries while continuing to serve their local business units.

As I contemplated this during my flight to Prague, I realized that I needed to offer something transformative that could unify and energize this diverse group. It had to be more than a technical solution; it needed to inspire and empower them. I envisioned a knowledge-sharing community where everyone could contribute and learn, a space where local practices could evolve into global best practices.

Additionally, I saw the potential for economies of scale. Despite their busy schedules serving local geographies, collectively, we could provide a shared service model. By establishing standardized data management and a common catalog of offerings, we could efficiently deliver data services across the Central and Eastern Europe region. It would be like a **swarm** model, where any member of the virtual team could execute data modifications from anywhere in the area.

Overcoming language barriers and the specificity of local data requests was challenging, but we successfully created a virtual team who were knowledgeable about each area's aspects.

The members of this team could step in for each other, providing efficient and high-quality data services. It was a simple yet effective model, and it outperformed siloed work within specific business domains. Data is a common asset across an enterprise, deserving of professional care and dedication. Having this virtual shared services team, along with tailored data solutions, also addressed the questions of *"Where is my data?"* and *"Who is in charge?"*.

The MAL solution we provided became a one-stop shop for many sales and marketing professionals, simplifying data access and quality monitoring. I encourage you to read the story of MAL ahead and, hopefully, this knowledge will be useful in your business and data environments. That being said, the virtual shared services team effectively became responsible for data management and associated data manipulations and processing.

This marked the beginning of a new era in data management.

The birth of MAL

MAL was a crucial concept within Microsoft's business framework, and was particularly relevant for businesses dealing with many business-to-business customers. It aimed to segment customers, focusing primarily on the most valuable ones.

This list was a hierarchy consisting of parent accounts and child accounts, with each geographical area initially developing its own list to emphasize important local customers. These local lists gradually evolved into a more global approach.

MAL served as a powerful tool for Microsoft's sales and marketing teams. It helped them concentrate their effort on the most valuable accounts and track various activities related to them, including marketing campaigns, sales promotions, and significant deals.

From a data management perspective, a significant challenge was maintaining the connections between branches (child accounts) and well-established top (parent) accounts. Ensuring that child accounts were correctly related to top-tier accounts was essential for accurately assessing the overall revenue generated by these top accounts. This task also involved handling issues such as duplication and dealing with malicious accounts.

However, at that time, there was no dedicated application for MALs. These lists initially existed as offline or semi-online Excel spreadsheets stored in different countries and regions, lacking central management.

Attempting to manage them solely within the CRM system raised usability constraints and other challenges, such as the following:

- Firstly, the CRM system didn't provide a direct connection to the revenue collection system, which was a separate system. This lack of integration made it difficult to consistently link account revenue data and other critical attributes, such as changing company names or addresses. To address this, we had to establish a bridge and maintain continuous links between CRM account definitions and those in the revenue collection system.

- Secondly, maintaining additional attributes specific only to MALs within CRM posed challenges. These attributes, such as assignments between account teams and aspects of parent-child account hierarchy, were essential for MAL but not suitable for CRM. Customizing CRM to accommodate these attributes would have been more complex than managing them within the MAL application.

As a result, we decided to store and manage many of these attributes, especially the account hierarchy, in the dedicated MAL application. This data would be synchronized with the rest of the data eco-flow, essentially making MAL an MDM solution for selected top enterprise accounts. The rest of the accounts remained managed in CRM. We facilitated synchronization between the MAL application, the CRM system, and the revenue collection system, ensuring data quality and maintaining the necessary data governance criteria and standards.

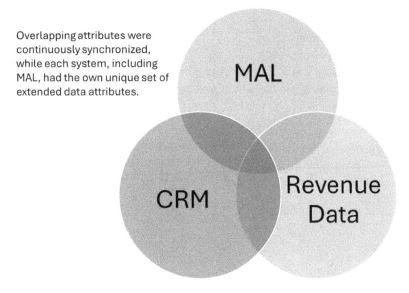

Overlapping attributes were continuously synchronized, while each system, including MAL, had the own unique set of extended data attributes.

Figure 1.1 – Data overlap between key business systems

One significant aspect of this work was managing the hierarchy between top parent accounts and child accounts.

Interestingly, we realized that there would be no single source of truth for this hierarchy. Legal views on how a company is structured and organized often differ from the views necessary for sales processes, especially for multinational corporations with branches worldwide. We needed to respect the sales view of the hierarchy to enable effective sales processes, even if it deviated from the formal legal view. This flexibility and alignment with the needs of sales and marketing were key to MAL's success.

The MAL solution was designed to be immediately relevant and useful to the business, not just accurate from a data perspective. It addressed critical business needs and gained traction quickly, helping drive data quality improvements and corrections. While we made certain trade-offs, such as building a custom application and hierarchy, ensuring the solution met the specific requirements of the business and provided the required flexibility was most important.

Next, let's dive into a few stages of MAL development and what each stage focuses on.

Development overview of MAL

This was an extensive process that unfolded in several key stages:

- **Stage one**: Our initial focus was to consolidate data from various offline sources spanning different regions. Our primary goal was simply to clean this data, preparing it for its initial release on the data platform. Of course, it also made it a very simplistic UI to operate.

- **Stage two**: In this phase, our aim was to centralize data availability on the data platform. We also introduced a more advanced user interface for data manipulation. This allowed users to perform tasks such as editing, adding new records, adjusting hierarchies, using preset basic workflows, and maintaining data accuracy. To safeguard the sensitive data involved, we implemented robust controls and security measures. Access to the data was limited to eligible users (primarily account managers) and specialized experts from teams of business and sales operations.

- **Stage three**: As we progressed, we began contemplating more advanced functionalities. These features were valuable but not immediately essential in the earlier stages. We also sought to integrate the MAL application more seamlessly into the broader Microsoft ecosystem and make it scalable, mature, and designed for many years of usage.

Let's discuss all three stages in the following sections.

Stage one

In stage one, our initial challenge was determining the components that should comprise the MAL. We undertook a comprehensive analysis of existing definitions and all the Excel worksheets across various regions.

Our aim was to distinguish elements with global relevance from those that were highly localized or specific to certain areas. This process helped us identify what would be suitable for global release.

In parallel with examining attributes, we started looking deep into the data itself. We embarked on a journey of deduplication and the establishment of a **single source of truth** at the subsidiary level, progressively globalizing the MAL. However, it's worth noting that not all regions initially embraced the project. Some (such as Japan and the United States) had highly specialized processes related to managed accounts.

We opted to concentrate on creating a product that could be swiftly launched and iterated upon in most regions, deferring more complex work and adoption challenges until subsequent stages.

In terms of data, a substantial portion was extracted directly from the CRM system.

We also integrated data from the revenue collection system and other business applications, including seller's compensation tracking and some licensing data. These efforts culminated in the creation of what we called a **golden record**. These records were clean, free from duplication, and met the criteria for data quality and content. They served as the foundational dataset for the application. When users began accessing the application, they interacted with this consolidated, globalized dataset.

Soon enough, the challenge arose to keep this dataset current and accurate.

Synchronizing updates made within the MAL application with the CRM and revenue collection system became pivotal. To facilitate this bidirectional synchronization, we developed a specialized API. Although this setup required some user education regarding the potential overriding of changes made in CRM or the revenue system during the next MAL data refresh, it enabled us to swiftly address business needs and implement what businesses were primarily looking for.

This marked the culmination of stage one.

> **The bare minimum**
>
> At this point, we had a small but functional data platform, region-specific MALs, certain synchronization mechanisms, and a global deployment strategy. This deployment allowed us to centralize data within a single storage space, accessible through a unified user interface.

Now, let's transition to stage two.

Stage two

This phase centered on elevating the user experience within the application. We introduced automated workflows and dispute resolution processes, encompassing tasks such as managing segmentation and updates to parent-child hierarchies.

We also initiated additional synchronizations with systems that could leverage the master data in the MAL for their specific requirements. Achieving the optimal user experience needed time and effort, given that this was a custom-built application.

At this stage, MAL became a global application used worldwide by the entire sales organization. Although some areas were investing more effort and control than others, overall satisfaction with MAL was already high.

It was a truly game-changing experience for the folks who, just a few months back, were operating on the Excel level! It was certainly a game changer for us as the virtual data team as it formed one of the core monetary investments and work focus areas for us back then.

Stage three

Moving forward to stage three, this phase brought forth substantial enhancements.

One noteworthy development was the introduction of a **Future Year** (**FY**) view. This feature allowed users to maintain the current account structure within the MAL while simultaneously simulating proposed changes for the upcoming financial year. This simulation held immense value for sales leaders, as it enabled them to experiment with the restructuring of account data for future financial targets.

At the finish line of the fiscal year, this FY view would supersede the current year view, effectively implementing the simulated changes. This process entailed intensive synchronization with our CRM and revenue collection system, which posed challenges due to the volume of updates.

> **Building trust**
>
> For our team of data professionals, this approach not only bolstered credibility but also encouraged the annual cleansing of data, ensuring a high-quality view of managed accounts for each fiscal year. It also established a repeatable routine for both data and sales teams, fostering collaboration and adherence to timelines.

In summary, the technical journey of constructing MAL unfolded in multiple stages, encompassing data consolidation, user interface development, and advanced functionalities. It required meticulous synchronization with existing systems and user education to navigate data overrides during updates. This approach not only addressed immediate business needs but also set the stage for enduring data quality and collaboration practices.

From a data perspective, the MAL project taught us the importance of focusing on what data is considered valuable and ensuring that the data perimeter doesn't become a limitation. We introduced recommendations and logic elements to help sales and marketing teams identify data that could be candidates for inclusion in the MAL but hadn't yet made it onto the list. This approach encouraged a broader perspective on data within the company.

Summary and key takeaways

By telling you the story of our initial data journey, I've unfolded three invaluable insights. These insights not only guided our path but transformed the way we perceived data within our organization. Even more importantly, they helped to address immediate issues with the data, win the trust of the business stakeholders, and set the foundation for future growth.

Takeaway 1 – becoming the change agent

Imagine a scenario where business units in your organization feel like islands, disconnected and isolated. This was our reality. My first insight is about becoming a catalyst for change – a change agent who bridges these disconnected units using data as a common language.

You don't need a formal mandate for this; all you need is the determination to influence and advise.

Over time, this influence will earn your trust, making you a trusted advisor. By raising awareness about the importance of data, you will ignite a spark for change. Invest in individuals who exhibit curiosity about understanding data challenges. Educate and guide them in the world of data.

Eventually, these individuals will become your stakeholders and key sponsors, driving the change you envisioned.

Takeaway 2 – discovering the killer feature

Now, picture this: you're on a quest to find the "killer feature" that will kickstart the transformation of your business through data. It might sound straightforward, but it's not. It requires deep empathy and a meticulous exploration of existing data problems. You need a willingness to tackle these issues with unexpected and innovative solutions.

Our story of MAL exemplifies this. We didn't just address our data challenges; we went a step further. We discovered a solution that not only navigated our data hurdles but also illuminated the path for others. It answered the question, *Where is my data?*, and provided the first steps in caring for data quality and fixing the most essential data issues.

Takeaway 3 – building the power of a virtual team

In every organization, there are individuals who deeply care about data, even if their roles don't explicitly involve it.

My third insight revolves around building a virtual team.

When building a dedicated team isn't feasible, assembling a ring of knowledge and data expertise is the next best thing. This team, lacking formal leadership or a hard mandate, becomes an incredible force for change. They unite to tackle real-world problems, much like the challenges we face with managed accounts.

They address the critical question of who is in charge, even if it's not official yet.

> **Transformation starts with you**
>
> In our data journey, these three insights reshaped our approach, transforming isolated business units into a harmonious orchestra, with data as the conductor. We learned that change starts with influence and that the "killer feature" can revolutionize your data landscape, and even a virtual team can be a driving force for change.

These lessons aren't just about data; they're about the power of transformation and the people who drive it.

In the next chapter, we will cover building a central data team and inventing a simple yet powerful marketing motto that made our lives much easier.

We Make Data Business Ready

This chapter is about initiating and building a data team, sometimes called the **Data Office**, as this is a joint venture between data professionals and business stakeholders.

We will be covering about gaining support from key stakeholders and business teams with a successful, unique motto that laid the groundwork for future data management, fostering alignment around a shared and straightforward objective across diverse organizations and departments. After all, who could oppose the necessity for "business-ready data" to achieve success in marketing campaigns, CRM utilization, or revenue recognition? The ability to convey this uncomplicated message and goal marked a transformative moment, uniting like-minded individuals from various sectors, and encouraging them to actively embrace **Data Quality** (**DQ**) thinking.

During this stage, a centralized data team did not yet exist, and the company had not committed to such an investment. Consequently, the concept of a virtual data office emerged, operating under the banner of the **Data Management Organization** (**DMO**).

In this chapter, we will cover the following topics:

- The power of one sentence
- Locally inspired, globally connected
- The rise of data management organization

The power of one sentence

In the preceding chapter, we delved into the early stages of Microsoft's journey toward becoming a data-driven organization. To be candid, those initial steps were far from smooth sailing. We encountered a multitude of challenges, not only in assembling a virtual community of data enthusiasts and partners but also in delivering on our promise to make a tangible impact on the business.

The story of Managed Accounts List stands out as an inspiring and comprehensive narrative. However, its inception was far from straightforward. While I won't delve into all the intricacies and hurdles we faced during its development in this discussion, it's worth noting that the journey from conceptualization to the first **Minimum Viable Product** (**MVP**) was time-consuming. Transforming it further into a pivotal application within the company was an iterative process.

Reflecting on our path and accomplishments as a data organization, one key factor looms large in my mind: the enthusiastic buy-in from stakeholders, particularly those in sales and marketing. Surely, many of them were on the forefront of DQ challenges, seeing and working with low quality data every day. Yet why would they trust us, why would they spend precious time supporting our initiatives? This support was vital for achieving our initial successes. It was a logical starting point since the individuals I interacted with in Prague were, for the most part, local data experts from various countries and subsidiaries. They played a crucial role as go-to data specialists, addressing basic data hygiene, resolving DQ issues, and managing data maintenance and updates. Their knowledge was deeply rooted in the unique challenges of local business operations and data.

However, our community lacked substantial connectivity, especially across geographical boundaries. Bridging this gap was essential, linking data specialists in Western Europe with their counterparts in Central and Eastern Europe, and so on, across the world. We were yearning for the wealth of best practices and diverse approaches that existed globally but were not readily accessible at a regional level.

Breaking down these silos became a priority.

So, beyond bolstering the virtual team of area data specialists and supporting newly established data communities in Central and Eastern Europe, I aimed to foster cross-regional connections. Our goal was to ensure we didn't miss out on valuable best practices or solutions already developed elsewhere that we could swiftly adopt for mutual benefit.

Concurrently, as mentioned earlier, it was crucial to keep our team engaged in continual learning, remaining open-minded and connected to regional and global capabilities. I wanted them to remain highly relevant to the local sales and marketing teams while evolving to meet our evolving business requirements. As our knowledge grew with each passing day, we began contemplating how to deliver greater value to the business.

It was one thing to connect across regions and learn about fantastic practices in various locales, but translating these insights into practical solutions for our business leaders was another challenge altogether. We had to be highly pragmatic and discerning in our approach, extracting what could be adopted while also thinking expansively and proactively.

We aimed to collate diverse practices and start structuring them. This process involved documenting locally proven data practices, data terminologies and dictionaries, business rules, keywords, metadata, FAQs, exceptions, and their resolution procedures. While we weren't certain whether all these practices would fit into our future strategy or merge into cross-regional capabilities, we were committed to capturing current knowledge and preparing for comparison, grouping, optimization, and more defined categorization.

> **Strategic assets**
> All these efforts eventually culminated in becoming the **Intellectual Property** (**IP**) of our DMO, a topic we will delve into more deeply in a dedicated way in *Chapter 7*.

Simultaneously, we realized the need to present our work and its impact more professionally to our stakeholders and business leaders.

We needed a statement that encapsulated our data mission, our ability to enhance the sales and marketing organizations, and our commitment to providing better data. This statement had to be bold and ambitious, resonating deeply with our business peers without being overly complex or theoretical.

It must bridge the gap between business needs and our capabilities. But how?

At this point, there were several teams working on DQ and data management across various geographic areas. However, these teams lacked comprehensive cohesion. In most cases, only the area data leaders were aware of each other's existence.

Here, my unique position came into play. I was the last area data lead to join the company, and I already had extensive connections across various areas due to my prior work in implementing global data cleaning processes. I had interacted with teams in the UK, France, Germany, Western Europe, the Middle East, the US, and more.

I observed how data issues or data wins were presented to stakeholders and how internal customers reacted to various business challenges. Sometimes they were highly supportive, recognizing our relevance, while at other times, they doubted the value of data and believed that alternative corporate-level initiatives were needed. Deep engagement and empathy were essential to navigate this landscape.

Inspired by a successful approach I had seen with the UK team, which focused on aiding marketing activities and processes, I decided to take a similar route.

The UK team specialized in the intelligent preparation of marketing data, and they had developed a motto that resonated with me: "*We make data business-ready.*"

This simple, powerful statement encapsulated our mission perfectly. It conveyed that our community was responsible for "making data" and effectively answered the perennial question of "Who is in charge of data?" While the term "making" might sound strange in the context of data, at that time, it signified the creation of something real and well understood, as we totally lacked robust data capabilities, platforms, or standardized data services.

This statement was instrumental during our experimental phase, helping us gradually move toward well defined and standardized data capabilities.

Even as we experimented with different approaches and solutions, it served as a beacon for our stakeholders, providing a clear and easily digestible representation of our mission. We introduced the statement *We make data business-ready* widely across our work and it became our guiding motto for several years. It united us with the business and their needs and proved effective in garnering support. We even put it in our email signatures and PowerPoint decks, incorporating it into our branding as much as we could.

Today, while data teams operate differently, with concepts such as data mesh and federated governance gaining prominence, I still believe that this simple yet powerful statement, along with the commitment it represents, can be a game-changer when there is a need to emphasize the value of data and make it more understandable and relevant to stakeholders.

We needed to start modestly, adapt to the organization's needs, and gradually evolve. This flexible approach allowed us to discover the most pressing business needs, learn about emerging issues, and progress step by step.

Did that lack of defined data strategy randomize us? I guess not, as "by default," we were reactive to what matters most and tried to capitalize on learnings and enhance our own data IP with every newly resolved business challenge. We had to build our approach and our effective data strategy from bottom up, adding every single win as continuous best practice and focusing our attention on where business priorities were.

As you know, back then, we didn't have a centralized data team, and our approach and success were based on being adaptable and responsive. Looking back, this proved to be the right strategy.

Here we see the early evolution of our data work:

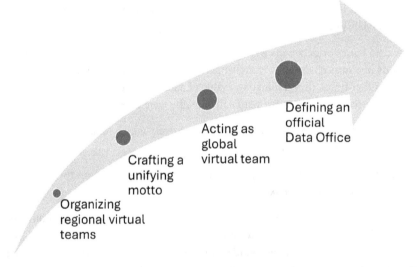

Figure 2.1 – Data work evolution

In less than 12 months from the starting point in our globalization and centralization journey, we established our first full data services catalog and a comprehensive data portfolio for the organization. But that's a story for another time – a bit later.

Business needs lead the way

The key takeaway from this experience is simple: aligning with business needs is paramount, and the journey often begins with addressing those needs as they arise. This dynamic approach allows you to fine-tune your offerings, adapt, and build credibility with stakeholders. Our commitment to making data business-ready, step by step, was instrumental in our long-term success.

Having one unifying and inspiring motto helped to connect various regional teams into a strong virtual community, cementing the foundations for the next stage.

Locally inspired, globally connected

A single sentence, "We make data business-ready," quietly sparked a steady data revolution within our global company. This phrase wasn't just an off-hand statement ; it became a powerful motto, a force that transformed our approach to data.

Something critical to note was that at the time, this simple sentence did more than unify and position the efforts of data practitioners within the company. It served as a universal replacement for what we now call a data strategy or data management strategy. Believe it or not, in those early stages of our journey toward a global, well-defined data approach, there was no centralized data strategy or data management strategy in place.

It may sound surprising, but it's true.

We had a corporate data team, and they did work toward enabling global capabilities and defining a much-needed, multi-year so called "Horizon" model for data applications, yet the actual usage of data was in the so-called "Field", or, in other words, the geographically based sales, marketing, and finance teams outside of Redmond Corporate Headquarters. They were the users and consumers of data, and we had no strategy to address their needs.

Moreover, every corner of the company, every subsidiary, and even individual business groups had their own unique perspective on how data should be handled. They each faced their own distinct data challenges. Sounds familiar for many, I guess.

We, as data practitioners, had a unique ability during this time. We could bridge the gaps between different geographical areas and act as the leaders of data practices within those regions. We focused on the practical aspects of data, delving deep into the operational side of things. Simultaneously, we were making substantial contributions to improving DQ and ensuring proper data maintenance to benefit the business.

That being said, in each geographical area, we encountered a mix of stakeholders. Some were fully aligned with and supportive of our mission, while others were skeptical or misaligned with the value of data.

In this challenging situation, what truly helped us was the universal language of data. Intentionally keeping ourselves outside of corporate politics, we made a first attempt to lead with data-driven decisions, visualizing DQ issues in front of our stakeholders while offering simple, practical follow-up solutions how to improve their experience with the data. When I say "universal language," I mean the language of data itself – factual data points, examples of bad and good data, and the impact of successful data initiatives. When we shared common findings and examples across different regions, it became clear that DQ challenges in the CRM, for example, were remarkably similar in France and Germany. Yes, local languages and practices differed, but the core data challenges were surprisingly alike. By using concrete data examples, we began consolidating our data management knowledge across regions, along with winning more and more trust with our stakeholders.

We transformed into hands-on data practitioners, deeply immersed in the systems. We could recap primary keys and unique IDs by heart, which helped us truly understand the data landscape within the company. We empathized with each challenge and data issue reported by the business, and we still had high empathy for any new data challenge that emerged.

> **Data strategy – keep it simple**
> In a way, our data strategy in those days was simple: be empathetic and ready to react to any new data challenge that came our way.

However, we surely knew that being only reactive wasn't the most efficient approach, and we aspired to shift toward being proactive. We aimed to be not only empathetic but also relevant, responsible, and highly accountable. We constantly searched for ways to innovate and elevate our data game.

One of our early solutions was the creation of a game-changing application known as Managed Accounts List, or simply MAL. We aimed to empower users to handle data issues and challenges themselves, promoting self-service.

The implementation path was far from simple, yet we started to harvest the benefits quickly after. This was the first successful reuse of something that was born as local but became global. Even though it was cumbersome and simplistic at the start, it made the right path and built the initial bricks for data literacy and a self-service approach.

Yet, we also had to keep navigating a maze of local processes while staying committed to addressing local needs. When I say "local," I refer to practices specific to individual countries, subsidiaries, or geographical areas. For example, data practices for updating the CRM in Poland could be vastly different from those in Russia, despite using the same CRM system. It may sound crazy, but back then, this was the reality.

Ironically, despite these diverse practices, all these CRM accounts created in a variety of ways somehow managed to function in the system. It's hard to believe in today's world of data governance and standardization, but it is a reality of business operations.

It was like running completely different data businesses in various countries and then attempting to create a unified approach across the entire region.

As we worked toward creating a universal CRM account creation process as an attempt for unification, for Central and Eastern Europe, we didn't stop there. We expanded our horizons to other geographic areas, such as France, Switzerland, and Germany. The beauty of the situation was the virtual proximity and trust that existed among our global data community.

While not everything was seamlessly united for global collaboration, we, as data practitioners, were well connected and supportive. We exchanged ideas, learned from one another, and presented new concepts in common forums.

Our goal was to elevate our local practices to a higher level, bridging regional gaps and eventually end up with global capabilities. Some were fully committed to this and others were a bit more skeptical. But overall, we all were aligned in the need to have a simplified and standardized process.

The question was – how exactly do we get there?

We coined the new motto for us - "Think local, act global."

Our local connections and relevance were non-negotiable, even as we pushed for stricter procedures and global thinking. We actively collaborated with businesses to enhance data collection and entry processes without disrupting data flows. At the same time, creating a standardized global approach wasn't an immediate option. Neither we, lacking a formal global data team, nor our business partners and users, without the tools and experience for easy global adoption, were ready for such a transition.

So, we found a middle ground.

We chose to begin with commonalities between different data processes, focusing on the 20 or 25 most common data requests, such as the previously mentioned CRM account creation and some other DQ validations. We created standardized forms and templates, sometimes backed by Excel-based tools, to cater to a wide range of user needs. We wanted them to feel comfortable but be more powerful in their work.

Let's look at a real-life example of what became a game-changer for us while being an ultra-pragmatic and simplistic solution.

Introducing a global request-tracking tool

This exemplary practice, originating in Australia, quickly spread across all regions. It marked a pivotal moment in our journey from local to global.

As I keep saying, we hadn't officially formed a global data team yet, but this shift in mindset and approach brought us closer together and kept us growing our global outreach.

The solution was simple – **Service Request Tracking Tool**, or in short, **SRTT**.

Originally built as a SharePoint solution for tracking various internal requests for data management and data manipulation, it quickly outgrew itself to become a powerful and standalone web-based application, with several automation workflows underneath.

The real value of this solution lies in the simplicity and affordability for the end users, while equipping the data teams with the benefits of consolidation, streamlining, and service request tracking workflow principles.

Here, we focused on a few fundamental pillars:

- The solution was positioned as a frontend portal for any type of data management requests/ DQ needs – aka a "one-stop shop" – and was open to any user in the company.

- Users were able to register themselves at the first log in and profile themselves for the most common type of data requests, business needs, communication preferences, and so on. This was important to understand the needs of different audiences and later do some analytics on who is coming for what kind of requests.

- It had a simple interface – a catalog of predefined forms to submit, with attached Excel-based templates (Excel was proven to be the tool that people were most comfortable with, which remains the case today).

- An ad hoc, non-predefined request form was possible too. We removed it later, as we matured, but it was crucial to have it at the start.

- Upon submission of a request, the user would receive a unique service request tracking number by email, along with continuous status updates – just like other service request apps and tools.

- A dedicated support/helpdesk alias was created shortly after, to help users with guidance and investigation support if they were stuck with something or something had been done incorrectly.

As you see, it was as simple as could be.

But this capability, being entirely focused on and dedicated to data, even though it was quite cumbersome and not highly intelligent, came with a few advantages and led us to make huge progress:

- First, we anchored all the data-related requests to one place, one portal where all the users were directed. This helped us to gradually address all the incoming users as a community, get them registered and profiled, and start to delve deeper into what kind of different data needs to exist in the company – across almost all the business groups. Later, this allowed us to also pivot initial data literacy and data fluency programs, with dedicated educational sessions, demos, best practices, and so on.

- Second, it was the path to building a single catalog of data services and data-related offerings. This is why I say it was important to be open-ended and non-restrictive with the scope and what we can take on. Only once we had learned more and were able to standardize our data services catalog did we further consolidate and remove ambiguous and non-standard requests.

- Third, in connection with the first point, we have a total addressable "market" of users, to whom we could centrally deploy more automation and new experimental solutions, gradually offer additional data domains, as well as have a full feedback loop and continuous enhancement of our IP and knowledge.

On the backend side, it was also a great win.

With predefined Excel-based templates, we saw fewer errors and mistakes as users were pushed to use defined metadata and taxonomy. We offered a variety of forms – from a very straightforward request, such as CRM account creation, to comprehensive multi-stage cascading data processing – the creation of CRM accounts along with contacts, activities, and opportunities in a single bulk data submission, all at the same time as one transaction.

Structured Excel templates were obviously perfect for easy automation – converting them into files ready for data upload, or later, for the API-based push into respective apps. It also helped fast-track data integrity across the key applications, as we were able to validate data from templates and "pre-apply" the intended changes in our sandbox data environment before the push to production systems. Plus, both us and the users had a single request reference number, which was easy to follow up and check at any moment.

> **Small steps with long-lasting effect**
> This led to the foundation for outsourcing opportunities at a later stage, along with establishing real-life sourced SLAs.

Was it a perfect solution? Nope, absolutely not. But it was a working solution.

The main disadvantage was totally weird data processing – something that we as the data team were always facepalming and ashaming ourselves, but for a long time, we had no better alternative.

As you read, users had to submit everything through Excel-based templates, with structured columns, metadata pick values, mandatory fields, and so on. So, the only real way to get those templates filled was to get the input data from the CRM or other systems itself, as the base for what is about to change.

Surely, net-new accounts, opportunities, or anything of that sort were coming directly from external sources, yet much of the day-to-day data manipulations, DQ updates, address and contact persona updates, and so on – all that often originated from an existing CRM – had to be modified in some way.

For single to dozen record changes, users usually would just do it by themselves via the UI, but once they need to change/update/modify more records, they would go for a bulk data submission request. So, the data would be copied out from the CRM, then posted into the Excel template and submitted to us.

And then the data team would do things in the reverse order – extract, validate/enrich, and push back into the source systems. Urrrgh! Yeah, certainly not the best data flow.

However, we weren't living in an ideal world, and we appreciated anything that worked for us and our users' needs.

Honestly, I don't believe that any of them truly liked the platform, but our satisfaction score (NSAT) was growing steadily through the years, starting from a miserable 99 at the beginning of that data management journey and ending with 180+ years later. Yet what we noticed is that even with all those limitations and difficulties, the solution somehow ended up being convenient and comfortable.

Once people were educated on how to submit, how to get help and assistance, and what to expect from the process, they were relieved and were actively collaborating with us in terms of feedback, suggestions, and outlines of their future needs.

> **Things that worked well**
>
> This was quite golden – and again and again underlined the importance of trust and relevance. Along with **Managed Accounts List** (**MAL**), this simple web-based portal became an epic catalyst for pushing local into global, mastering centralization and standardization, and building an even stronger brand for us as the data team.

At first, we were a virtual team; only later did we become a physical team – that's the story we will be unveiling throughout this chapter.

Moving ahead

The company's strategic move to consolidate its IT teams into a global unit, known as Microsoft IT, was unfolding simultaneously.

This transition helped facilitate our shift to a more organized structure. It wasn't just a change in conversation; it was a shift from local teams to a unified global team responsible for specific data domains.

Looking back, it was more than mere coincidence; it was serendipity that these changes occurred just as we were poised to elevate our data game.

We were almost ready, perhaps more prepared than any other team within our IT peers, to make this shift toward becoming a truly global organization. Remember, while we hadn't formally established a global physical data team yet, our virtual community of data practitioners was exceptionally productive. We collaborated effectively as data champions, but this moment of transition was still comprehensively different. We were evolving from a loose network into a cohesive global team. The early introduced toolsets such as MAL and SRTT helped to enforce the positioning and enablement for our audience.

This transformation gave birth to the DMO – I cover this important moment in depth through the next section of this chapter.

Our mission remained crystal clear: *We make data business-ready*. But now it had to be carried out on a global scale.

We were intensely customer-centric, having come up through the ranks alongside the local business communities, understanding their pain points and witnessing the importance of data. We knew that data issues had real-world consequences. This was not just a theory for us; it was practical, hands-on expertise. This commitment and deep understanding of our role within the business, coupled with the realization that our power lay in the collective knowledge of our community, drove us forward.

As our internal customers began to see us, the virtual data team, as the truly global and responsible data team, we knew we were on the right path. Nothing could deter us; the only way was forward. The company's shift from decentralized IT to centralized shared services further bolstered our data agenda, accelerating DQ improvements; but, as was said, it was simply underpinning our internal readiness.

We aimed to create a unified back-office with data engineering, data operations, and data support ecosystem. This marked a significant shift in how we operated. This wasn't anymore just a local arrangement with friendly local data experts; it was a global team effort. And neither did we focus on providing local solutions; we aimed to offer global capabilities. We continued to navigate the complex world of data, introducing standardized forms and templates, and, most importantly, driving home the message that data was a global concern. We launched early efforts on data literacy to reinforce this notion.

Our team's transformation was mirrored by the company's shift to a centralized IT model, giving us the organizational structure we truly needed.

We were now poised for global expansion, to create a worldwide service delivery model, and to radically improve the "state of data" in the company. As we were transforming from a loose virtual community into a cohesive global team, we knew that we had the foundation, the commitment, and the knowledge to become the truly global data organization we had always aspired to be.

The stage was set for our data journey to enter a new, even more remarkable phase.

The rise of Data Management Organization

When we embarked on the journey to establish a new global and official organization, designing it effectively from the outset was paramount.

However, the reality was far from simple.

We had a pre-existing workforce spread across various geographic regions, and this complexity came at a significant cost, an exceedingly high one. It was evident from the beginning that this newly forged global organization couldn't merely be a conglomeration of existing teams placed under one physical umbrella. We needed to make some challenging decisions and navigate difficult trade-offs.

Let's delve deeper into the challenges we faced and how we tackled them.

We initiated this journey with several geographical areas, each led by individuals in pivotal roles, like me as the area data lead. These leaders often had on-site teams, typically complemented by one, two, three, or more full-time Microsoft employees dedicated to supporting their mission. This setup was typical in mature and well-established regions such as Germany, France, or the UK.

In contrast, there were areas where the bulk of the data work was handled by local contractors or even a bit of outsourcing. There were also exceptional cases where teams possessed not only data management skills but also robust local data engineering capabilities, developing applications, solutions, and platforms.

Deciding how to unify these diverse components into a cohesive global organization was far from straightforward.

Future-focused skills and expertise
Our challenge was to construct a team that could operate globally while still harnessing the rich expertise of local specialists in each area. This posed the question of how to build a team that could overlap these two worlds, capitalizing on local knowledge and catering to the unique requirements of different regions while enabling ongoing growth.

Our decision, which we'll discuss in detail, was to focus on the future.

We recognized that the existing model, though effective so far, would become prohibitively expensive to maintain. Managing a multitude of local contractors across different subsidiaries, despite their exceptional knowledge, would be financially unsustainable.

The logical path to optimization was outsourcing, particularly in lower-cost regions. However, given our global journey and our limited understanding of common processes across regions, it was premature and inefficient to aggressively pursue outsourcing.

We needed to buy time and establish a stable core data offering first.

We experimented by outsourcing certain well-defined processes but encountered swift and painful setbacks. Although we didn't achieve immediate success, these experiences taught us a valuable lesson: our understanding of the ownership of data management capabilities in a global context was still in its infancy. We would later absolutely succeed in outsourcing, a topic I'll explore in a dedicated way in the *Chapter 6*.

Hence, from the inception of our new global DMO, we had to make the tough decision to part ways with most of our experienced contractors. Instead, we focused on building a core team of *full-time employees (FTEs)* who would lead the change, learning on the fly as they orchestrated our global efforts.

This transition from having a large pool of contractors to a handful of FTEs was unexpected and posed a challenge to our scalability. Until then, many of our local contractors had effectively functioned as full-time employees, concealing the extent of their work. Microsoft later introduced new contracting and outsourcing policies, emphasizing standardization and strategic outsourcing.

Nonetheless, we adapted to our circumstances.

Our budget for the newly formed global data team simply couldn't accommodate the existing contractors, except for some located in lower-cost regions such as Central and Eastern Europe. While I was pleased to witness my team becoming a strategic focal point for global delivery, I was equally concerned about how we would fulfill the data needs of the entire Microsoft ecosystem with a team originally designed for a single geographic area.

In terms of organizational structure and principles, it obviously felt comforting to maintain a mental connection between employees and their geographic origins, even as we embraced the concept of going global and adopted a shared services approach. The alternative approach would have been to entirely disconnect employees from their geographic ties and immerse them in global delivery, focusing solely on a global understanding of new needs and objectives.

> **Tough, yet critical-to-success decision**
> Although there were concerns about the latter approach, we opted for it, clearly separating individuals from their previous roles and extending them into new global delivery positions.

This was met with discomfort, stress, anxiety, and a fear of failure among employees. From an organizational standpoint, it posed challenges, especially since we had to significantly reduce the team due to the departure of contractors, all while assuming global data accountability.

Yet, from a business perspective, not that much had changed – and that was good.

Yes, we introduced new people responsible for global practices, but the core business needs more or less remained constant. It is just that now we needed to find commonalities across different data processes; promote standardization, automation, and data insights; and strive for global excellence.

As data ceased to be treated as a local concern and began receiving proper global attention, we embarked on the task of documenting everything, including local exceptions.

This was about data leadership, change management, and a progressive journey. As a team, we were strongly committed to finding better solutions. We understood that achieving economies of scale would require us to outsource data operations. Our data solutions, such as MAL and SRTT, were making data more accessible to business teams, and they were starting to rely on us to handle data issues, often behind the scenes.

However, despite the difficult transition and the high-pressure with new roles and responsibilities, we went with what felt right, even though it was a demanding shift.

We believed it was necessary for the efficiency of data management, offering fresh learning opportunities, new roles, and fresh perspectives from the standpoint of this entirely new data organization. We leaned heavily on our managers, urging them to prioritize the well-being of their teams. The strong sense of community we had cultivated in the past days helped alleviate some of the anxiety and set the stage for success.

> **Becoming global wasn't easy, but totally worth it**
>
> In summary, the geographically based team transformed into a global entity, albeit without local contractors. Individuals who were once responsible for specific regions and familiar stakeholders suddenly found themselves responsible for global delivery. They had to adapt to new roles, acquire new skills, and establish new connections across the company. They also had to work diligently on improving their English language proficiency, as prior to this change, English was only partially relevant as a communication language within their respective regions.

Our new roles and capabilities offered a comfortable dual-faceted appearance of "primary" and "secondary" responsibilities:

- The primary role involved leading a specific data capability or set of services and engaging with a global audience of stakeholders.

- The secondary role required supporting or shadowing someone else in their primary role, providing an added layer of expertise and backup while the primary role delivery remained highly accountable

The ability to learn rapidly in compressed timeframes was crucial to our success.

Often, we had to acquire knowledge in mere hours, not days, to address concerns or business escalations from regions where specific data practices or knowledge were absent, or where processes had been standardized at a global level. The learning curve was steep, both for us and our internal stakeholders, who had to adapt to this new reality and understand that proximity to an office did not necessarily correlate with local demand or needs. Our sense of professional community, highlighted in *Chapter 1*, played a pivotal role in facilitating this change, ensuring we moved in the right direction and achieved our goals.

While we encountered challenges in managing costs and delivering during the transitional phase for about half a year to a year, our new setup, focused on globality, created an environment of safe learning without judgment, allowing us to adapt and deliver on our mission.

My own transformative moment during this period involved shifting my focus toward the global team, global data treatment, and the future of our team. It meant letting go of the comfort of our previous area data lead role and embracing a truly global perspective.

This shift was fundamental and contributed significantly to our eventual success, as subsequent chapters demonstrate. We encouraged ourselves to look ahead rather than dwell on the past, to be proactive and transformative, and to live the data agenda we all aspired to achieve.

My personal story – Data Management Organization announcement

It was an ordinary mid-week, hard-working day in the Munich office – except for one thing.

It was my birthday.

Being even busier than usual and running from one conference call to another, I was totally off track with incoming emails and just dreaming of a nice, lovely, and quiet evening at home – being alone and away from my family, unfortunately, I still had a deep inner respect for celebrating my birthday, but deferring celebrative mood towards the end of the day.

There were still several hours before the end of the day, and one of the key things I was yet to learn was about a planned announcement of a new organizational structure. Plenty of rumors were circulating, all of them pointing toward a kind of shared services principle, along with more centralization than ever before.

I had no specific expectations for anything, especially for my geographical area and my direct scope of work. I thought that the things here in the CEE area were deemed to be so much immature and just starting, so I believed it would be crazy to change the operational setup so early at least comparing with other, much more advanced and matured areas. Only a few months back, we had finished hiring for area-wide roles and were now carrying out several business visits across the area, learning about the regional and country-specific pain points, including those for DQ and data management routines.

In other words, I was deep into operations and daily challenges, not spending too much time chatting about the rumors and what they could mean for all of us. And even thinking of the opportunity to finally establish a central data team, one that would be formal and clear, was far off on the horizon. We had only discussed that opportunity very recently and briefly; hence, I was not yet expecting any actual action to happen in that direction.

An emerging request for an urgent business meeting came up from one of the renowned data leaders in EMEA, with whom we worked very closely, and coincidently, I had just recently shared with him a lot of progress and updates about how successful we were in Central and Eastern Europe with our data community, data champions, and the cross-country resource utilization for the "common good" of the entire area.

Surprised and curious, I answered the call and delved into the discussion:

Data Leader (DL): "Aleks, I need your help. We are optimizing external resources (aka contractors) across all the geographical areas and I need your input. Think of criticality to the company, adaptability for new challenges, deepness of experience, and flexibility of minds. And, yeah, we need to stay within the budget, and the budget is tight."

Aleks: "Oh, OK, not a very inspiring conversation, but work is work... Got it, how much do we need to optimize for?"

DL: "We would need to let go of about 85% of the current worldwide community of contractors."

Aleks: "What????! You are kidding me! Impossible – the world will collapse, and we will be swamped by the sea of business escalations from the very next day!"

DL: "Yeah… maybe, or maybe not. Look, with this new central data team, as you have seen in the announcement, we are proposing to take a major step forward, and now you, as one of the team leaders, need to make the best judgment for the success of our organization design. Please, take this as an opportunity."

Tons of thoughts were running in my mind – *Central data team? One of the leaders? What is this all about? Did I miss something crucial? Or is this a bad birthday joke?*

It certainly wasn't a birthday joke.

Apparently, the announcement of global shared services had already been made and communicated via email, which I missed as I'd been busy with calls, and this announcement also included the formation of a new central data team, with a worldwide mandate. Effective immediately.

I got to learn about my new role as manager with direct reports from France, South Africa, Japan, and even Thailand. What a change, and what a truly global step!

This was beyond exciting and surpassed any expectations in terms of how quickly the official formation of a global data team would happen. While we clearly were already going that way and building trust with stakeholders, maximizing the power of the community of data champions and data practitioners and implementing some early global solutions, it felt still overwhelming, unprecedented, surprising, exciting, and worrying – all at the same time; and we had to act quickly.

It's one thing dreaming about global capabilities and global influence on data and another to suddenly co-own this capability and be the person behind the highest service delivery expectations from worldwide users.

The good thing was that the design of the organization was exactly around those guidelines that we all steered toward and worked hard to prove in the months preceding the announcement.

All that implicit elevation from locally minded, virtual team members to global data citizens working tightly together, along with early consolidation attempts of core data services and the introduction of pilot solutions such as SRTT and MAL outside of originated geographies – all these played a pivotal role to the design of the org – and eventually, an equally crucial role in the success of that first central data team.

We managed to preserve and re-purpose most contractors in Central Europe and the Middle East, and we got a truly global team of full-time employees – all were highly experienced data professionals across the whole world, and together we were officially named the Data Management Organization.

We had an exceptionally talented team, with great data fluency and problem-solving skills, with most people already being in the company long enough to know how to use it for our benefit.

Now, all that remained was to deliver.

So, simple, right? But where to start and how not to fail?

That is what the next chapter is about – consolidating and evolving our new footprint.

Summary and key takeaways

By telling you the story of our initial data journey, I've unfolded three invaluable learnings. These insights not only guided our path but transformed the way we perceived data within our organization. I hope these will be helpful on your journey as well.

Takeaway #1 – crafting an inspiring motto for transformation

Imagine a scenario where your business needs and IT/data delivery appear disconnected, lacking that vital mental connection.

In this chapter, we delved into the importance of a powerful motto or slogan that resonates deeply with the key stakeholders – and with us.

At Microsoft, we knew it was not just about delivering facts and figures; it was about capturing hearts and trust. By creating a compelling motto that bridges the gap between business needs and data delivery, we won stakeholders over.

Even amid delivering the most relevant and powerful solutions, don't underestimate the impact of an inspiring motto – "the power of one sentence."

Takeaway #2 – scaling from local to global with trust

In our journey, trust proved to be an invaluable asset, propelling us from local success to global excellence.

The core principle here was to maintain absolute relevance to business needs.

Small, iterative improvements, sometimes seen as temporary or even rudimentary, can have a tremendous impact when they directly address stakeholder needs.

There was no actual, real-life pressure to over-engineer if your users were satisfied. While aiming for process and operational excellence is important and opens a path for innovation, embracing an ultra-pragmatic approach often leads to victory.

Takeaway #3 – the formula for a centralized data team

Ever wondered what it takes to transform into a central, dedicated data team?

It's a combination of local trusted relationships, high relevance to the standing business needs, and a global challenger mindset. And a little bit of luck, perhaps.

Building a tightly knit community of data professionals who are all well connected and share a common vision was key to leading. Moreover, having a compact portfolio of straightforward yet impactful data capabilities, such as MAL and SRTT as in our previous examples can be the catalyst for one of the most potent enterprise transformations.

This lesson, from my view, underscores the importance of simplicity and a shared sense of purpose in driving significant change within any organization.

The next chapter will take us through the first hard work carried out by a centralized data team – inventory and simplification of all data functions.

Thousands to One – From Locally Siloed to Globally Centralized Processes

In this chapter, we will reflect on our transformative journey in which we evolved from 12 local data teams into a global data management powerhouse. Each region presented unique challenges with distinct data workflows and business requirements. Initially, our localized approach was effective, but the transition to a global scale necessitated a fundamental change in our processes and consolidation strategies.

We'll review these strategies, along with easy and relevant examples, in the coming pages.

We will start with a pivotal example of this transition – our benchmark CRM account creation process, which merged various local practices into a unified global procedure. As we downsized and globalized our team, the focus shifted to streamlining and optimizing operations. The **Service Request Tracking Tool (SRTT)** emerged as a crucial tool in standardizing service delivery and gaining insights into complex request patterns. This tool helped enhance user experience and encourage adoption as the primary submission method for any type of data-related request.

Our approach respected the frontline experience and maximized productivity, even at the cost of additional effort on our part.

Overall, we will walk through the following key aspects of our process consolidation journey, while evolving into a true global central data team:

- Evolving from localized to global operations
- Integrating local practices into a globally executable framework
- The challenges of transitioning to a global team
- Balancing local nuances with global standardization
- The role of simple yet effective tools in optimizing service delivery

- Streamlining operations for a leaner, more effective team
- The transition from a variety of services to a consolidated, singular, comprehensive catalog – what we called the "Book of Work"

Let's start at the beginning of our journey.

The opening story

Moving from local to global was tricky, and not just due to process consolidation needs and other significant delivery-oriented tasks. Having great methodologies, supportive management, and trusted relationships with stakeholders played a vital part.

Not everything went smoothly from the beginning, though. While I praise the adaptability of our team members, we struggled with landing the change with business stakeholders. Let me reflect on an episode that seems funny now but, at the time, was a tough call for action, with tangible learning at the end.

My weekly team meeting started with one of the members reporting the resignation of a valued contractor. This highly skilled and experienced lady directly supported several full-time employees in our journey toward the global footprint. She was in one of the smaller subsidiaries in Europe and had reported a certain local tension recently. I jumped immediately into the direct conversation, trying to understand and resolve the case and save the talent for us.

Aleks: "Hey, how are you? What's the matter there?"

Contractor: "The local marketing lead is bombarding me with a lot of work that isn't in our service remit, and also the local folks just stop by my table and give me work to execute. I'm trying to push back and direct them to the global service offering, yet they insist, saying basically, "You sit here, you are part of our office, you get paid by us – and with this, you first will need to do what we demand, and only afterward can you go back to your global playground." I'm stressed, I'm unhappy, and I'd rather quit than be at a point of conflict all the time."

Aleks: "Okay, that's tough, I understand. Please give me a few days to sort this out. Meanwhile, if you feel tired and demotivated, please take some time off and try to recover."

I was pretty devasted by how she was being treated. My first reaction was anger and I almost jumped into writing some harsh escalation email to that marketing lead, along with the country **General Manager (GM)** and a few other folks.

But then I paused a bit and wondered why the local business folks ended up with such a perception. Something was missing in this puzzle. It couldn't be just that brutal and unintelligent, even if we had screwed up with our change management communications (which I presumed we had not, as other subsidiaries hadn't reported any issues).

I decided instead to call the local IT manager to possibly get some more context.

Through our conversation, I realized a few key things. First, the subsidiary folks worked very closely with each other, almost like a family business, and this deemed artificial separation of data work hit them badly. Second, the whole local team shared a lot of local perks – company dinners, awards, team-building events, and so on.

Obviously, our person was fully included in those benefits and activities, and she enjoyed them. Yet at the same time, this inclusion contributed to the perception that she was working for local needs, and hence her global role was a kind of secondary affair. Now, I could fully imagine the actual situation. For all of them there, it was truly hard to smoothly distinguish between local versus global, professional versus social relationships, and remote manager versus local next-to-you leader.

I ended up flying to the subsidiary and taking time to build a personal connection with the leadership. By explaining to them the broader context of our work, team organization, and global shared service principles, along with continuous support for local tweaks, I created a shared understanding of our dilemma. This opened the path for a solution.

To make life simpler for local folks and our team person, we decided to relocate her within the office, joining the IT team corner. It was a simple gesture, yet this relocation helped. Furthermore, we jointly presented to the local office a few educational sessions about the global data capabilities we had, raising their literacy, and building excitement about that unique local connection they had to such a powerful global team. The image and perception changed dramatically. Now, she seemed like the global data expert, "luckily" co-located within the same geo subsidiary, with a span of knowledge far beyond the local domain.

It was a classy win-win scenario and a working example for us of how to marry global and local dimensions into one multi-dimensional view.

Five inventory perspectives

In our previous chapters, we reviewed our journey tracing the transformation from a local data team to a global powerhouse. We explored a bit of our history and touched on our tactical maneuvers. As we embarked further on this global endeavor, we confronted a multitude of complex, highly customized processes. It's worth re-emphasizing that each geographic region boasted its distinct data workflows, intricately intertwined with indicative business requirements.

In the era of a localized workforce, our approach truly thrived, rooted in our dedication to providing exceptional experiences for the local stakeholders. We were all about understanding those nuances that made our local business stakeholders succeed.

However, we hadn't given much thought to the idea of globalization. So, we took steps to elevate some of the local data practices, selecting the most effective among them and adopting them on a broader scale as global practices.

For instance, I previously highlighted the CRM account creation process, which we thoroughly crafted by integrating various local practices into a unified global procedure. Yet, as we transitioned into a global team and significantly reduced our workforce, we encountered the pressing need to optimize and streamline our operations.

> ### Going global
> Operating on a global scale with a leaner team demanded a reinvention of our methods and a fundamental shift in our "what" and "how."

This task was no walk in the park. Not only did we have to continue delivering our existing services but we also had to simplify our future portfolio, aiming to construct a comprehensive, singular catalog of data services across the company.

At the time, this idea was still in its infancy, a distant aspiration amid the massiveness of highly customized requests, each accompanied by urgent business needs. These demands often required immediate action within our systems, with little time for deep analysis or understanding of the underlying reasons.

Then came the SRTT – a game-changer.

As simple as it could be (but with structured forms and templates), the SRTT offered the much-needed framework to standardize our service delivery and gain insights into request patterns, including sophisticated, unique requests. Our primary goal was to make the tool universally accessible while comprehensively understanding all request types and special cases. We were still managing a diverse array of sometimes similar requests, but our aim was to enhance user-friendliness and encourage users to adopt this tool as their primary submission method.

Acknowledging that the frontline experience could be cumbersome and time-consuming, we treated incoming demands with the utmost respect, maximizing end users' productivity, even if it meant investing extra effort on our side.

Simultaneously, the request funnel enabled us to analyze processes in the background and progressively consolidate our services.

For example, our CRM account creation templates ranged from basic account setups to comprehensive templates that included account, contact, opportunity, and activity creation. Some templates extended to facilitate the simultaneous creation of multiple objects in one go. We intentionally maintained high template fidelity and a broad range of offerings to cater to our diverse user base. This even included an open-ended request option, where users could submit any data-related request, providing detailed descriptions and securely attaching data files. We would then analyze these requests and commit to dedicated **Service-Level Agreements (SLAs)** for each specific case.

During our initial inventory efforts, which spanned various channels for executing local and global processes, we encountered a plethora of similar yet distinct processes.

However, a swift decision to eliminate them wasn't feasible. Our success in establishing a centralized data team hinged on our ability to remain highly relevant to business users and rapidly enhance data quality. Consequently, we embarked on a comprehensive inventory undertaking, categorizing data management and maintenance processes into five distinct channels or groups. Next, we are going to review all five groups in detail.

One-stop shop

The first aspect we'll delve into is the SRTT. This tool played a pivotal role in our data management journey. It provided users with forms and templates, offering multiple submission avenues while guiding them on the most efficient approaches from our perspective. It also simplified the data submission process, encouraging users to do some preliminary work on their end, ultimately accelerating data processing on our side.

As we closely monitored the tool's utilization and the changes within our systems, patterns began to emerge.

We discerned which forms and templates were in high demand compared to those with lower utilization rates, although they still held importance. Gradually, we initiated a plan to retire certain forms and templates. To facilitate this transition, we implemented change management strategies, ensuring that users were prepared to switch to alternative submission methods or data preparation processes. After several months of careful work, we achieved significant standardization of our procedures.

Previously, I mentioned our open submission form, which allowed us to accommodate ad hoc, infrequently needed requests. We fully recognized the importance of maintaining flexibility in our future offerings. After our first year as a global team, we substantially reduced the number of templates and forms. We further refined them to align with specific business domains. These included managing and maintaining master data in CRM, handling revenue collection adjustments and reconciliation, onboarding external data sources into our primary systems, managing marketing-related activities, and performing routine data cleanup tasks, often initiated by users.

Eventually, we phased out the open form submission feature when it became clear that no new requests were coming through. This indicated that we had successfully captured most recurring requests, which we referred to as "reactive work."

Aligning with role experiences

The second area we focused on during our analysis was **role experience**, or **RolEx**. These user experiences were designed to cater to various user roles within our organization, spanning sales, marketing, finance, licensing, operations, and more.

When employees logged into Tier 1 systems and applications, they were provided with role-specific access tailored to their responsibilities. Our goal was to ensure that each role had access to the right data, presented in a manner that minimized confusion and maximized efficiency.

We extended this approach to data by analyzing the common data modifications or requests associated with each role. For instance, we examined what data operations were crucial for an account manager and what data they needed to accomplish their tasks effectively.

This exploration also shed light on how different roles intersected and influenced underlying data. We didn't stop there; we chimed in on special roles or edge cases.

One example was the *Business Sales Operation* role – essentially, a power user role with the authority to make data adjustments on a geographical area level. Individuals with this role wielded significant responsibility for revenue, **Lead-to-Order (L2O)**, and **Order-to-Cash (O2C)** processes.

Aligning our data processes with these critical business roles was paramount.

Corporate applications and tools

Our third area of analysis centered on the landscape of primary applications, tools, and systems from a corporate-wide perspective.

We not only considered core solutions, such as CRM, revenue collection, and finance/billing, but also custom-built applications that played vital roles in our business. Take, for instance, the *Managed Accounts List* application, which acted as a bridge between CRM and revenue collection while serving as a master source for top-tier accounts data. It facilitated dual-direction data sync but also introduced challenges such as data overriding and conflicting updates.

Our approach involved identifying data gaps and suggesting root-cause fixes within these systems. However, we realized that due to constant changes and a diverse user audience, users in many roles still sought our assistance.

This led to a mix of data fixes and demands for system-level improvements. We collaborated with our corporate data engineering teams to address these gaps, bottlenecks, synchronization issues, and more. Our goal was to create a clear roadmap for feature development, ensuring that users receive the necessary guidance to work with data effectively, and ultimately, preventing messy and inconvenient daily workflows.

Analyzing these corporate platforms not only simplified user experiences but also enriched our catalog of roles and role-specific data needs.

It prompted innovative ideas, such as developing dedicated apps or tailored data processes for specific user roles. A notable example was the need to continually adjust customer segmentation based on revenue profiles. We established a package of analytical processes and a dedicated application, backed by a robust background operational process and managed by our central data team. This application identified missing revenue transactions and incomplete or erroneous data and hence was effectively influencing accurate customer segmentation decisions. Users could review recommendations and make informed decisions. This bespoke solution significantly impacted revenue accuracy, seller compensation, and up-to-date customer segmentation, demonstrating the power of agile data services.

In essence, our journey here involved a comprehensive examination of broadly used tools, roles, and systems to create a harmonious and efficient data management ecosystem that aligned with our evolving business needs.

Shadow IT

Our fourth area of focus was what we commonly referred to as **shadow IT**.

This term emerged from local investments made by business leaders or specific groups that were somewhat in the shadow of the global IT infrastructure. Initially, this was presented as an IT infrastructure problem, with sometimes outdated or locally favored solutions sporadically resurfacing. For instance, some teams might have local solutions for marketing data processing or specialized applications for local business approvals.

The challenge of identifying shadow IT cases persists even today, especially with the global availability of platforms such as Power Apps. These tools empower local teams to create their own applications, addressing exact needs in a self-service manner. To address the challenges here while retaining the benefits, a proper application governance process should be set in place, along with continuous scanning and security mitigation for new applications – something we had missed in the early stages.

Due to the absence of a well-structured governance approach at the time, we ended up with a massive list of local solutions and applications, often rapidly developed in various places. Many of these apps interacted with data or manipulated copies of data, later attempting to integrate changes into the main sources or **Line of Business (LOB)** systems.

To make sense of this complex and poorly documented portfolio of applications, we embarked on a comprehensive analysis. We aimed to determine which processes could be considered globally suitable and integrated into dedicated data services. Often, we discovered that certain applications or functions were developed in isolation, lacking an understanding of how they fit into the global data and application ecosystem.

Roughly half of these shadow IT applications and experiences were deemed to be global fit, either as dedicated applications or as new features awaiting implementation in the global environment. The other half were considered redundant, unnecessary for global use, poorly constructed, or requiring immediate retirement for security and privacy reasons.

Analyzing this space was a challenge due to the constant flux of the portfolio and the continuous discovery of items. However, it allowed us to uncover various unauthorized uses of data, identify data copies and stale solutions, and, importantly, learn why these apps were created in the first place. We recognized significant gaps in data fluency and data fidelity, leading us to set a new standard and focus on fostering a data culture within the company.

This then involved ongoing training and education for our users and the establishment of a community of initial data stewards and experts in various business segments who would help train new employees.

Background work

Moving forward, our fifth area of inventory was proactive (background) data processes.

With the data intake tools we had in place, such as the SRTT UI, we started addressing reactive requests from the business users in a more proactive manner. This approach allowed us to put on the hat of data stewards and serve as role models for data quality. We improved data maintenance and health routines by monitoring incoming requests and acting firmly without waiting for specific triggers.

For example, we noticed that we often received requests for CRM account creation originating from data feeds in the revenue collection system. These feeds detected revenue above a certain threshold but couldn't match it to an existing account or customer.

These transactions then were held as orphaned records, which was fine for revenue collection in total, but problematic at the individual record level. These requests were often derived from naming errors or data-matching inaccuracies. They could also represent genuinely new customers for Microsoft, such as entities with no previous engagement with our sales and marketing teams. We began actively monitoring data injections into the revenue collection system, preemptively creating CRM accounts based on monitoring results and extensive research.

This was just one example of our attempts to gain control over our inventory of local requests, leading to standardization, automation proposals, immediate improvements, or proactive fixes.

The next steps

Matching the output from these five inventory areas with the actual data integrity on the ground enabled us to comprehend the "state of data" across the company.

We combined role experiences, identified data needs, assessed gaps between global Tier 1 IT systems and additional capabilities (both legitimate and shadow IT), and formed an initial portfolio of data services.

This central, globally accessible portfolio, operated by our team on behalf of business needs, served as a data "plumbing" system, addressing critical fixes and changes to maintain data health. We needed to keep our data in a healthy state, enabling background deduplication processes, data cleanup and purging, and more.

While forming the portfolio, we critically evaluated what truly mattered. We differentiated between "must-have" and "nice-to-have" capabilities. Sometimes, we could envision a data service but didn't prioritize it within the data catalog. For instance, CRM contact deduplication, while important, was considered too complex to implement efficiently at the time.

Hence, we prioritized standardized and commonly demanded capabilities for our shared, global data catalog. This catalog represented available data services within the company, enabling users to request data-related executions or results to be performed by the data team in the background. It wasn't a traditional data catalog as known in modern data governance, but a catalog of data services (not to be misunderstood!).

To summarize, the combined outputs from these five inventory areas, approached from both top-down and bottom-up perspectives, led to the identification of a distinct list of data management activities across the globe.

In total, we identified over 1,000 different activities, processes, functions, or data applications actively interacting with and modifying the company's data. Interestingly, this aligns with the period when we truly transitioned into a global team. This wealth of information presented a unique opportunity.

Think about this for a moment: more than 1,000 different data-related activities impacted our core systems worldwide.

They appeared diverse across regions. Optimizing this inventory was crucial to creating a robust global portfolio, emphasizing the shared nature of data across regions.

It underscored the importance of treating data holistically and uniformly, regardless of local interests or previous practices.

Our next challenge was to reorganize these 1,000+ processes into a handful of well-defined global data services, highly efficient and standardized. These services would be centrally executed and available for global consumption. In the following pages, I will delve into the approach we took, explaining how we achieved a remarkable optimization outcome. We ultimately reduced the initial inventory of 1,000+ items to a streamlined list of 72 company-wide data services.

It's an exciting journey, isn't it?

Consolidation paths

Obviously, the consolidation wasn't easy work. Yet we knew what we wanted to achieve – a clear set of well-defined and broadly demanded data services, spanning data operations, data applications, and data platform-driven solutions. This type of upgrade would be massive in terms of technology but would also impose an outstanding challenge in terms of change management and uplift of user experience.

It is like when you know something is hard but totally worth it – you have no other choice but to do it. So, let's see how.

Getting started – streamlining from over 1,000 data services to 72

In the massive world of data management, where complexity and volume often reign supreme, it's crucial to employ logic and methodology to streamline operations.

Imagine having to transition from over 1,000 processes to just 72 data services while ensuring no compromise on impact, audience engagement, or purpose. This formidable task is precisely what we tackled, and I'll take you through our journey of how we achieved it.

To remind us of context, we initially identified more than 1,000 different processes, and ultimately, we streamlined this overwhelming list down to a lean and agile portfolio of data services that could operate globally. Moreover, we also ventured into deploying data applications, or, as we would refer to them today, data products.

So, how did we navigate this monumental challenge? Let's delve into our strategy.

After compiling the initial inventory, we realized that the road ahead required us to take *four distinct paths*, or more aptly, four distinct buckets, to convert these inventory items into future solutions. These can be categorized into three primary buckets, each serving a specific purpose, and a fourth one designed to handle exceptions and special cases.

Naturally, as we combed through the inventory, some items were redundant or didn't align with our global approach. However, we couldn't simply discard them. We needed to find a way to continue servicing these ultra-specific local services and localized versions of existing services.

These considerations played a vital role in shaping our future approach.

Within the inventory, we also discovered true duplicates and applications that performed unnecessary data modifications. Some were relics from a time when local businesses were unaware of more efficient data-handling practices. Our strategy involved a gradual phase-out, merging of capabilities, or complete removal of these redundant elements from our service portfolio.

Now, let's explore these four different buckets where we identified pathways for continued operations and optimization. These buckets were as follows:

- Applications
- No-code solutions
- Data platform solutions
- Exceptions

Let's look at each in more detail in the following subsections.

The first path – data enhancement through applications

The first major direction was to address data gaps, challenges, and issues through improvements and modifications in the existing application landscape.

This engineering-centric approach is often the preferred choice, especially for a software company like ours. For instance, if we identified deficiencies in CRM functionality or flaws in data ingestion processes for revenue collection and management systems or other Tier 1 systems, we would initiate discussions with corporate data engineering teams. These discussions led to the joint development of roadmaps, resource commitments, and release plans to rectify these issues.

In theory, this approach seemed smooth and professional, but we quickly learned that it wasn't always the most effective strategy.

In practice, though, addressing data challenges with software engineering in an environment with low maturity posed immediate problems.

It didn't provide the quick fixes that the data team needed or remove existing pain points from data execution. Furthermore, it often led to design flaws. Hence, alongside long-term roadmaps, we also considered short-term solutions such as building specific applications or enhancing existing ones with temporary functionality.

These were like patches or quick fixes to meet immediate needs. Prioritization was based on the urgency and criticality of resolving issues. Our philosophy was clear: if a solid long-term solution wasn't viable, we wouldn't hesitate to deliver short-term fixes or temporary solutions.

It was an effort-intensive approach, and it sparked numerous debates at the executive level.

The dilemma revolved around whether to prioritize agility and address immediate business pain or stick to a more traditional, long-term engineering approach. Over time, we leaned toward addressing immediate demands first, with simple and quick solutions. Only when the most pressing issues were resolved did we contemplate comprehensive, future-oriented solutions.

This approach wasn't universally applicable but it aligned with our experiences.

We found that mitigating immediate business pain was often more crucial than crafting elaborate architecture or giving IT teams the luxury of extensive planning. Our business operated at a rapid pace, with ever-evolving requirements and constant new demands. There was little to no time for in-depth analysis and the creation of well-defined development roadmaps.

In the later years, this philosophy became even more ingrained in our approach, along with a clear understanding that data is different from software.

The rapidly evolving business landscape demanded quick answers, making monumental, rigid solutions or lengthy design and architecture processes impractical. Striking the right balance between business demands and engineering capabilities became paramount. Engineering teams sought to build robust solutions with a focus on design, stability, and performance. In contrast, our business stakeholders emphasized ultra-fast delivery, streamlining everything they considered insignificant, and prioritizing time-to-market and critical task completion.

From a data perspective, our central team found itself mediating between these two priorities. We advocated alternative, non-engineering-based solutions, such as Power Apps, over traditional approaches. We actively educated both parties – businesses and engineers – about the importance of and difference between such data demands and sought pragmatic compromises. This role as intermediaries played a vital role in our data journey.

So, that covers the first path of our strategy. Now, let's move on to the second path, which involves exploring no-application, no-code solutions.

The second path – no-code solutions

This often proved to be the most convenient and quickest path to establish *data operations* or *specific data services*.

> **What exactly is a data service?**
>
> It's a measurable, impact-aligned, and KPI-driven delivery operated by the data team, either solely or in partnership with the business team. This data service operates on a repetitive, continuous basis, making it accessible to the entire company or dedicated stakeholders.

These services were agile and flexible, allowing us to experiment and learn extensively about data domains and evolving business needs. They often served as prerequisites for permanent solutions in the application space or as data products on the data platform. In essence, we piloted data requirements through data service operations, assessed outcomes, and then made informed decisions about the next steps.

It's important to clarify that, at the time, these services reflected popular service delivery and service operations concepts but were tailored specifically to data. They weren't exactly what we now know as DevOps or DataOps, but they laid some early foundations, particularly regarding flexibility and adaptability.

The deployment of these services followed a pattern.

After initial setup and introduction, we would decide whether to maintain them as permanent data services or, in some cases, transform them into data products or data applications. This transition occurred after thorough refinement, clarity on KPIs and expected outcomes, exception-handling mechanisms, business continuity plans, cost analyses, and considerations for monetization.

Monitoring usage, success rates, and user feedback played pivotal roles too. While a few services were eventually phased out due to cost or operational complexity, these were exceptions.

For example, consider the **Venture Integration** (**VI**) work we often performed. Microsoft's continuous acquisitions necessitated the integration of data from newly acquired companies into our existing ecosystem. This data integration, or VI as per the official name, involved fuzzy-matching external data with our own data across diverse domains, with a strong focus on customer master data. It was essentially about harmonizing master records and transactional domain data, albeit in a denormalized schema.

What made this integration complex was that it had to be executed in real time, allowing the acquired company to continue business as usual while ensuring complete data integrity and parity with Microsoft.

This included establishing joint co-selling strategies, go-to-market plans, and unified revenue reporting and recognition mechanisms, all while complying with various regulations and fair competition standards.

Initially, we launched this as a service – a dedicated data service within our data operations team. We assembled a mix of full-time employees, including data engineers, data solution managers, outsourcing leads, and business experts. They worked on defining the core service propositions and executed the first release as an agile service with custom SLAs.

With each new request, we tailored SLAs more specifically based on volume, complexity, and additional requirements. Ultimately, we delivered seamless integration of third-party company data into Microsoft's native sources. It may sound like a project, but we deliberately classified it as a service due to its operational nature, SLA-driven execution, and substantial reuse of existing expertise.

This approach garnered significant success and demand. However, we realized that it was evolving into a continuous pipeline of similar requests. While we were eager to assist, we needed to transform this model, either by converting it into a self-service or by turning it into a live data product that offered reusability, accessibility, and regular updates.

Crucially, it had to maintain automated, high-accuracy data integration. Our maturity in data operations was instrumental in achieving this transition. The knowledge we gained from operating as a service, mitigating data gaps, ensuring data integrity, responding promptly to user queries, and resolving data discrepancies was vital for a successful shift from data service to data product.

This second bucket, data service operations, emerged as one of our most successful strategies. It provided invaluable opportunities for experimentation and an in-depth understanding of our data landscape, including various domains, data quality, and data health across diverse sources. This *continuous data operations* approach facilitated not only our operations but also our learning about data-related challenges in the company.

Our educational efforts didn't stop at internal teams; we continued to educate our business partners and users.

Effective data management requires collaboration between those who provide the service and those who consume it. Through this ongoing partnership, we learned more about data, existing data flows, problems, and challenges within the organization. Simultaneously, our stakeholders gained insights into the data solutions we were providing, enabling them to harness data more effectively and contribute to data ownership and literacy.

This symbiotic interaction was crucial in our journey toward optimizing data services. It ensured that data remained a shared responsibility and an asset for the entire organization.

The third path – data platform solutions

In our exploration of data management strategies, we've already covered two fundamental aspects: data applications and data service operations.

Now, it's time to delve into the third aspect, often overlooked but equally critical – data platform solutions.

Contrary to popular opinion, we didn't initially view data platforms as the ultimate solution to our data challenges. While we eventually ventured into developing data platforms – transforming from classy data copies to data lakes, and even into structured and analytical elements of data lakehouses, and later, growing and embracing the concept of Data Mesh – we understood that going all-in with data platforms in the early stages could be counterproductive.

Given the immature state of our data environment, even achieving success with a simple data warehouse project seemed like a true miracle. So, we opted for pragmatism, concentrating our efforts on creating a data environment that could address the core needs of data management and very basic data analytics. It made possible many of the data manipulations and data operations we needed, yet it was more like a dynamic data sandbox, strengthened with data security and data privacy controls. Eventually, with formidable continuous evolution, with the help of data architects and exceptional contributions by our own team members, it became a full-scale data platform with typical platform elements. But our start was a very simple SQL-driven solution, building all the additional capabilities on the way to our evolution.

But then, why did we even consider data platforms during these initial stages?

Well, during our inventory process, we encountered complex domains and significant data quality challenges that neither data applications nor data service operations could handle adequately. This led us to the conclusion that we needed more intricate and domain-specific solutions to meet these data demands and enhance data quality in the long run.

The already-mentioned VI work serves as a prime example. Initially launched as a data service, it provided invaluable insights that eventually allowed us to convert it into a data product – albeit one that was built on a data platform. I'll delve deeper into the core design principles of our first platform a bit later.

> **When is the time for a data platform?**
> For now, it's essential to grasp that the need for this platform stemmed from the necessity of tackling multi-domain data challenges, rather than simply adhering to popular enterprise architecture or engineering directives.

This isn't to argue in favor of an immediate platform built as part of addressing business needs, nor the opposite. Instead, it illustrates the magnitude of the choices we face and the need to respond to demands with the most suitable capabilities.

To underscore the significance of this aspect, consider another example – the channel revenue reporting example. As Microsoft ventured into the Surface device business, it became evident that we lacked certain capabilities typically associated with hardware producers, such as interfaces with partners and distributors. Initially, we relied on an external SaaS provider to process and feed this data. While sufficient for the time being, it wouldn't support our business's growth and scalability.

Consequently, we needed to bring this operation in-house and develop our solution.

This situation posed a unique challenge. We already had experience addressing specific data needs with custom-built solutions (recall the famous Managed Accounts List application). However, this case was more complex, involving numerous new data domains such as supply chain, partner incentives, inventory, and new operational principles. We stepped in and leveraged some existing data services and created a web-based UI for our partners and resellers.

But that wasn't enough.

The data from channel reporting required validation against hundreds of business rules, data enrichment and integration with internal key systems, and extensive business intelligence capabilities for generating reports on sales, operations, incentives, forecasting, and more.

We soon realized that a dedicated data platform was the only way forward. This platform acted as a central hub for channel revenue, supply chain data, CRM data, partner information, and distributor and reseller details, and featured robust data quality capabilities, real-time processing, and revenue reconciliation. It gradually evolved into a bit of a data lakehouse solution, housing both raw and converted data along with extensive analytics capabilities.

The key takeaway here is that one size doesn't fit all and, sometimes, a universal solution is the most cumbersome due to numerous trade-offs.

In our case, we needed to consider not just a data platform solution but also a highly segregated environment. This allowed us to customize data processing for emerging business needs without impacting the architecture and performance of existing data solutions.

While it was a costly endeavor, it was a justified one. Years later, the data mesh approach would emerge and blur the lines between these distinct approaches by incorporating multiple platforms under seemingly one platform umbrella.

The fourth path – handling exceptions

Returning to our strategic paths (aka buckets), let's discuss the fourth and final one – exceptions.

As a global team, we were avid proponents of the 80/20 rule, which we frequently employed. While I'll elaborate on this principle in *Chapter 8*, let me provide some practical context within our inventory and consolidation work.

So far, we've discussed the inventory from five distinctive angles and three primary execution directions. However, some exceptions didn't fit neatly into these categories. These exceptions often originated from rare data domains or areas where we lacked sufficient knowledge to determine the best course of action – whether it should be an application, a data service operation, or a platform solution.

For example, consider our involvement in philanthropy and sustainability business efforts. We embarked on a journey to assist philanthropic initiatives at Microsoft in managing and utilizing their data more effectively.

We started with data operations, delivering a quick fix through a dedicated data service, and learning as we progressed. Over time, this evolved into a more automated application. Yet, we recognized that, especially concerning sustainability initiative (**Environmental, Social, and Governance (ESG)**) and evolving needs for sustainability reporting, we would require a vastly different solution. While still centered on data and improved data outcomes, the complexity of this challenge demanded an entirely different architecture.

This need culminated in the creation of a separate platform for sustainability, outside the remit of our team. This platform eventually matured into Microsoft Sustainability Cloud, complete with a Sustainability Manager BI solution.

The key point here is that we never shied away from tackling new data challenges, even when they were entirely unfamiliar. Typically, we would start with one of the three buckets and gradually progress into a hybrid solution, embracing a learning path and the "fail fast" principle. Our openness to new challenges, coupled with a global mindset centered on aiding our stakeholders and users in managing data better, fueled our growth and expertise across various domains.

From a planning perspective, predicting effort and accommodating unexpected demands were always challenging. However, this ambiguity was an integral part of our daily lives, and we couldn't fathom not addressing the company's need for high-quality data. In the realm of our work, we consistently rose to the occasion, responding to data challenges with determination and maximum adaptability.

Enabling globally but with a local twist

In the previous chapters, we embarked on a journey, unraveling the complexities of constructing a robust global data management framework.

We delved into the following essential foundational elements:

- The initial inventory
- Setting the paths for future-state data processes
- Addressing the rapid growth of demand for data services

These elements formed the bedrock for our aspirations of functioning as a global team.

Following this, we discussed our strategic approach after completing the inventory and our decision to split our future-focused efforts into several strategic paths.

Among these paths, we defined those three main avenues, and we also considered a distinct approach for managing exceptions.

Next, let's go deep into the practical implementation of our strategies and the critical roles played by technology, processes, and, most significantly, people – our team of dedicated individuals.

This is a classical and renowned trio (people, processes, and technology); however, we will look at them in reverse order.

Technology – the cornerstone of global data management

Our journey begins with technology – not to suggest its supremacy over processes or people but to underline its paramount importance.

We quickly realized the need for enhanced global capabilities to instill confidence and ensure the scalability of our efforts. This enhancement was essential to effectively manage the outcomes of our inventory and the methodical categorization we had undertaken.

We recognized that implementing global processes while maintaining relevance to local data needs and specific rules and exceptions required the establishment of a repository of rules. This led to the creation of an internal **Data Governance Repository** (**DGR**), acting as a shared resource between our team and stakeholders. We carefully documented and preserved known business rules, special exceptions, and specific keywords. These keywords extended beyond language barriers, ensuring our fuzzy matching technology operated accurately across various linguistic nuances.

The data quality rules/DGR was a continuous project, requiring regular updates and maintenance. This sustained effort ensured the accuracy and fulfillment of this repository, guaranteeing the effectiveness of our search results and the ultimate precision of fuzzy matching technology. Additionally, we actively curated a list of words and keywords to be excluded, creating a blacklist for terms that were inappropriate or incorrect. This process targeted the elimination of undesirable terms from every record and table we encountered.

One of the most powerful aspects of these early Data Governance efforts was the transparency achieved between the repository's contents and vocabulary and how these elements were perceived by our business users and stakeholders. This transparency allowed both our team and our stakeholders to collaboratively maintain the repository's accuracy.

Even as we moved all our Data Governance efforts to Microsoft Purview in the later stages, we maintained a vigilant watch over local specifics, unusual wording, or emerging exceptions, either eliminating them from the data or ensuring compliance with the recorded and stored keywords.

As you might have noticed, we emphasized the need to stay relevant, an essential factor for both global and localized capabilities.

This was especially significant in countries where typical efforts significantly diverged from the common baseline. Some of the most distinct differences were observed in powerful economies such as China, Japan, and the United States. In these regions, we encountered numerous examples illustrating the importance of adapting to locally differentiated processes and specific rules for success.

The second aspect of enhancing technology in the data application space was the development of two additional critical capabilities – namely, *data uploads* and *data matching*:

- **Data uploads**: This capability was conceived as a universal feature that allowed us to extract data from the data platform or directly from source systems, make necessary modifications, and efficiently push it back through APIs. This essentially offered almost real-time data reflection with robust error processing. It allowed us to ensure data integrity across key systems such as CRM, revenue collection, and data applications such as *Managed Accounts List*.

- **Data matching**: We invested in an in-house solution to create a reliable and versatile fuzzy matching engine. This engine, operating exclusively within our data team, became a significant asset. It enabled us to fulfill a wide range of demands, from processing marketing leads to executing complex venture integration tasks. This capability was highly dependent on data match accuracy and was instrumental in various scenarios. Whether we were merging and acquiring companies, aligning data from external sources with existing Microsoft data, or responding to emerging needs such as philanthropy, our fuzzy matching engine played a crucial role in these efforts.

Processes – the core of data management

Transitioning from technology, we delve into the core of our global data management efforts – the processes that emphasize our journey.

We've previously highlighted the pivotal role of data service operations, which served as a driving force for industrialization and the transformation of our inventory outcomes into actionable data services. This approach laid the foundation for a well-qualified portfolio of data capabilities and data services accessible through a unified and published catalog – broadly known as the **Book of Work** (**BoW**). This BoW was made in a user-friendly way, with extensive descriptions for each of the offered services, along with impact and intended usage, audience, exceptions management, quality, success and cost controls, and much more. It served as the basis for all of our users to understand what we do and how, and for us, it represented a summarized *helicopter* view of the impact we deliver.

In addition to operational capabilities, we recognized the significance of providing comprehensive support to our internal customers and stakeholders. This led to the establishment of support services such as the global data management helpdesk capability, featuring a classical multi-tiered approach and additional escalation paths. These pathways facilitated fast-tracking urgent demands and prioritizing critical-to-business requests. It's essential to note that most of the data service operations and helpdesk support were eventually operated as outsourced capabilities.

Balancing local and global aspects was a consistent theme in our processes, ensuring tight integration of data governance and rules repositories into the BoW for data service operations. We also had to create a multitude of standard operating procedures and conduct extensive data literacy initiatives to convey the best practices to our sales, marketing, and finance teams.

Furthermore, in the following years, we developed a comprehensive data literacy and data fluency program, which significantly contributed to fostering a data culture within our organization. Initially, our focus was pragmatic, addressing areas where users faced the most significant challenges. User feedback played a pivotal role in shaping these initiatives, resulting in improved user experience and a higher perception of service delivery.

The success of these efforts formed the foundation of our robust data culture.

People – the pillars of success

The most critical component of our journey was undoubtedly our people.

While we share this perspective from the viewpoint of our data team, it's crucial to acknowledge that our success wasn't solely dependent upon our data expertise but also our alignment with a broader community of exceptional Microsoft employees.

Our team comprised passionate data professionals with an in-depth understanding of data. They were committed to paramount data quality and possessed a profound affinity for analytics and qualitative evaluation. Their firm dedication and avid appetite for learning allowed us to adapt quickly to new technologies and data domains.

In the initial stages, our focus revolved around foundational skills, encompassing technical proficiency and change management skills, complemented by highly specialized role definitions.

This approach allowed team members to excel in their primary roles and evolve into cross-skilled professionals over time. Team members developed core expertise in their primary roles while also engaging in secondary areas of responsibility. Gradually, through cross-education and skill-sharing, our team became completely cross-skilled, interconnected, and versatile.

This combination of technical acumen, operational proficiency, and business understanding was a true breakthrough. The multifaceted nature of our internal data team empowered us to build a robust data culture across the company.

It allowed us to engage effectively with various business units, external partners, and customers.

Our deep understanding of data and practical mindset drove the data culture, which became the foundation of our data strategy – one built on trust, high value, and transformation. Being distributed across various locations in Asia, Europe, the Middle East, and North America completed the need for diversity and inclusion, along with multi-cultural awareness and the ability to discuss and resolve any sort of emerging issues across the world.

In conclusion, the success of any enterprise is inherently tied to its people. In our case, our exceptional team members championed the cause of data culture, fostering trust, and paving the way for transformative and innovative data management.

In the chapters ahead, we'll explore how this passion for data led us to not only improve existing data but also develop new data products and innovations, creating company-wide revenue-generating opportunities for the future.

Summary and key takeaways

Let's look at a few key takeaways from this comprehensive chapter. While the scope of our work was huge and even scary to start with, breaking it down into a few highly specific and well-defined initiatives helped us to stay focused and motivated and accomplish the work efficiently.

Takeaway 1 – approaching the inventory from five diverse perspectives

This highlighted the complexity of localized processes and emphasized the need for streamlining operations as the team transitioned to a global approach.

The introduction of the global SRTT played a significant role in standardizing service delivery. The continuation of inventory efforts involved categorizing data management processes into five perspectives: global request tracking analysis, role experience, corporate applications and tools, shadow IT, and proactive data processes.

The analysis of shadow IT revealed a need for application and data governance and a focus on fostering a data culture within the company. The last area, background data processes, emphasized a shift toward proactive data maintenance.

Takeaway 2 – paths to consolidate effectively

Transitioning from over a thousand processes to 72 data services required strategic pathways.

First, addressing data gaps through existing applications was an option but was not always the most effective.

No-code solutions such as data service operations were agile and ideal for experimentation. Data platforms were necessary investments for complex multi-domain data challenges. Handling exceptions involved navigating unfamiliar territories, adopting hybrid solutions, and embracing adaptability and learning.

Responding to unpredictable data demands requires a dynamic approach and a true commitment to data quality.

Takeaway 3 – people, processes, and technology

In the journey toward constructing a global data management framework, a magic trio did the trick:

- Technology was crucial in managing global data effectively. A data quality repository, which contains known business rules and exceptions, was vital. Regular updates and maintenance ensured accuracy and relevance. Fuzzy matching technology should be language-agnostic, accommodating linguistic nuances – and many more examples.

- Processes are key. Data service operations were fundamental for industrialization and the transformation of inventory into actionable data services. Support services, such as a global helpdesk, expedite urgent demands and prioritize critical requests. Well-written and qualitative documentation and data literacy initiatives are essential for conveying best practices.

- The absolute success of data management efforts relies heavily on highly dedicated and motivated individuals (people). Building a cross-skilled team with technical proficiency, operational know-how, and business understanding is essential. A robust data culture fosters trust and eventually transforms data management faster than any technology or process.

Ultimately, technology, processes, and people are all intertwined, forming the foundation of effective global data management and business transformation.

To address the most emerging data challenges and build powerful long-term solutions, we had to use a variety of approaches – that's what our next chapter is about.

4

"Reactive! Proactive? Predictive"

Data quality (**DQ**) problems can't be put on hold, especially when business teams struggle to do their tasks due to data issues.

This means the first requirement for mitigating a DQ-related issue is always urgent, and the quickest solution is to react by offering on-demand data management services.

As data office teams become more experienced and as data challenges and business needs become clearer, there comes a point where a proactive approach to DQ becomes necessary. However, it remains important to continue addressing reactive tasks.

Moreover, as proactive and reactive capabilities are used over time, they lead to the development of predictive recommendations for data problems and solutions. Ideally, this is handled behind the scenes by businesses, so they don't even have to deal with DQ issues themselves. These problems are then automatically identified and resolved without causing disruption.

The key questions and skill sets we are going to address in this heavy experience-based chapter are as follows:

- How to quickly fix the most critical and comprehensive data issues, and what to focus on the most in the early stages.

- Evolving from reactive to proactive data services – what it takes, what to consider, what to avoid, how to deal with growing scope, ecosystem, feedback loop, and correlation back with reactive work.

- Best practices for predictive data maintenance – surfacing key issues, applying **Machine Learning** (**ML**), using recommendation logic and tunable engines, and enabling users to act on critical feedback. This also made us ready for AI very early in the game.

Addressing urgency

In this section, we are going to focus on several data enablement and support initiatives that were provided by our team to our beloved business stakeholders.

With our scope of work having a growing nature, along with the evolution of the data-related work itself, it became clear that we needed to split these DQ initiatives and data services into three very broad, yet distinctive categories.

These categories coexisted at some points in time, but they also represented a somewhat natural evolution of how a data team should react to the needs of the business for highly qualitative data.

The three categories of data enablement and support were as follows:

- Reactive data services
- Proactive data services
- Predictive data services

This is the way they appeared chronologically and, as we have said, this represents a natural evolution of doing data delivery work. If we compare them all in a single view, we will see the immediate differences in implementation complexity:

Service Type	Time to market	Maturity of know-how	Span of control	Costs and efficiency	Business impact
Reactive	Fast	Little to none	Highly scoped	Intense	Limited
Proactive	Moderate	Moderate	Broad	Moderate	High impact
Predictive	Slow	High	Broad	High Intense	High impact

Table 4.1 – Implementation complexity of data services

> **Maturity path**
>
> The common path is started by reacting to a data request, then optimizing your data flows and data services by being more proactive with data fixes up front, before finally moving to the most advanced model, which is the predictive data management model.

So, let's start with the first category, which is *reactive*, so named because this category was created as a quick response to emerging business needs.

These services initially appeared in our consolidated **Book of Work (BoW)** as part of the catalog of everything that is deemed necessary in the organization.

These were the most high-demand workloads for specific and highly tailored data management or DQ requests. Most of this work was typically quite straightforward.

The top focus for our data team, apart from fulfilling those requests, was also to ensure scalability and to ensure there was a good level of support given to the end users and business requesters in adherence to the progressive SLA, along with leading **Key Performance Indicators** (**KPIs**) and improvement targets.

We focused on continuous education of the business stakeholders about new ways of doing this work better or optimizing further, providing them with their own space to learn how to prevent such reactive data requests. Also, we constantly tried to optimize that space to ensure that the execution was the most streamlined, qualitative, transparent, and effective.

> **You must be a no-drama person and have the ability to quickly manage the risks**
>
> The truth is that with this reactive delivery, you don't need much change management or much leadership, yet at the same time, you need to have a lot of empathy and a rational mindset, plus sometimes some crisis management skills.

Most of these reactive data requests came either from data operations or from data applications when users were unable to accomplish certain work. Much of this work was outsourced quickly, as soon as we were able to stabilize its delivery and ensure that there was a good understanding between the demand and the expected outcome – these two factors jointly became the ultimate enabler of outsourcing work.

To name a few examples, we had CRM master account creation and other object creation in the CRM system done in a highly authoritative way, which needed to be done as a complex and cascading workload that was only performed by the data team. The reason for not allowing users to do this themselves was a lack of maturity and data governance, paired also with pretty complex execution on the data side of the house – for example, in the background (not only did the CRM entry have to be completed with compliance to various rules but data also had to be synchronized with the revenue collection system, the managed account list, and so on).

This reactive type of work was also related to data integration efforts, which were often involved in processing certain external data sources and matching the data from there with the company's internal data, either as part of marketing delivery or as part of data or company acquisition. All these examples were already largely covered in the previous chapters, but I wanted to mention them here as the most typical examples of addressing business urgency with data delivery.

What else do we need to consider here?

I think one of the most important aspects of reactive service response is to see the number of requests that you can gradually convert from front-office work into some kind of back-office work. We will cover this in the next section in more detail.

> **Don't say yes to everything**
>
> One of the things that was very critical for us was to be thoughtful and not commit to the incoming work automatically.

We paid a lot of attention to always evaluating requests in terms of potential data silos, unintentional data damage, and other potential risks for the company. We also protected ourselves from falling into any kind of immediate action or even a kind of panic mode – especially if high business pressure was exerted on us.

As in cybersecurity, every time you feel you are getting pushed to accomplish something quickly and without much consideration, you should do the total opposite.

Pause and think. Think and pause.

Clearly, the demand and criticality are there, but what is the right action here on the data itself?

This truly needs a better investigation. Often, even seemingly straightforward fixes lead to unpredictable cascading effects – because this is data, and data has a lot of integrity and is reused across the company.

Our response to high business pressure to quickly deliver something was to think about the data as the most valuable company asset. And, in this sense, I felt that the data team should always stay in control of this type of internal request and truly be able to evaluate and provide valuable guidance to the business requesters or, sometimes, to engineering teams. Who else then should be the guardians, if not data professionals?

The data team is the best team to consult on what's viable to do with data and what's probably best to avoid. This "guardian angel" function played an important role in that we could filter some of the risky ventures that our business stakeholders would probably go for simply because they weren't aware of the risks. For them, some of the innovative and data-related initiatives seemed natural, and they fell into a kind of entrepreneurial path while underestimating the potential negative and long-term impact on the value of data, or the risks associated with data oversharing and data privacy.

As for us, we were aware of the growing risks associated with exposing our data to some risky adventures or stepping into certain business operations that wouldn't be scalable afterward.

> ### Having controls is essential
> Even today, with Data Mesh in place in many organizations, I wonder how much of these controls are embedded into the partnership between federated owners and data team/data platform providers.

Ideally, there is a need for an open, trusted, and continuously used channel of communication and two-way consultancy to prevent unpleasant and unexpected data faults, while endorsing and supporting the drive for innovation from the business data stewards.

Back then, we had to serve in this function of control, as well as the consultancy and education of the business.

> **Golden rule**
>
> The golden rule was that before we commit to anything, we must reach a common understanding of business goals and the state of data.

If we do not commit to and instead reject those requests, we also should strive to reach a common understanding of why we did so, what are the working alternatives, and whether we could help the stakeholders to re-approach the challenge – but now in a more informed and prepared way. Obviously, the latter was an important part of the overall data fluency and data literacy of the company and largely prevented a repeat of these types of situations as described previously.

Another thing here is to understand from a data team perspective that we often still have to react quickly. Although this never made us happy, obviously, at the same time, we realized you couldn't blame anyone for being unaware of the data or data processing limitations, or for asking for data modifications or data crunching activities that were not recommended.

In those early stages, we couldn't and shouldn't expect our stakeholders to hold that type of data expertise and data literacy even if we had several proactive, extensive education discussions and other communications.

My first piece of advice here is to be a thoughtful leader.

If you have received data to deal with that is labeled highly critical by the business and you have been in discussion about this already before with them, yet it still catches you unexpectedly, in terms of how low the business understanding is, then it is time to hold for a minute. Then, do the due diligence and the work requested. Once the work is accomplished, only then talk to the businesses about how to do it better next time. We clearly found that from the perspective of business continuity and the ability to act with relevance, it's not the right moment to delay the execution of something important and open the topic for debate instead. It is critical to solve something where the data team could be the most helpful, instead of debating or finger-pointing.

My second piece of advice is to continuously communicate with your business stakeholders, with your end users, and even with your own data team.

Anything and everything about how you do the execution, what the recently noted best practices for data management or best practices for DQ are, the ways to consult and reach out for some help before any requests, and so on are all routine aspects of data team delivery, and they are critical for your stakeholders to understand. However, they will tend to forget them quickly, hence why constant communication is crucial.

Also, we need to communicate the opposite: what the data team does not recommend doing, where the data team found some issues with data processing or data updates, data cleaning initiatives that were delayed, or anything else like that that you end up owning as a service. But you want to be as proactive and communicative as possible to prevent anything from going wrong with the users' and stakeholders' understanding.

Having full transparency between data teams and stakeholders is ultimately a trust builder, even when things might go wrong on either side of the house.

Let's get proactive

Let's take the next step in our experience and tap into proactive data services and what it means to be proactive with data services.

In the previous section, I thoroughly laid out the path that we'd been considering, as we would learn about and investigate a lot of demands for data modifications from the internal business groups, based on the incoming reactive requests that we received for data creation, data maintenance, or related data cleanup activities.

We would try then to convert those requests into a more intelligent and more proactive approach. In other words, we wouldn't wait for the business users or the stakeholders to come to us with a defined DQ ask but, instead, learn from already-existing requests, aim to anticipate them, and try to be proactive.

On the other hand, we also were looking through the data itself, especially everything in our sphere of control: mainly CRM data, marketing data (to a certain extent), revenue data, licensing data, and product data. All these data domains were examined deeply, taking the perspective of "fit to Data Quality" and overall data health standards.

By "standards" here, I refer to the most widely used Data Management Association, abbreviated as **DAMA**-developed approaches to DQ. Namely, I mean the following key dimensions:

- **Data Uniqueness**: Absence of duplicates
- **Completeness**: Whether we have a full, expected definition of data
- **Data Accuracy**: Especially on company naming and address data
- **Data Validity**: This is controlled via taxonomy and a metadata dictionary
- **Timeliness**: The last update should match business expectations
- **Data Consistency**: How good the data integration is across our domains

Not surprisingly, we immediately saw plenty of defects in the data.

> **Be empowered**
> We also clearly saw things that we should just go in and fix without waiting for any business input and without even having any learning history from reactive requests.

To give you an example, we found a lot of data in the CRM system that was entered in a rush or was imported into the system without powerful operational governance or quality controls. And so, that data, while not being complete garbage, still lacked a lot of important attributes, or it was just not accurate enough, or it was heavily duplicated.

For all these types of defects, we felt that we could just go ahead and fix them. We didn't need any formal approval or any formal remit from anyone to do it. We also found some integrity issues, which, again, we fixed without waiting for a formal request or business input. Additionally, we thought about some of our more regular processes, following data life cycle goals. I'm mentioning this here explicitly because the data life cycle is different for different types of data. For example, the data for a customer master account definition won't change that often, while the contact data for the same account might expire much sooner.

Here, we had to implement different perimeters and different cycles of data cleanups to address the diverse speed of data being changed, evolving, or even being updated by the external business inputs, such as marketing or sales campaigns, which naturally will detail and validate the data while being in touch with the customers.

On this forensic and experimental journey, we learned a couple of things, and that's what I want to share here.

The first lesson was surprisingly not positive at all.

If you remember my example in previous chapters, I said that we, as good listeners from the data team, received a demand from the business users to create an account in the CRM, based on the inputs we saw being ingested in the revenue aggregation system.

You might recall that we took this as an opportunity to streamline and develop a quick fix, instead of waiting for our stakeholders to submit requests to create a master account based on the incoming revenue. Instead, we would have a process with a type of background intelligence, where we would just regularly scan the revenue aggregation system for newly created revenue allocations that weren't yet explicitly linked to any existing CRM account.

Nice, isn't it?

So, we set up an automated procedure that would take the qualified data (specific criteria-based data) from the revenue system, enhance it, and enrich it to the highest possible extent. Finally, it would automatically create a new master data entry in CRM and link it with the revenue system. Wow, such an automated routine!

We were very proud of this newly automated process, which eventually fixed the data flow gap between two key business systems! I mentioned this example a couple of chapters back as an example of data teams simultaneously listening, but also actively monitoring for improvements, automation opportunities, and small innovations.

What appeared shortly after was shocking for all of us for a while.

I was in a perfect mood. For the last few days, we had been bombarded by compliments from our management and our sister IT teams because of the recent breakthrough in automated master account creation based on incoming revenue criteria. After years of reactive and cumbersome work, we finally had a fully automated and highly efficient workflow. It was the win we had been waiting for for years, and it was only possible due to our deep expertise, extensive business knowledge, and leadership.

I enjoyed drawing some lovely slides outlining the increased speed of go-to-market and also increased *time back* to the sales teams (we used the latter one as a key productivity measure), along with further opportunities for automation and data intelligence, to increase the accuracy of our CRM and revenue data. We were about to present this fundamental win to our Corporate VP and then ask for additional investment.

Suddenly, a chat window popped up from one of my team members. I was eager to respond as she was one of the experts responsible for launching the automated account creation system. "*Just in time,*" I thought, "*I need to ask her for a few metrics to precisely reflect our latest numbers, prior to an upcoming read-out to the VP.*"

Team member (TM): "Hi Aleks, how are you? I have something to talk about."

Aleks: "Sure, all is good. Happy to, and I need from you a few metrics about our recent launch – we need to be sure we sell this story hard!"

TM: "Well… listen, I know it sounds strange, but I have a feeling that we need to stop this process immediately. I think we are doing more damage than good to the business…"

Aleks: "What do you mean?! We have tested it, we have a sign-off from key leaders, it works perfectly, and everybody is happy! Where did you get these concerns from?"

TM: "I've spoken to a few account managers locally, and they said their sales leaders are escalating the urgent need to meet and revisit the account pipeline management as the current system view doesn't match their planning snapshot and resource allocation anymore. They report the unexpected appearance of thousands of accounts, which breaks their revenue baselines and makes it impossible to manage… and it only started a few days ago."

Aleks: "Hmm, when exactly would you say it started?"

TM: "The day we launched our process."

Long story short, we had to put the new process on hold and deep-dive into what happened and why this eagerly anticipated process was a failure in real-life deployment.

The reason for this was that we didn't fully understand the way our business sales operations were managing their accounts, along with the mapping between which accounts were being served by which account teams and how that was aligned with sales territory definitions, segments, industry aspects, and so on. We had a simplified view of this, but not the exact view.

> **Ensure you have a full picture**
> We had totally missed that in our approach and broke the business process, as we were focusing purely on the data, and focusing on that proactive automation and data auto-enrichment.

The process that we were so proud of received a lot of negative business feedback over the next few days. Our dear stakeholders were sincerely surprised by those new accounts suddenly popping into the system overnight without them knowing why, and without them pre-approving and pre-allocating the respective account team resources to manage all these newly created CRM master accounts.

What was the best way to act in this scenario, then?

We realized that, in our case, the right action would be to find the new records while actively monitoring the data perimeter, and then to enrich and recommend that data for consideration to the business stewards, while giving them the power to make an informed decision at the end. Creating new accounts as the master data in the CRM was not the right decision.

On the other hand, the monitoring efforts we put into the incoming revenue records were incredibly important and crucial for the company's sales business long-term success. This alone later led to the development of critical revenue allocation/aggregation capabilities that had an exponential positive impact on us.

This became a learning experience for us, and we made it our focus thereafter to move toward the "Recommendation" principle and try to do all the necessary background work with enriching and monitoring data, but then allow the last step to be owned by our business users so that they could decide whether they want to proceed with our recommended action or make a different decision over the earlier identified and presented decision to their review data.

It was a fundamental decision to aspire toward recommendation-based services, not only from the capability perspective but also from the notion of giving more ownership and more hands-on accountability and control to the actual business users. This will enable us to move more to predictable services and eventually to decentralize data efforts (we will cover this in *Chapter 5*), and later even into the data mesh architecture.

We will see that empowering businesses to make decisions themselves about the data, while having all the technical and data capabilities to support their decisions, was fundamental and crucial for the long-term success of data management evolution.

Now, let's get back to the second thing we learned, which we learned when we set up proactive services.

As I've mentioned, a lot of that proactive work was about basic and fundamental DQ improvements within the data domains and DQ dimensions we had embraced. These improvements were mostly guided by the six DAMA DQ dimensions we mentioned previously. We introduced a number of automatic scans for data health and applied immediate corrections to the data. In connection with learning that we should not be in too much of a rush to apply corrective actions, we deliberately decided not to proceed with these auto-fixes on a daily basis. Instead, we decided to follow more rigorously with the actual rhythm of the business in the company. We created a well-defined and scheduled rhythm of quarterly cleanups during which data would be scanned and fixed automatically on a very transparent and predefined schedule. We also had to have an approved business scope for what would fall into the DQ clean-up activity in every segment of the business and domain. In other words, we introduced quarterly cleanups where the actual execution date would be connected to the business rhythm, typically to allow the business to get ready before big campaigns, massive sales marketing initiatives, long-term planning circles, and so on.

For example, the moment the sales and marketing team stepped into the data analytics and planned their next quarter or next year, they counted on the data in the systems to be as accurate as possible at that moment.

To launch this approach to clean-ups, we had to agree on many conditions, and we had to empower our tools and systems with the ability to quickly correct the data while retaining full traceability and monitoring of what actually we have corrected. This was in case there were some open questions or unexpected behavior of applied corrections. If this happened, we could either roll back those changes or tweak certain fixes, or even certain individual records.

We also found that doing this on a quarterly basis with upfront high visibility and highly predictive user experience to the business groups really was a game changer. These quarterly clean-ups became something that the businesses relied on a lot, and they always came to us to validate that we were ready for our next cleanup. They would wait for the clean-up to be completed before taking an analytical snapshot of the data and moving forward with their planning.

The downside of this is that you are taking some accountability out of business hands in the sense that people will start to become a little bit lazy with their daily tasks or daily jobs of keeping DQ high. They start to feel that even if they don't do this accurately, on a day-to-day basis, then the "magic will happen" anyway, and, by the end of the quarter, we will be able to pick up and correct erroneous records and ensure that the quality is still high.

> **Data requires constant care**
> This obviously had some pros and cons, and we couldn't allow the perception to grow among the users that data was processed only in a rhythmical cycle, and that no attention to DQ was required in between the clean-ups.

At the end of our experimentation path, there was a lot of data usage on an everyday basis by the business users, and they saw the consequences of not paying attention to what had recently been corrected and improved. So, we had to find ways to strengthen the inner discipline while continuing to support and enable the users with an awesome data experience.

The approach we chose was to push for higher in-flight operational governance over the data. We made a so-called "operational data governance" program to ensure that we facilitated the highest quality of data when it is entered, or in daily maintenance, while also not restricting our sales and marketing business with heavy prerequisites or show-stopper requirements for data entry and maintenance. We'll talk more about this in *Chapter 10*, where we discuss how these early activities helped us to become successful with more heavy-lifting data governance efforts at later stages of our path.

For now, to summarize, we learned two key things by implementing proactive services:

- First, there was great potential to apply highly deterministic DQ fixes that were in line with standards defined by **DAMA** for DQ dimensions, and I feel generally we succeeded with this

- The second thing we learned was that before doing something new and innovative, it is vital to consult your stakeholders so that they are involved in decisions and are not only the beneficiary

We will capitalize on this much more as we move on to the next section of our story, predictive data management, and we will learn how to make the most out of this topic.

One thing that is also probably worth adding is that at some point in time, we thought about an alternative approach.

We thought about *a simultaneous fix of all the possible defects at the single record level.* In other words, in this approach, we would not go by the quality dimensions and apply data fixes based on one of those specific dimensions, for example, going after data de-duplication of customer master accounts first, and then looking at data completeness on the same records, and then looking at data accuracy, and so on.

Instead, what if, even if we encounter a single defect on a record, we immediately stop the process and validate this entire record for all possible associated defects and fix them all at that moment, and only then move to the next record? By doing so, we would not come back to the record within a noticeable period, thereby reducing the overall amount of clean-up effort and achieving greater homogeneity of clean data.

We carefully evaluated this process by doing several DQ scans and pilot projects and, in the end, we decided not to proceed with that idea. The main reason for this was the real-life entropy of the data and the fact that it would change too often and hence would need to be updated too often, too. Even if we had processed data fixes previously at the record level, there was a very low guarantee that these fixes would be sustained long enough to be of any use.

However, it was good to test it, and it was an important practical experience. It might work well elsewhere, with more controlled and predictive updates. In a way, it also helped us to focus on those quarterly/monthly cleanups rather than trying to spend too much time fixing the day-to-day accuracy of the data. Not ideal cadence though, as you need data to be qualitative at any time, hence we made extra operational data governance controls while trying to facilitate everyday discipline on the quality, completeness, and accuracy of data entry and data updates.

To sum up, we met the most important of our business expectations, along with being efficient with our computational resources. It was just sufficient to run it on a quarterly (and sometimes monthly, or on a special schedule) basis, perhaps with a few exceptions here and there.

Achieving higher understanding and buy-in from business users and stakeholders in terms of their expectations from the data team at any given moment was critical, and those scheduled DQ cleansing activities did the job and had the impact we wanted. Clearly, it was far from an ideal approach to any known data architecture, yet it was still the closest to real-life business needs while allowing the data team to have a stable, reliable, and repetitive execution workload. Again, the pragmatic way won over a better way.

Path to predictive data management

Let's continue the evolution of our data services. We discussed reactive services first, where our data team was in a position to simply react by providing necessary support for the businesses whenever a DQ issue or a data need appeared.

We've talked about proactive services too, and how we turned reactive into proactive, albeit with some failures and learning along the way.

We went by the twofold path, where, on one side, we analyzed what we learned from our reactive requests, and then tried to convert those reactive requests into proactive data fixes, whenever it felt viable. On the other hand, we also identified a number of very deterministic and straightforward fixes of the data itself, which we could just do fully on our own remit, following the standard definitions of DQ dimensions. So to say, there were data fixes that just needed to be done... period.

We've also mentioned the third direction of this, which we decided to call *predictive*. We may think that predictive and proactive are kind of the same, but the way we differentiate them is that predictive services would have much higher intelligence built into the data processes and/or services.

Looking back, we saw that our proactive services were a rather bulky, blanket type of approach where you have a massive DQ issue or some persistent DQ fixes to apply, and we pursued it in an "all-or-nothing" way. Much of it could have been turned into an almost fully automated process with a sense of regularity and continuous monitoring of the DQ perimeter for newly appearing defects, while constantly fixing existing, well-known defects in an automated way (and surely also fixing the root causes of them).

The preceding approach was very successful in many simple workloads, and we gave examples of our quarterly cleanup activities for the CRM data.

Similarly, we got good traction with the revenue recognition system by just doing highly deterministic de-duplications or enriching/augmenting the missing attributes via direct updates. These processes worked well, and we got great credit from the stakeholders on the actual state of data after the fixes were applied.

Soon, though, we realized that to be able to act more intelligently and powerfully, we would need a different approach altogether.

On the one hand, we had to become much better at anticipating where data issues could be. This meant that we stepped back from simply automating data requests and data fixes, and instead, we looked more deeply at the root causes. We would anticipate the existing issues and new gaps in our data ecosystem forming a constant inflow of DQ challenges to come up with a highly predictive understanding of where, when, and how we would encounter certain types of data issues, which eventually would need to be fixed so that the businesses could thrive on trusted and accurate data.

On the other hand, the more complex and the more intelligent the solution or fix, the less we would be able to fully decide on the best action by ourselves or rely on and apply a given set of business rules.

In other words, to provide the solution for complex data issues, we would need to be in consultation with the users of the data and be able to determine the most accurate and correct approach, besides already having a lot of our own know-how and experience. We needed an interactive and closed-loop partnership with the business stewards, with constant upgrades and uplifts of our joint knowledge and applied approach.

The hope was that by doing so, we would achieve multiple benefits:

- Primarily, we would learn more about complex defects and, gradually, we would also learn more about how these defects were eventually best fixed by knowledgeable people. These results would directly empower the ML principles applied to the identification of the defects, and hence, we would be able to proceed faster with either the recommendation of a fix or even with the direct fix of a given defect.

- The second benefit would be to have greater involvement of the actual users and owners of the data. This would allow them to start to learn about the fixes applied, the state of data, and the decisions that we took ultimately and jointly to fix our company's data. This would help us to get a more practically educated business community that had not only heard about DQ issues but was also a solid part of problem-solving DQ issues. We would be more focused on learning what the desired state of the data should be and what kind of techniques need to be applied to get the data in the right form. Long-term, this would help to elevate many of our business users into the role of the data power user or eventually to the role of a fully-fledged data steward and data advocate within the business communities.

- Thirdly, and importantly, the given approach provides us with more universal recommendation-based data capabilities, where we can use and reuse predictive principles along with the business rules and ML models to investigate any type of data, validate it from various data health and quality improvement perspectives, and then provide recommendations on how the problem can be solved. These recommendations are then either approved or rejected by the business stewards, allowing a learning feedback loop as part of the ML execution.

Almost any kind of enterprise data could be fed through this flexible approach, allowing a unification of the logic and UX appearance for the users, while being configurable in the core logic engine.

This approach could also be applied to and executed on a variety of business processes, not just for data but across the portfolio of growing business and data applications.

We will be able to gain much more efficiency with this technology, enhance and stabilize our IP, and provide a broad range of enterprise business users with simple and friendly recommender-based solutions that hide the complexity of data issues on the frontline while being able to address the most complex data issues.

Clearly, it will be less cumbersome and less frustrating compared to the previous practices of having a bunch of reactive services and proactive services on the table.

So, how did we turn the page here and move into advanced, predictive processing?

We started with a relatively simple domain, where we saw the emerging business need for a while, but we had no simple solution to provide.

You might recall that, a couple of times in the previous chapters, I mentioned the need to keep CRM data fresh and accurate, especially for business contacts.

When you think about the typical CRM customer account, especially for enterprises, you will have a number of contacts, or contact personas, associated with this account. They could be technical decision-makers, business decision-makers, CXO leaders, and others with whom our sales team will be working or interacting.

Keeping this data fresh and up to date was always a special challenge.

In particular, when we encounter duplication of the data at the account level and while applying the de-duplication, we will always reach a point when we also have to de-duplicate the related contact data. That will be much more difficult as we wouldn't have any external reference for the right data.

In other words, if we have a person named "John Smith" on one account and another person named "John Smith" on a duplicate account, and if we apply de-duplication logic and merge these accounts into one, it won't be easy to tell and decide whether it is the same persona (i.e., the same "John Smith") or whether it's actually two different personas who are working in that company.

Of course, having an email address always helps, but what if you have an email address for one account and a phone number for the other? Also, we wouldn't automatically know whether that contact was still an actual contact for the given account at all, as it might be outdated and not refreshed on the system. Surely, the more attributes are associated with this person (such as email address, phone, address, last activity, last update, and job role), the more likely that you will succeed with the accurate identification of a person.

Thinking beyond this challenge as an initial data accuracy challenge, we will constantly see an evolution of this contact data, which happens in the outer world but might not be reflected in our systems. An example could be that same John Smith getting a promotion in the company and being reclassified from a technical decision-maker to a business decision-maker, which changes the way this data should be classified in the CRM; it also changes the way this is perceived by our sales and marketing analytics and how our sales team should be aware of the people who work on the customer side on this account.

We realized that there is no easy way to do any kind of data magic here without the involvement of the account teams. Yet pushing the account teams to be fully accountable for the accuracy of the data and simply hoping that it's in their interest to keep this data as accurate and up to date as possible would be false hope and overkill.

The middle way would be to identify a moment when data was just updated and then pass it to a recommendation engine, which would run in the background of the CRM and, in parallel, we would constantly monitor what we got as the last update in CRM, for the whole perimeter of **Business Decision-Makers (BDMs)**, **Technical Decision-Makers (TDMs)**, and CXO level contacts.

The idea

The process would monitor many of the system attributes and how this data appears in the CRM, when it was last updated, and when it was last used in any communications by the account teams. It would also check the appearance of this data in the public space, such as looking at LinkedIn or connecting to the Outlook account of the account managers and seeing whether they still used these contacts.

Plus, when corporate emails were bouncing back, meaning that the person had probably left the organization, we would also add that data for monitoring the behaviors around the key contact data.

Based on all these techniques, the engine then would recommend a certain action. Then, these recommendations would be sent in a very simple way, through a basic and friendly UI (originally created as a standalone UI, but later simply integrated into the CRM experience) to the end users.

The system would trigger those defined simple questions and recommendations, going to account managers and account teams, and validating whenever a recommendation was accurate and correct. It would simply ask for "Yes" or "No."

Later, we enhanced the "No" answer with an optional comment note, but we knew that by design and to get any real traction here, we must be very simple. Yes, we would absolutely love to collect more information and turn it into a kind of micro-survey, but then we wouldn't have any real traction from our ultra-busy target audience. We had to live with a discrete minimum of data and figure out internally with additional data mining and data analytics why a recommendation was declined. We analyzed this gradually, expanding our analytical coverage in depth and breadth, step by step, with a limited initial scope.

We started with the small pilot in a couple of geographical areas where we saw a combination of good and bad data, along with highly motivated account teams supported by upper business management, who truly wanted to see progress on the contact information availability and accuracy in CRM.

Going with a very focused and targeted launch in a few regions was highly successful.

Quickly yet progressively, we moved tool deployment to more and more regions until we managed to release it almost as a worldwide capability, albeit still realizing that we would not be able to provide accurate recommendations in every geographical area. And that was fine. That was another aspect of being relevant and being honest, and not trying to implement technology in some places just for the sake of technology while realizing that there is not enough data or not enough readiness for success.

Despite these few places where this contact recommender didn't work or was not able to be launched, we still gathered distinctive proof for this approach.

We did know it made sense, and it landed well with the businesses. This prompted us to launch more of these recommendation-based, predictability-focused data capabilities. Eventually, we launched a couple of very powerful capabilities that were based on the same logic, yet went far beyond the refreshing of CRM contact data.

One of them was co-selling with partners, where Microsoft would share a co-sell opportunity pipeline with our partners and then search and match existing customer definitions to see whether we were working with the same customer on the same (or maybe similar) opportunity.

This operation space was highly ambiguous due to sharing and integrating data across the ecosystems of the partners and Microsoft, but it had a massive impact on sales and high execution priority for operations. We focused on providing a recommended action in the shared data space and shared visibility, which could then be jointly taken by a partner and our assigned partner account manager.

The key here was not only to provide highly accurate recommendations along with an accurate match with the data submitted externally by the partner to us but also to be very mindful of the volume of data to process. Since we've been talking about thousands of requests flowing daily into Microsoft from our partners and being able to accurately identify the right recommended action, learning from feedback and then trying to predict the behavior next time was very important.

Another capability where we also gained extensive traction in the company with this recommendation logic was monitoring our incoming revenue for accuracy and predicting where and when the revenue would land on customers' accounts. Again, we used the same logic: we would try to maximize the existing knowledge if duplicate records and unqualified or badly qualified records appeared in the revenue system, and it would be a task for us to provide the best possible recommendation on whether this data should be fixed or merged, or a different action.

That helped our sales and business operations teams to realize that there are often critical gaps in revenue flows and they have a great capability in place, a quick and responsive system that learns from their action and continuously improves.

The background work

In the background, we, as the data team, would be actively monitoring the decisions the sales team was making for these recommendations, along with continuously monitoring new defects and new challenges in that space. We would tweak and fine-tune the engines for the highest efficiency and do this in regular releases, as well as take proactive input from business teams about where we should focus the most, or address the latest business rules around revenue segmentation and classification.

A wonderful effect from a technology perspective is that all three examples (one for the contact accuracy in CRM, another for the accuracy of the co-sell process, and the final one about the revenue attribution) were powered by the same engine in the background, with a highly similar data architecture and design. The data domains were very different, but from the technology perspective and from the way the business rules were made configurable, and how easily we were able to move from the first example to the second and then to the third, we achieved a completely different level of scalability and technical innovation.

It was an absolute breakthrough compared to where we had started not long ago with highly customized, reactive data processing, or even with some automated, highly customized, and not-so-easy-to-adjust automated background proactive DQ processes.

Nowadays, I would say that of course a lot of these predictable data processes will become AI-driven, and they are already becoming AI-driven as we speak. I see this as one of the most wonderful low-hanging fruit, where applying AI validation to data and using AI-provided recommendations to fix data defects is one of the most powerful capabilities.

We will see this absolutely thriving going forward, as AI will take on more and more automation and intelligence, and recommend more immediate, interactive DQ fixes, especially in master data or data that has a good external reference (or that is part of an LLM model). AI will also learn about existing and common data models and data processes across different data providers and disciplines, democratizing referential data availability and discoverability, while keeping it refreshed, accurate, traceable, and up to date.

This is a big advantage compared with human knowledge, where we would not normally expect someone to know a variety of different database designs and the principles of data storage and data architecture, and even table-level and attribute-level setup across CRM, ERP, finance, and other popular solutions. From an AI perspective, all this know-how could be just a fundamental part of LLM training and acquired common knowledge.

Summary and key takeaways

There are so many great takeaways from this chapter, so let's try to group them by the three main evolutional aspects of data services enablement and delivery.

Takeaway #1 – addressing urgency and data demand, with quick and impactful actions, to win the time for the next steps

- **Initiate with a reactive approach**: Prioritize urgent business needs with an empathetic crisis management mindset while ensuring support and efficient escalation paths.

- **Strategic outsourcing**: Move defined and precise processes to outsourcing, ensuring meticulous execution and adherence to SLAs.

- **Managing co-impact and triggered actions**: Anticipate cascading actions resulting from operational decisions, highlighting the need for a data playground or data sandbox to navigate complex requests without further complications.

- **Effective response strategies**: Establish an in-house SWAT team for immediate response, conduct thorough due diligence to fully comprehend requests, communicate extensively with stakeholders to ensure mutual understanding, and avoid unproductive debates that delay resolution. Communication and proactive updates play a critical role in maintaining smooth operations and averting potential disruptions.

Takeaway #2 – add proactive capabilities, converging from an initial and reactive approach to a solid set of data services

- **Transition from reactive to proactive**: While a shift to proactive measures seems intuitive, the practical implementation can be challenging. Balancing the need to address numerous tactical data improvement opportunities while avoiding an exhaustive fix is crucial. Implementing periodic scheduled clean-ups aligned with business cycles proved effective. Integrating business insights with data management efforts further enhanced the predictive capabilities of DQ and data management.

- **Striking the right balance**: The challenge lies in prioritizing data improvements without overwhelming the system. Quarterly or monthly clean-ups, transparent to the business and aligned with the **Rhythm of Business (RoB)**, served as a practical solution. Despite its architectural limitations, this approach effectively showcased the value of ongoing data maintenance, facilitating the background management of clean data.

- **Leveraging business involvement**: Sourcing demand from reactive scenarios and learning from successful proactive RoB initiatives led to the development of predictive DQ and data management strategies. By incorporating business insights and critical inputs, the data team successfully transitioned toward predictive data maintenance, emphasizing the value of data-driven decision-making.

Takeaway #3 – path to predictive data maintenance – as your maturity grows, you will be ready to tap into the next evolutional step

- **User input is key**: The path to predictive data maintenance involves close collaboration with users and corrective actions based on recommendation logic

- **Start small**: Our contact data cleaning, integrated with the CRM, evolved into powerful co-sell and revenue correction processes, showcasing the power of data capabilities

- **Learning from everywhere and the feedback loop**: Flexibility and a continuous feedback loop in the logic-based engine led to enhanced accuracy through applied ML

- **The future is AI-driven**: Balancing AI-powered insights with continuous learning is crucial for sustainable and effective data management

Before we jump into the AI-powered future, let's look, in the next chapter, at so-called data domains and their business ownership, and how they are used to drive data accountability and the federation of effort.

Part 2:
Build Insights
to Global Capabilities

In this part, we continue the data journey, now introducing powerful and proven capabilities such as a **domain-driven approach** and business and data stewardship, along with defying, advancing, and preserving the company's specific data intellectual potential. At the same time, we showcase how fostering an effective framework based on the **Pareto 80/20 principle** helps to navigate all kinds of data challenges. We will also cover outsourcing and in-sourcing options, and why they matter in the complex world of data delivery.

This part includes the following chapters:

- *Chapter 5, Mastering Your Data Domains and Business Ownership*
- *Chapter 6, Navigating the Strategic Data Dilemma*
- *Chapter 7, The Unique Data IP Is Your Magic*
- *Chapter 8, The Pareto Principle in Action*

Mastering Your Data Domains and Business Ownership

In this chapter, we are shifting gears and will be reflecting on our journey in a fast-forward way. The establishment of a highly efficient, global, central Data Management team marked a significant achievement. This team caters to thousands of internal users daily, operates on a specialized data quality platform, and enables both proactive and predictive data management while ensuring accessibility.

Initially, this achievement was gratifying. However, challenges arose with the increasing complexity of data issues and new domains demanding attention. The costs of maintaining this expanding platform, adaptable to changing business needs and new functionalities, began to be too expensive. Despite stakeholders' satisfaction and willingness to cover rising costs, it was evident that a change in strategy was needed for sustained success amid these evolving challenges. But what was this change in strategy?

Let's dive deep into this together in this chapter by addressing a number of interesting dilemmas and covering new concepts. These are the main topics of this chapter:

- The path toward domain thinking
- Defining data and business domains

The path toward domain thinking

In *Chapters 3 and 4*, we reflected on the extensive range of services we've offered to our business audience. We embarked on this journey with reactive services, prioritizing the immediate satisfaction of business needs. This approach was foundational, setting the stage for our evolution into proactive services, where our aim shifted to staying ahead of potential data quality issues and proactively addressing them before they impacted our users.

This progression led us to the advanced stage of predictive data management, where we excelled in anticipating data gaps and challenges, enabling an intelligent, learnable, and repeatable response.

The implementation of these diverse services marked a pivotal moment of success within the company.

We were particularly effective in resolving the most intricate and concerning data issues, adeptly responding to the need for high-quality data. At this moment, we sensed a shift in our approach – from revolutionary strides to a more evolutionary pace. This was made evident by a significant reduction in urgent, demanding issues, and a notable increase in business enablement and satisfaction with our data services.

Our strategy of regular data clean-ups, combined with targeted applications (such as a **Managed Accounts List (MAL)** and **Service Request Tracking Tool (SRTT)**, among many other tailored solutions), had a profound ground-level impact. Furthermore, our predictive services, grounded in recommendation logic, amplified this impact, utilizing our established data foundations.

Despite these advancements, we soon recognized a growing demand for our services, especially as we ventured beyond our initial focus areas, such as sales, marketing, and revenue data.

We began exploring new knowledge domains within the company, such as supply chain management, device channel sales, the Microsoft Philanthropies business model, and the intricacies of mergers, acquisitions, and venture integration initiatives. This expansion brought into focus the scalability challenges of our data engineering and data operations, a concern that persisted even when we had plenty of resources.

The growth in the portfolio of work and its impact fueled the wish to split responsibilities and return some of them to the business. We made a solid step forward by building partnerships with business users, growing their data literacy, and using predictive data management, along with the introduction of the concept of data domains – business-oriented, data-oriented, and hybrid domains. With the creation of virtual teams and data views that were portrayed in a domain-specific way, we eventually nailed down the approach.

This was a true "aha" moment – as we fast-forward to a crucial point of this realization, we found ourselves celebrating recent successes yet simultaneously contemplating the need for a radical revamp of our data management approach.

Our services operated more efficiently than ever, evidenced by exceptional KPIs and soaring business satisfaction. However, we faced the challenge of evaluating two significant areas for our future positioning and success:

- The first area centered on managing expanding *data domains*, where the intersection of data and business needs required a more reliable and scalable approach. As we ventured into new business areas, we had to consider constraints such as team size and centralization, which affected our capacity for growth and the ability to respond swiftly to evolving data needs.

- The second critical area was *ownership*. Our strategic vision was that we would start by recognizing limits and defining new accountabilities, then continue with building a joint understanding of business and data domains and, most importantly, initiating the transition of data accountability back to the business, while being reassured of the business users' increased involvement in the data stewardship role. The final phase in our vision involved us stepping back to focus on strategic cross-domain initiatives. Our discussions in the previous chapter highlighted the growing role of business users in our predictive data maintenance, a development that emerged as users became more involved in data practices. Here, the future partnership between data professionals and business owners hinged on deepening co-involvement. We envisioned a scenario where business users transition from mere participants to actual owners of data, sharing the challenges of data quality and management and gaining clarity on future data prospects and needs.

State-of-the-art data management

At this point, we had successfully established a highly efficient global Data Management team. This team, operating on a specialized data quality platform, provided a range of data services to various internal business units, catering to thousands of daily users. The underlying data platform enabled proactive and predictive data management and ensured widespread data accessibility.

Yet, as we expanded, we faced complexities arising from new business challenges and new knowledge domains. These emerging tasks demanded attention and resolution, and the costs associated with maintaining and evolving our platform began to strain our budget. Despite our stakeholders' satisfaction and their willingness to cover the increasing costs of ownership and maintenance, we recognized the need to adapt our approach.

A new strategy was essential to ensure sustained success amid these evolving challenges, prompting us to rethink and innovate in our quest to continue delivering exceptional data services in a dynamic business environment.

Defining data and business domains

As we progressed to the next stage of our data management journey, we were tasked with devising a strategy that would not only address scalability challenges but also chart a course for our future collaboration with business teams.

This called for an evolution in our approach – timed to overlap with our recent achievements – where we successfully enabled significant advancements in data services.

That being said, our growing portfolio of work, bolstered by increasing reliability and popularity within the organization, began to create a snowball effect.

The extensive ownership of data services, coupled with the escalating demand and the expanding scope of our platform, started to overwhelm our capacities. We had evolved into a central team managing global data for the company; with each success in tackling critical data quality and discoverability issues and leading data innovation efforts, the workload became increasingly challenging to manage effectively. In a way, we were victims of our success.

We found ourselves at a crossroads, necessitating the redistribution of responsibilities –essentially, planning to return them to the business units from which they originated.

Well, that sounds surprising.

Let's revisit this entire scenario to have the full context. This idea might seem counterintuitive at first glance, but we'll delve deeper into the details and the precise thinking behind it.

Our partnership with business users – the end consumers of our data – has always been exceptional. You might recall our emphasis in previous chapters on aligning data leadership with business needs. Now, boosted by our efforts in data literacy and education and our deeper involvement in predictive data management, we saw an opportunity to reassess our operations. We questioned whether there was a way to shift more ownership to business data stewards, allowing us to concentrate on specialized, innovative data challenges.

We considered a few options:

- Expand our own team
- Transition the core of everyday work to another team
- Transfer the execution of daily operations back to business teams

The first one was the least realistic, primarily due to work scope and focus considerations – we really didn't want to become a bottleneck in our daily execution processes.

Another option was to delegate our responsibilities to a different operations team within the company, who were less mature in data management but capable of maintaining ongoing data operations and service delivery. This would free us to focus on areas requiring advanced expertise. However, upon further reflection, we concluded that a more radical change was needed – transferring data management back to the business units. This might sound surprising as we had previously centralized these functions to streamline and enhance data capabilities for business users, with the exact purpose of relieving them from time-consuming daily tasks.

Nevertheless, the more we contemplated the successful realization of our ambitions with data, the clearer it became that ultimate accountability for data should reside with its users. The central data team would continue to facilitate cross-company data standards and broad data accessibility, but the true value and application of data would be best determined by business users themselves.

Recognizing and accepting this truth led us to the next challenge: organizing this transition realistically, considering our past experiences.

> **Empower the business teams**
>
> It was crucial to truly empower other teams, understanding that a mere transfer of our current data operations and engineering tasks to business units would likely result in dissatisfaction, failure, and productivity loss.

We addressed data significantly differently than the business teams. Our approach to data was holistic, addressing interconnected challenges suitable for a global operations model. In contrast, business teams were typically only focused on specific business lines, utilizing data within their unique contexts.

For instance, sales and marketing teams often work closely, sharing customer data but focusing on different aspects of the customer journey. This operational model is common across many enterprises, indicating that empowering business units with data ownership requires defining clear, naturally bounded areas of responsibility – or, in data terminology, the data domains aligned with those respective business functions.

As we examined the concept of data domains, we aimed to organize our work around these domains, fostering ownership among data users in each area. This was way before the announcement of data mesh architecture; our goal was to find a new common ground for scaled partnership with the business community, and not to re-architect the platform.

So, what constitutes a data domain? We identified two main approaches: *business-oriented domains* and *data-oriented domains*, with a possible third – a hybrid model combining elements of both. To be clear, there is no right or wrong approach to implementing any of those domain tactics – rather, it is about identifying the most suitable one for a given business case or based on data availability. For example, when building data products, depending on how big the scope of the data product is, it could span across several domains or, conversely, be sharply focused on a single domain. Let's talk about the main approaches in more detail:

- **Business-portrayed domains**: These mirror business functions and data usage, aligning with the enterprise's organizational structure – for example, domains (such as marketing, sales, revenue reporting, and credit control) overlapping with data domains and sharing entities (such as customers or partners). The primary focus here is to match data usage with business functions, such as splitting the revenue domain to reflect different business group needs.

- **Data-oriented domains**: These focus on the end-to-end usage of specific master data entities and their related objects, such as customers, contacts, products, or opportunities. This approach acknowledges the overlap and multiple appearances of a single master data element across various business contexts. In our case, we combined these appearances under one master data domain, recognizing differing operational uses across the company.

- **Hybrid (matrix) domains**: This approach intelligently combines business and data domains, creating exclusive domain combinations due to specific usage or uniqueness. In our case, we prioritized data ownership, adding business domain considerations. An example is MAL, which combines strategic customer accounts with revenue data and its own unique attributes, forming a distinct hybrid domain. Everything that would qualify as a kind of *thing in itself* – meaning an end-to-end business process supported by underlying data – would likely end up as a hybrid domain. Besides the MAL example, we could have similar cases such as **Customer and Partner Relationship Management** (**CPERM**), which represents a defined perimeter of customers and partners whom we surveyed about their satisfaction with Microsoft, and maintaining that data almost as a dedicated data mart. This can be thought of as data resulting from regular surveys filled out by customers and partners. This data remains connected to the master definition of the customer or partner account; however, since it has been significantly enriched and augmented, it would now have too many and too specific attributes to fit anywhere else. Further along this path of exploring hybrid domains, the majority of data integration solutions (data products) would typically span across several business and data domains, resulting in highly denormalized and tightly connected data views.

The following figure is a visual of the different domain approaches:

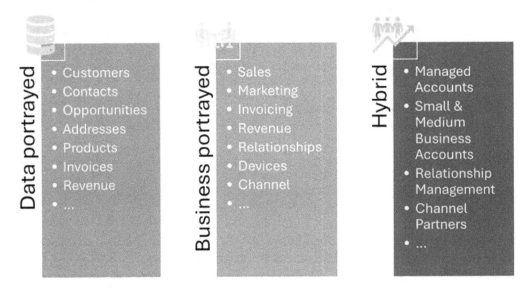

Figure 5.1 – Domain types and underlying data examples

As we embarked on this journey of domain organization and empowering business units with data stewardship, we were paving the way for a more collaborative, effective data management landscape. This new approach aimed at harnessing the strengths of both our central data team and the business units, fostering a partnership that recognized the unique value each brought to the table in managing and utilizing data for the company's success.

Broad use of data domains

Exploring the concept of data domains deeper, particularly in relation to hybrid domains, we recognized their alignment with certain characteristics of data products. Our initial focus was on establishing domains as a foundational layer, serving multifaceted purposes ranging from data governance and security to facilitating easier data analytics. Interestingly, we even developed a set of data products that exactly matched our data-oriented domain definitions. This approach was designed to simplify the discoverability and consumption of data from our platform, while distinctly separating the paths for data product development versus domain ownership.

But why was this approach so significant, and what were the real benefits?

While the upcoming data mesh design concept was a tempting factor, our rationale was beyond just embracing modern architecture and rather was focused on business enablement with a user-friendly view of the data. We were driven by two highly impactful objectives, aiming to achieve the best of both worlds in terms of the partnership between business and data teams, as follows:

- **Virtual teams for hybrid domains**: We established virtual teams that mirrored the structure of hybrid domains. These teams included our dedicated **Subject Matter Experts** (**SMEs**) and business owners/stewards, forming a knowledge center of excellence for specific areas, such as MAL or CPERM. Envision these teams as pods, where data team members with expertise in specific data domains (such as customer, revenue, or relationship management) worked closely with business owners and data stewards. This collaboration provided a shared data foundation, equally accessible and useful to both data and business professionals, with business stewards assuming the role of domain owners.

- **Views unified by domain-portrayed data**: To support these virtual domain teams, we created views unified by domain-specific data. For example, when Microsoft acquired GitHub, we had to quickly establish a joint co-sell process between these two business entities. The resulting solution was a connected data product that focused on co-selling as the ultimate business goal while spanning several data domains across both GitHub and Microsoft data estates. This allowed teams to observe their specific data in a consolidated, consistent, and interrelated manner. The structure resembled a snowflake or hub-and-spoke model, where key subject data was positioned at the center, surrounded by all the relevant data dimensions, correlations, connections to other domains, and essential metadata. This setup enabled a holistic view of data, making it easier to understand how different pieces of data interacted and influenced one another within and across domains. Key business outcomes with a complex underlying structure, such as revenue, co-sell, and customer experience, are usually great examples of hybrid domains.

By adopting this approach, we aimed to empower and connect both data and business teams. The virtual teams for hybrid domains fostered a deep understanding and ownership of data, ensuring that domain expertise was leveraged effectively. Meanwhile, the domain-portrayed data with its unifying view provided a comprehensive business perspective on data, enhancing our ability to make informed decisions and drive meaningful insights.

> **Hybrid domains connected understanding**
> This strategy was instrumental in bridging the gap between data management and business objectives, creating a more integrated, efficient, and effective data environment.

The following figure shows an example of the overlapping domains, surrounding the unified view of Revenue as the ultimate business goal. In this case, we see overlapping teams composed of data SMEs and business stewards from different business groups (**Small-to-Medium Businesses** (**SMBs**) and

MALs) collaborating within the joint domain space of Revenue, while at the same time managing their own specific domains and attributes.

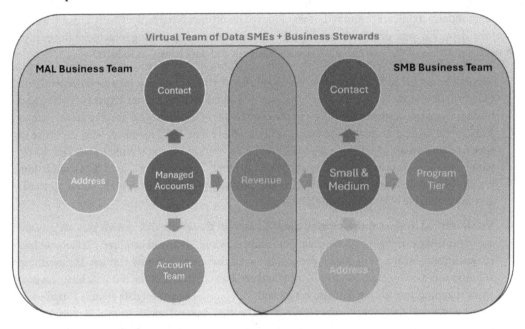

Figure 5.2 – Collaboration model between virtual teams over domain-portrayed data

In our data architecture framework, as delineated by the domains and their definitions, we intentionally designed overlaps in certain areas while keeping others distinct and somewhat separated.

This approach was intentional, aiming to unify the understanding of data consumption at a high level between business owners and the data team. We envisioned a scenario where both parties would view the same *business need + data* within a combined domain. This alignment would allow for a clearer comprehension of the data challenges within a specific domain, facilitating better planning and strategy development.

> **Finding similar patterns**
>
> Portraying unified data entities as data domains created a bridge connecting similar data usage patterns across various business units within the company. This structure provided us with a holistic view of the cumulative impact on the underlying master data.

It's essential to emphasize that while this was a crucial aspect of our data architecture, it was even more pivotal for the organization of people and data. The formation of cross-disciplinary virtual teams, or pods, operating with shared business objectives and a unified view of the data foundation was a critical alignment point. This framework helped business users become more acquainted with the necessary data, progressively leading them toward genuine ownership.

From the data team's perspective, we approached customer account usage as a singular master data domain of *Customer*, which was contextually applied in various applications across domains such as *Sales, Marketing, Sales and Marketing*, and *Revenue*. Our team's expertise and SMEs delved into diverse examples of data usage, exploring variances in workflows and the context of extended attributes and comparing data life cycle patterns. We also scrutinized associated data quality issues that arose at the intersections of these domains, along with other edge cases or instances where data integrity was compromised.

As we progressed, this comprehensive understanding and domain expertise would lay the groundwork for scaling with a certified *data product* approach – we will cover this in *Chapter 11*.

Ownership – business teams versus the data team

Progressing in our data management evolution, we acknowledged that, despite our successes, we were not faultless superheroes.

There were limits to how far we could stretch our service excellence and our capacity to address every emerging data issue. It became evident that we needed to become more selective in our approach, redefining our accountabilities and introducing new responsibilities for the business teams. This selective approach was critical in maintaining our effectiveness and focus.

The work we had done in defining a joint understanding of business and data domains, coupled with establishing a physical layer of domain-driven data views, achieved more than just innovative visualization of data challenges for our stakeholders. It helped us maintain a concentrated pool of knowledge within each domain. This deep domain knowledge was pivotal in driving next-level improvements that were sharply focused and ultra-tailored to specific business needs. It also engaged business users more deeply in stewardship and data ownership roles.

To accommodate these flexible needs, we occasionally had to further customize our approach.

For instance, we split the *Revenue* domain into sub-domains for SMBs and large corporate businesses. Although the underlying data schema was largely similar, the combination of business processes, data usage, and life cycle varied significantly between these domains, necessitating dedicated virtual teams for each.

This unification of the data team with business stakeholders through shared domain-portrayed data views imposed operational principles and shared data knowledge. It was a clear articulation that we were all in the same boat, working toward common goals and benefits. Simultaneously, it laid down a foundation for further role separation and distribution – a vital consideration toward our goal of shifting the workloads.

As business data stewards grew more knowledgeable and experienced, we felt confident in granting them more control, ownership, and powerful solutions. Where we once chased down business rules from stakeholders, developing extensive documentation and system controls, key business users now came forward with new or updated rules, enablement principles, and controls.

Being in the driver's seat

Empowered with self-service applications and rule-based, recommendation-driven predictive data solutions, they effectively combined key controls over emerging business needs with their primary roles in business delivery.

This empowerment and education shifted them away from the operational gimmicks and escalations of the past.

It was a defining moment for both sides to re-evaluate our potential and strive for a different, more ambitious setup in our partnership.

This shift also enabled us to step back from frontline roles and focus on two major aspects:

- Transitioning ownership and controls to business teams where feasible
- Concentrating our efforts on strategic cross-domain initiatives, such as global federated data governance, data-mesh-operated platforms, and driving innovation from our data

A milestone

As we prepare to explore the tactics and dynamics of executing these principles deeper, it's important to recognize the strategic significance of this directional shift and the need for a comprehensive learning curve to achieve success.

It had been a few years since we faced high demand for data quality and the need to provide robust service care to enable business partners with clean and reliable data, without distracting them from core business capabilities.

We took the lead in those days, earning the title of *the team that cares*, with responsibility for data quality in front of our business partners. We covered the importance of being relevant to business needs, internal leadership, and the change management skills needed to establish solid data foundations in the company in previous chapters.

But a couple of years later, we were considering handing back these well-established controls and data services to our business stakeholders.

This was in response to the need for scalability across new business domains and the growing difficulty for a centralized data team to handle every aspect of daily data management. Outsourcing and the development of a modern, established data platform, combined with sandbox environments and innovation capabilities, played a significant role in our success. However, this perspective represented only one side of the coin – our view as the data team.

Despite our stakeholders' satisfaction and willingness to cover additional costs, we needed to create a new immersive reality where they could take over much of the day-to-day work.

But how would they manage?

Our stakeholders were content with our services and even willing to fund any incremental costs incurred by our central data team. We could have easily secured additional funding and resources from the board of executives, given our impressive KPIs and the tangible benefits of our work.

However, we recognized the necessity of scalability and innovation with more comprehensive data capabilities, prompting a call to action for business stakeholders. To achieve this, we had to create a desire for change on the business side. As change management methodology teaches, significant shifts start with fostering a desire for change. Our strategy here was threefold, highlighting domains, controls, and assurance as key areas of interest for our business partners.

> **Elevator pitch**
>
> Our *elevator pitch* message was straightforward: "You know your data better than us, so how about we give you full control to operate it, assuring you that things won't fall apart and we'll still be close by?"

We emphasized the deep knowledge business teams had gained about their data and how our domain-portrayed views and hybrid domains ensured mutual understanding. The focus on "full control" meant handing over necessary resources (including access controls, data apps, operational scorecards, and reporting) to the business teams, encouraging them to take ownership. The assurance aspect was built on the trust we had established, providing comfort that we would continue to support their data needs while shifting to more powerful capabilities.

As we prepared to implement these changes, we faced the challenge of upgrading our operating principles.

After our efforts in centralizing and globalizing data management, it was time to decentralize and empower business partners to take control. This required a new set of change management practices and a redefinition of operational principles between teams.

The shift-left principle

We adopted the **shift-left** methodology, focusing on getting closer to our customers and defining matured data and business domains. We also pivoted this principle using the **data as a supply chain** approach, modeling the end-to-end data flow between us and our business stakeholders. This model aimed to optimize data flow and enhance our partners' ability to manage these controls effectively.

The real need here was to upgrade our operational principles. As we were shifting from a centralized to a decentralized approach and started to execute the aforementioned shift-left strategy – focusing on well-defined, mature domains – we had to take a number of strategic considerations for this approach. We succeeded by balancing knowledge retention and giving full control to business domains while striving to ensure a positive impact without unnecessary complexities. This once again underlined the critical importance of change management in implementing new operational agreements.

From inventory and consolidation to predictive data management, our journey has been about centralizing efforts. Now, we were at a milestone where we needed to decentralize our shared efforts in data management and enablement, requiring a shift in our approach to empower business teams to take the reins.

The general shift-left custom framework looked like the following in our case:

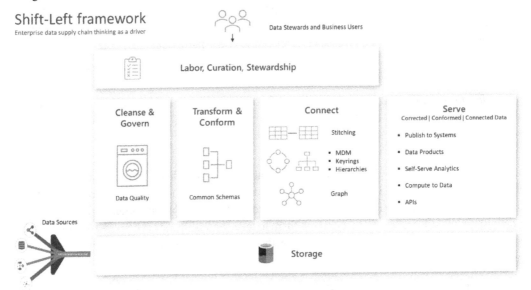

Figure 5.3 – Shift left framework for data processes (source: Karthik Ravindran)

Adopting the shift-left approach and applying the outlined template raised several key strategic questions that we needed to address thoughtfully:

- **Identifying suitable domains**: Determining where to start was crucial. We looked for domains that were mature in terms of data and had established and successful partnerships with business teams. These domains were typically more self-contained, with embedded operations and minimal connections to similar domains. We also prioritized domains that presented end-to-end data flow opportunities to minimize gray areas and initial handholding efforts. The size, complexity, and criticality of the data, along with the importance of business continuity and data sensitivity, were also key factors in our selection process.

- **Defining the scope**: One of the most challenging aspects was determining the scope of what would be transitioned to business ownership. We debated between limiting the scope to frontend capabilities, such as business control over operational scorecards, and including a portion of data engineering to enable basic maintenance and small changes. Each domain required an individual assessment to determine the appropriate scope, keeping in mind that core platform capabilities, such as data pipelines, transformation, security, and access controls, would remain centralized.

- **Budget and vendor management**: Moving portions of data operations to business ownership meant revisiting the management of outsourced vendor-driven delivery and budget responsibilities. We decided to maintain strategic contract ownership with the data team while allowing individual business groups to manage their purchase orders and budgets. This approach provided flexibility for business partners and retained strategic oversight for the data team.

- **Retention of centralized functions**: Cross-domain work and platform-based capabilities (such as strategic data governance, centralized metadata and taxonomy orchestration, data product development, and global data quality controls) would remain central. This ensured that technology-intensive and broad capabilities stayed with the core team.

- **Machine learning and analytics**: While the center of excellence for machine learning and analytics would remain with the data team, domain-specific operational analytics would be transitioned to business ownership. We aimed to avoid being locked into a provider role and instead provide learning support and best practices to the business data steward community for machine learning and analytics usage.

- **Business Intelligence (BI)**: Our approach to BI, particularly Power BI, was always driven by stakeholders for stakeholders. As BI at Microsoft was considered a commodity, this aspect would not see a significant change.

The challenge here was to ensure that knowledge and expertise within these virtual data and business domains were not lost during the transition.

We needed to balance giving full abilities and controls to business teams by retaining our core data experts and **Intellectual Property** (**IP**) for broader company benefits. The key was to acknowledge that while knowledge was moving, people were not. The outsourced delivery side, including data operations and engineering, would transition to business ownership, but not our core data experts.

As we envisioned these dimensions in our shift-left design, our focus remained customer-centric.

The true goal

Our goal was to streamline and empower business users with knowledge and abilities, not to simply offload work. The new operational agreements initially felt complex and less intuitive. Any change in a stable environment is typically met with skepticism, and this was no exception. Leadership and ample change management were crucial in this transition.

The benefits for business data stewards were clear: more control and flexibility, allowing our team to focus on innovative capabilities. We maintained a realistic view of what could be transitioned, especially in cases involving data science and software engineering. Each *shift-left* scenario was approached individually, with a common evaluation methodology but tailored to the specific maturity of business data stewardship.

For example, the aforementioned CPERM domain was an ideal candidate for this approach. This hybrid domain involved a complex process of data gathering, enrichment, and preparation for customer satisfaction surveys, followed by data processing and integration. Our team's involvement had been integral to this process for years, but under the *shift-left* approach, we looked to transition this responsibility to business teams.

We designed a comprehensive framework for this transition, automating and simplifying routines for data selection, extraction, and secure transfer to vendors. We have developed new data products and governance controls to empower business data stewards to manage this process from end to end. An outsourced team was dedicated to serving this specific work, overseen by one of our SMEs.

Within just 60 days, the entire scope of work was successfully transitioned to business ownership. Our role shifted to on-demand consultancy and periodic follow-ups to capture new learnings and paradigms. Regular meetings between business stakeholders and our team ensured alignment, addressed any challenges, maintained the benefits of interoperability, and increased productivity on both sides.

This transition was a testament to our adaptability and the trust we had built with our business partners. It represented a significant milestone in our journey, showcasing our ability to empower others while continuing to innovate and lead in the data space.

Summary and key takeaways

Incorporating what we learned from our experience, we've identified several key insights that have profoundly impacted our approach to data management and business collaboration at this point of our evolution.

Takeaway #1 – integration of data and business domains

The first major insight was the realization that defining data domains (such as *Customer*, *Contact*, *Opportunity*, and *Product*) in tandem with corresponding business domains (such as *Sales*, *Marketing*, and *Revenue*) leads to a more holistic and effective data management strategy.

The real power emerges at the intersection of these two domain types, giving rise to hybrid business data domains.

In these hybrid domains, both the data team and business stakeholders share the same perspective on data. The data team brings an added advantage with a fully consolidated and unified portrait of the data domain, ensuring that all stakeholders are on the same page and that the data is represented in a way that is both comprehensive and forward-looking.

Takeaway #2 – empowering business ownership with data

The second insight revolves around the thriving nature of business ownership when aligned with domain-portrayed data.

This alignment fosters a clear connection between business priorities and the data team's capability to provide a consistent, unified, and forward-looking representation of data.

It's not just the data itself that catalyzes this shift – the formation of aligned virtual teams, comprising both business data stewards and our data SMEs, is absolutely crucial.

These teams are where the desire for data excellence and ownership is kindled, creating a productive environment for transferring much of the data accountability back to the business side.

This partnership cultivates mutual understanding and shared goals, leading to more effective and efficient data management practices.

Takeaway #3 – evolving operational principles with shift left

Our third insight concerns the need to continually refine the operational principles that guide the collaboration between the data team and business stakeholders.

The implementation of the shift-left approach was a pivotal part of this evolution.

On one side of this approach, we have a community of well-educated business data stewards, fully focused and empowered within their respective domains. On the other hand, there is a mature data team that embeds change management values in its core functioning.

This dynamic creates a powerful momentum for establishing true business data ownership. It enhances scalability and boosts the performance of the data team, allowing for a more agile response to changing business needs and a more strategic allocation of resources. This dual focus on education and empowerment results in a more resilient and proactive data management environment, where business teams are equipped to take ownership and make informed decisions, while the data team can focus on strategic initiatives and support.

The next chapter is about scalability and managing risks with outsourcing and insourcing and finding the balance between the two.

6

Navigating the Strategic Data Dilemma

The need for outsourcing arose early on our path to driving data at scale. As soon as our team became even slightly global, we faced scalability needs, along with the requirement to reduce running costs. We already talked about this in previous chapters.

Much as expected, the early attempts were met with more failures than successes. We made all the mistakes that most enterprises would in their path toward outsourcing. Namely, we wanted it to be quick and easy and require minimal effort in terms of knowledge transitions from our side while finding that suppliers seemed to magically pick things up. These expectations of the company were exactly in line with any common "sales pitch deck" of any major outsourcing partner – for example, they will shadow the delivery and operation, and soon after, they will perform like a symphony orchestra. All you have to do is sit back, relax, and enjoy the array of benefits.

Needless to say, the aforementioned has never worked that way. But we did learn from early mistakes by course-correcting and working our path to success differently. Now, I want to invite you to read our story and share certain key learnings.

We are going to cover the following in this chapter:

- Where to start and what is truly important at that point – an unconventional and bitter truth that everyone needs to acknowledge before committing to outsourcing.

- The smart balance between what to outsource and what to keep in-house, and how far to go with outsourcing. Almost everything is possible with a great delivery partner – yet it is ultimately your decision where to draw the line.

- The data operations part of delivery is the most significant portion of outsourced work, closely followed by data engineering. This "yin-yang" tandem has proven its value in the tandem operations model, thriving with joint, collaborative, outcomes. Any attempt to go with one or the other quickly fails – let's review why.

Setting up a global outsourced data operation

As mentioned, our path to outsourcing started early. Actually, way too early.

The first attempt to scale and simplify local data work by transitioning to outsourcing was already in the works back in 2007. At that point, we only had isolated regional data teams, with very few common connections. The outsourcing direction was directed by corporate teams, selecting a major and renowned supplier to pick up the work. Ironically, I was on the supplier side, while at the same time co-leading early **Data Quality** (**DQ**) and data management work at Microsoft as part of another project.

We were motivated and energized but inexperienced and had a hard time tapping into business relevance. The local sales and marketing teams, who were mostly struggling with DQ and data issues, were totally happy with local on-site resources doing the work. Now, if this had been a couple of years prior to data office creation, we would have embraced the virtual global data team, later upgrading to a formal global data team. This was a classic example of bad change management – little to no awareness, no desire, and the absence of knowledge and relevance. The ability was kind of there, in theory, but again, with only ability and lacking all other key aspects, you won't get far.

That's exactly what happened. After a year of intensive tryouts and numerous interactions with data folks, we officially concluded that the approach was dead, useless, and nonsensical for the operational conditions of Microsoft.

Personally, I was happy in a way to reach this ending, as I also experienced the complete absence of readiness on Microsoft's side to operate through outsourcing agreements, along with an unwillingness from the supplier side to customize the processes and invest more in educational aspects, by potentially raising desire and appetite from the local business teams.

Attempt #2

Just two years later, we faced a totally different story. But before then, we had another attempt, prompting us to ponder the possibility of achieving success through outsourced data operations.

It was my third month in the company, performing the area data lead role, and gradually getting to know the area, the people, and the data challenges.

A friend messaged me asking for help and consultancy on some new, prospective project in France, where he was facilitating the work from a top-level perspective.

Friend: "Hey, I wanted to talk to you about your possible support and involvement."

Aleks: "Sure, no problem! What's up on your side?"

Friend: "We are implementing outsourced data operations, with France being the pilot subsidiary."

Aleks: "What...?! We shut down the previous work not that long ago! Why are we falling into the same trap again? You know this simply won't work – the business isn't interested, and the suppliers are heavily underestimating the complexity and precision needed for the data work. Data isn't the same as business processes and data also isn't software. Data is less structured and with tons of ambiguity."

Friend: "I know, but look, the situation is different now. We have a small supplier, and they are committed to dealing with any complexities and customizing the approach as far as would be needed. Also, France has well-established standards of data work and the folks in the outsourced operations will speak French and be co-located onsite. But I need your help with launching this and overseeing the first few weeks of delivery – knowing all your extensive experience."

Aleks: "Well… I don't know. Of course, we can give it a try, and yes, we have plenty of learnings from previous work, but I still have reservations about how suitable the whole idea is, and how we will manage the business involvement."

Friend: "All I'm asking is to give it a go – help them launch the work and stay current for a month or so. And by the way – they have an excellent lead PM for this work and the French data team is ultra supportive."

Aleks: "OK, I see. I will book myself a flight to Paris then."

After an intensive week onsite in France, we launched a group of data cleanup and DQ enforcement services, with an outsourced (or rather, nearshore) operational principle.

The start wasn't smooth at all, even with truly great support from the French data community and a high tolerance for mistakes made by the user community. We hoped that, gradually, things would get better – that we would stabilize the quality and eventually succeed with the initial goal. The first month slowly turned into the second, then the third. Following the original agreement, I had to step back from immediately overseeing the work due to other priorities, just consulting from time to time with the supplier's PM.

I certainly noticed the progress and the absolute commitment to make this real. Yet, the whole thing was too slow to make traction, and periodic waves of negative feedback from end users were not making life easier.

Seven months after starting, the work was minimized and then put on hold, alongside worsening relationships between delivery and the end user community.

This marked the second massive milestone in failing to outsource data operations.

I was sad it didn't work, despite the enormous efforts we put into it, and I promised myself to never get involved in this type of work again. Although the outsourcing trend itself was getting bigger and bigger, we clearly couldn't find the right approach and the powerful traction required. I didn't blame anyone; we were just a company that wasn't made for dealing with outsourcing. I let it go for the time being, focusing on the immediate teams we had to scale delivery, especially local contractors who seemed to be an excellent fit for what we needed in the data management operations space – with next-to-the-business placement, excellent data skills, and competitive pricing.

Yet the road had more curves than I thought.

Count to three

About a year after the attempt to launch France-based outsourced work, we were again struggling with scalability and costs – but now on a worldwide level. The rapid development of global capabilities, paired with great adoption by business teams, required us to consider the next steps quickly. The question of whether we should consider outsourcing arose again. This time, we were really driven by the hard necessity to offload work and establish business continuity for data operations across time zones. And there were a few critical issues to address:

- First and foremost, our data process's maturity was low. As the existing work was done by a legacy, highly educated, and highly performing team, not much was documented, standardized, and formalized. It was more of a case of "tribal knowledge," as my manager would call it, than a well-defined understanding of how to manage DQ at scale.

- Second was the lack of a suitable outsourcing partner. It seemed that we had tried both options already – a global and highly renowned supplier and a boutique-type small, local, and handy one. None of us were sure what else we could try.

- Third, and finally, we had no change management in place, so no willingness from our business users to accept the outsourcing approach as the next "try-it-out attempt" for real-deal delivery.

All these aspects were fundamental and interrelated with each other, so it would probably be smart to approach them all together in a connected manner.

Where to start?

We started by documenting the existing work, along with standardizing it.

Remember our story of "1,000 to 1" from *Chapter 3*? That's exactly what was happening in those days – and while the primary purpose for this consolidation wasn't related to outsourcing as such, it tremendously helped to fast-track the path of global outsourced data operations.

Finding a suitable supplier was a lucky occasion and perhaps deserves a dedicated story. But what was most crucial was finding a mid-sized experienced company with a high specialty in data processes and data-management-related operations that was also interested in exploring new and different locations for their work, outside of India and preferably closer to Europe. That itself was a good potential match already for the criteria, and now, considering the proximity of our Europe-heavy global team, having a solid, suitable location for the future delivery center would make a lot of sense.

Thinking also of cultural aspects here and evaluating the ability to capitalize on cultural similarities between the teams, being in the same time zone, and the physical proximity for short trips and engagements – all of this suddenly lined up as a wonderful, connected proposition.

Addressing the last aspect was the easiest – we simply decided to add a set of folks to a dedicated team to manage the landing of the initial launch, along with continuous engagement, understanding of changing demands and new requirements, managing relationships, and end user satisfaction.

We called them *data engagement managers*, and this remained a dedicated role for a few years up until we got maturity and, with that, the ability to incorporate those functions into operations delivery roles. By the way, this is where we deviated a bit from our global-only approach, as these engagement roles were set up as area-specific (US, Latin America, Europe, and Asia). This was important for building true comradery and engagement with our stakeholders – especially due to the magnitude of change we were bringing in.

This preparation work was happening in parallel to our day-to-day delivery, and most of my involvement in those days was around the aforementioned process consolidation, the introduction of global centralized capabilities such as SRTT, MAL, and Global Helpdesk – all that work still being mostly powered by our contractors.

As we were hyperscaling that entire demand for DQ and data management, we started with a slow and embedded approach to outsourcing – basically, bringing outsourced folks into our regular delivery – to let them learn through practice and get their hands dirty. Obviously, we started with well-documented and relatively easy processes, with lower risks for business escalations and focusing more on the volume aspects and less on the qualitative and complexity dimensions. This work was mostly done from India, with just a bit of added capacity from our newly established delivery center in Warsaw, Poland.

Soon, though, we made it to the point where the next logical steps would be to start outsourcing complex, multi-step, and multi-stage processes, with extensive need for local languages, analytical and comprehensive approaches, and the frontline appearance of the outsourced personnel.

In other words, they would need to become us – emulating the highly experienced team of global data stewards, executing advanced data management practices from end to end, and being fully responsible in front of the business stakeholders.

Well, that was a good challenge to address.

Taking the driver's seat

It was around early December, three weeks before Christmas, yet we had no time to cheer about the upcoming holidays. Generally, the days were very intensive back then, since many year-end transactions were happening, often requiring us to support business users with plenty of handholding and agile distribution of work between the team members.

Never before had we felt so critically the need to have trusted, capable, and reliable support for our delivery. The outsourced processes were working well but were limited to relatively simple things – and most importantly, they were all back-office jobs, while we were struggling with business-facing delivery. People who would not only be capable of executing well-defined processes for DQ and data management but also could be empowered to engage on the frontend, analyzing and understanding the business demand, often with some custom requests and highly important specifics within the dataset – that absolutely could not be missed. For sure, we were pursuing our goal and direction for global standardization and simplification, yet we knew it would take a while to reach, and meanwhile, we would need to support the business needs, offering localization of global data capabilities.

My manager wanted to talk in our one-to-one about an opportunity, and I was certainly curious to know more.

Manager: "Aleks, I want to talk about your career progression and some opportunities. But first – you know, we have these outsourced data operations we have finally launched. What's your honest opinion about that?"

Aleks: "It works but in a limited way. It's useful, but I'm sure we haven't cracked its full potential yet. The recent incubation of work in Warsaw, Poland, sounds very promising – especially if we were to incorporate previous learnings from launching data operations a few years back."

Manager: "Why do you think Warsaw could be very promising?"

Aleks: "Well, we need a kind of unusual approach to outsourcing. We need people who can perform magic with data and understand the business just like us – while not being us. And being consistent in their own identity, yet fully aligned with us on the cultural side and how business works. I believe we can get that type of talent in Poland. Agile, smart, confident, communicative, and next to us in terms of proximity, cultural fit, and willingness to learn. Yet – in outsourced operations."

Manager: "Sounds good. What about you helping to build these capabilities there?"

Aleks: "No, thank you. I've been working on these attempts for a while, and I've said to myself – that's enough. Plus, now I have important priorities in our data operations delivery and simplification that can't be compromised."

Manager: "Right, but what about if you become an end-to-end owner of all the outsourcing work, along with data operations delivery? This will connect the dots between onsite and outsourcing and it will give you the autonomy and budget to operate and adjust our contracts as necessary – and where necessary."

Aleks: "Hmmm... tempting, kind of..."

Manager: "Ahh, I forgot to mention – this will certainly secure a promotion to the next level for you. If successful, of course."

Aleks: "Let's talk about this, then! :)"

The third entry into outsourcing was finally truly successful for us as a team and made a long-term, impressive impact, often becoming a lifesaver in the days ahead. I'm not trying to pretend I was an outsourcing god, but I had some ideas in mind for how to make the whole setup more effective and competitive. The team was also eager to provide more input, learnings, and essential aspects that must be addressed in our next approach.

Importantly, the outsourcing supplier company was absolutely committed to supporting the reforms, working hands-on with the detailed plans and revisiting our existing contracts to develop new ones, which were harder for them to deliver, yet were raising the overall bar for delivery and thus setting us up for success in the years ahead. Both the leadership on their side and the delivery-level analysts and project managers were extremely supportive and open to learning and trying new ways of collaboration.

We have learned a ton from each other during this 10+ years of the data operations journey, and looking back, I can't imagine how we would have gotten to where we are today without that incredibly talented and innovative pool of data professionals from India, China, Poland, and Singapore.

Before we delve into those foundational tactics and learnings, here are a few key metrics to illustrate the scale of work we have got as managed service outsourced operations:

- More than 350 people in data operations and 50+ people in data engineering at the peak of delivery
- The entire data "Book of Work" was supported by outsourcing, with not a single process to be left out as an exception
- Data platform engineering, maintenance, and support were run by an outsourced engineering capability, including all data apps and data products
- All major European languages were covered, along with other key world languages, operated either from India, Poland, or China (and later Singapore) with a 24/6 "follow the sun" delivery model
- Frontline delivery for not only Microsoft's internal employees but also external partners, including marketing events, exhibitions, and webinars
- Go-to-market enablement for critical internal projects such as **Master Data Management** (**MDM**) implementation or external company products such as the launch of *Microsoft Unified Support*

This was a long story, yet I hope it set a good stage and managed a certain level of expectations in regard to how the path to outsourcing could look in a modern data setting. The next subsection is about summarizing these learnings and making sure they are practically applicable.

Our wins – embracing outsourcing as a key enabler

Embarking on the journey to establish a global outsourced data operation involves several crucial learnings and principles.

Here, I will depict some core wins and capabilities we learned as we built our outsourcing strategy.

One must approach this mission not as a mere delegation of tasks but as a strategic partnership. We wanted to partner and provide full enablement, rather than focusing on pushing over the execution and taking us off the work. It's vital to start slowly, yet with a firm commitment to success. This commitment will lay the groundwork for scalability and long-term benefits. We learned not to hurry but to be patient and invest in education. It paid off across many deliverables later, as people on the outsourcing side felt confident that they knew our business, our needs, and the way we work.

Assessing the best candidate processes for outsourcing was obviously very important. Here, again, we played the partnership card – we aimed at understanding their perspective to enable effective execution, and not to blindly perceive our objectives. In essence, whatever would be in the outsourced work scope had been decided and designed, tested, and incubated together, and then we would celebrate the success together, too.

Building trust and partnership

A successful outsourcing relationship is based on mutual trust and respect. It's about being much more than just a demanding customer – it's also about embracing plenty of intelligence and empathy.

Think of establishing a partnership where small wins are celebrated and failures are seen as learning opportunities. It was utterly vital to get there.

That approach cultivated an environment where outsourced teams felt valued and empowered. At the same time, it raised our self-awareness and control of the natural tendency to micromanage and, instead, encourage independence and accountability.

Our teams worked closely with each other on all levels, from analysts to executives. We sincerely wanted our partners to succeed with this work, and we utilized our culture, shared values, and energy to get them on the same page.

Educational foundations

Invest heavily in education, both process-specific and general.

This includes educating the outsourced team about the company's business model, culture, terminology, relationships, and, crucially, the key players and certain company politics in the air. We documented a lot, but even more, we presented live and recorded these live presentations for future reuse. We also made a number of visits to outsourcing centers, meeting and engaging with our business audience, taking questions and feedback, seeing how they work, and then adjusting our education approach accordingly.

Ensuring that the team understands the essence of their work enables them to articulate their roles with honor and a desire to do their absolute best. Remember, these teams are often far away from the latest trends and may lack comprehensive end-to-end know-how of the business changes, re-organization, and most recent guidelines.

Despite these limitations, their commitment to excellence and willingness to adapt and scale our processes was invaluable and was matched by our commitment to continuous education. As a specific example, we saw a mistake in a reply from a support/helpdesk analyst, so we checked whether our provided guidelines were still accurate, only to find we had failed to update them, which had led to the issue.

Documentation and pilot projects – essential tools

Documentation and pilot projects (we called them incubation projects) are non-negotiable in establishing a successful outsourced operation.

Expect scenarios *not covered in the documentation* and provide clear guidance for these instances. We know that we can't document everything – hence, having crisp, unambiguous guidance of what to do and how to act when there is an exception is ultra important. The best practice here was to simply ask to stop the execution of work, put a hold on to any further execution, and call for supervision or advice from our **full-time employee (FTE)** leads.

This is beyond simple – yet we learned the hard way a few times, and actively applying this *stop-and-ask* principle saved us from far more severe escalations and money loss.

We covered even the most basic aspects that might typically fall under "common sense." Remember, common sense can vary widely across different cultures and backgrounds, hence it is smarter to specify precisely what and how something needs to be done. Another great practice we had was involving outsourcing teams in the incubation of new or modernized work and letting them design the workflows that work best for them. While we would provide steering and capabilities, the formal execution would be developed and wrapped up by outsourcing folks. And exactly the same outsourcing resources would later push the deployment from incubation to production, to ensure zero gaps in between.

Fostering quality, upskilling, and collaboration

We aimed to create a culture that encourages quality and invests in upskilling resources toward the next level of expertise: data stewardship.

One might say that it's not a customer's job to do this. Well, I would say it depends.

We had a number of upskilling initiatives carried out by the outsourcing partners themselves, and this is how it largely should be. However, in our case, as a technology and innovation company, we saw many new capabilities coming in front of us rapidly, and we wanted our partners to be among the first to use them. In the end, the initiatives provided a clear benefit back to us in terms of productivity, while also allowing us to learn how our most modern technology works and anticipate the future of customer success.

Encouraging the outsourced team to engage in open analytical queries and provide input that enhances the existing process was another major path. We noticed incredible motivation and a challenger mindset in outsourced teams when dealing with such ideations, hacks, or prospective projects. Often, we would learn new things by ourselves and about our processes, as well as being presented with ideas on how to deliver better. Outsourced teams, being on the frontline of delivery, would excel with nuances that we either were not aware of or were not considering seriously enough.

Finally, by the time we got both data operations and data engineering work outsourced (and to different suppliers), we had to come up with a strategy that virtually merged data operations with data engineering under the "same room concept."

We wanted a kind of DevOps approach that takes data engineering and data operations as end-to-end accountability, yet the challenge was with work being done by different suppliers. Consolidation under one supplier was not an option; therefore, we created an imaginative "shared room," where either data operations or data engineering folks could enter at any time. Now, imagine being in that room; we would foster a kind of close partnership between fellows, which eventually led to more cohesive and efficient outcomes. People were not acting in silos; there wasn't an "us versus them" mindset or any kind of finger-pointing.

Choosing your approach

The choice between incubation and fully industrialized processes, offshore versus nearshore, and selecting specific locations for specialized services is of strategic importance. There are known common trends and recommendations, yet I would strongly suggest adopting a highly individualized approach here, aligned with the company's business objectives, culture, and expectations.

It's crucial to find the right talent and cultural composition that align with specific business scenarios. Avoid generalizing; what works for one scenario may not work for another. For example, in our case, we found the winning composition where India-based resources would perform a lot of well-grounded and mature work, including data engineering, and they would also provide maximum business continuity and coverage across time zones. To be clear – the work there wasn't straightforward. Nope. It is about the maturity and stability of certain deliverables, ensuring a smooth ride and nimble handling of critical-to-business capabilities.

At the same time, we realized that Poland-based operations were a fantastic fit for direct engagement with users and partners, with the cultural aspect taking the lead – by appearing more open to ambiguous situations where extra guidance would be needed. Any kind of research or forensics would also be a great match, resulting in us piloting all the incubation work in Poland before productionizing and landing in India. This is a well-known paradigm of nearshore and offshore capabilities complementing each other, and in our case, it worked perfectly, with an intelligent choice of locations and bulletproof reliability.

Contracts and KPIs – the triple-A approach

One of our massive wins was adopting a multi-year contract strategy with KPIs focused on overall success, not just standard and common SLAs. We took the bonds rating principle as inspiration and developed our own comprehensive scorecard.

Our triple-A approach included a weighted scorecard emphasizing the combination of SLAs, regular satisfaction score (NSAT), year-over-year cost savings, the number of incubated and delivered innovations, and the impact of those innovations on production. This approach ensured a holistic assessment of the outsourced team's performance, emphasizing the overall end user experience as the key, avoiding falling into pitfalls of either "quick, but low quality" or "on budget, but with no innovations."

It is tricky to demand excellence across all the dimensions of delivery, so it was important to discuss intensively the weightage of certain indicators and agree on them between us and the supplier. On the other hand, this type of scorecard was extremely objective by showing simultaneously the strengths and weaknesses of delivery.

Navigating challenges and pitfalls

Outsourcing is not without its challenges. From **Business Continuity Process (BCP)** experiences to handling and unpacking "watermelon" KPIs (green on the outside and red on the inside), there are numerous pitfalls to be aware of.

Advocating for outsourcing costs as a strategic investment into the state of data – rather than a temporary expense – is difficult for many to comprehend. This demands executive buy-in, strategic relationships between the companies, and a willingness to constantly evolve the work by challenging the status quo. Still, even with a high success rate of delivery and undeniable major improvements, the success might be fragile and fail under the pressure of cost savings or similar situations.

Keeping intellectual property safe, managing retention rates, and navigating the transition between vendors are all complex yet essential aspects of outsourcing successfully. We experienced all of them on our path, yet none of them pushed us off track and demanded we reconsider our overall approach.

Trust and open partnership are what make it thrive. Even in challenging situations, when dealing with critical escalations, navigating resources, or budget cuts, it is crucial to stay honest and transparent, standing for each other's success and looking to the next day with confidence.

Now, as we've summarized the key wins that come with an effective outsourcing approach, let's take a deep breath and think about the next possible steps in the outsourcing journey. Certainly, this will involve overall optimization, increasing cost efficiency, driving higher impact and user satisfaction, and much, much more of those usual steps that would be targeted as the next logical goals.

However, what if we step back for a second and take a "helicopter" view of what we just navigated?

Evolution of outsourcing and insourcing

As you reach a certain level of outsourcing, you will likely ask yourself two important questions:

- How far should you go with outsourcing data-related work?

- Opposite consideration – what are your criteria for insourcing it back?

Our experience was precisely the same. On the one hand, we were highly satisfied with our outsourcing delivery for both data operations and data engineering. On the other hand, we started to challenge ourselves to think, "*What is the evolution of this work? Should we only think of continuous, lean improvements, such as automation and various efficiency gains, or are there more powerful capabilities that could be outsourced? Yet, to play devil's advocate, we need to evaluate the risks associated with outsourcing even further – and what if we already went too far?*"

To test this hypothesis, we decided to take a bit of an unusual direction – we opened a new location for outsourced data management work in… Singapore.

I believe that all of you, even those with minimal experience and knowledge of outsourcing, would certainly be aware that Singapore is one of the most expensive places to operate. In this sense, it sounds strange to position Singapore as an innovative outsourcing destination – yet, it is an amazing talent hub. Let's look at the story behind this.

While visiting our outsourcing location in Dalian, China, we encountered limitations in its setup and fit for the future. Originally set to cover major Asia languages, the center delivered this promise and built a strong trust within the Asia-based business community. However, with the upcoming shift in technology introducing more advanced requirements for outsourced data stewardship, languages were becoming the prime criteria. Yes, we would still need the language coverage for Asian markets, but even more, we needed to elevate our game with advanced analytics, data governance, and data science all being embedded into data operations delivery.

Poland was the obvious location to consider and keep enhancing, and our supplier was fully aligned with this direction. However, there was no solution for what to do with outsourcing in Asia. Ideally, we should be able to combine both the language needs and the requirements for the modern tech stack among highly educated talent.

A lead delivery partner from the supplier side and I were sitting in the hotel in Dalian, talking through various options on how to unpack the next steps for outsourcing in Asia.

Partner: "I think Shanghai is a great option, Aleks. Remember we did this already before and now the talent availability is so much more evolved there."

Aleks: 'Well, we shall certainly consider that. But learning from our experience in Poland, I would love to have the outsourced center somewhat close to our own folks. It really fast-tracks the learning and ability to outsource complex tasks. But, I guess that won't be possible."

Partner: "Let me ask you this way – is there any place in Asia at all that would fulfill your requirements?"

Aleks: "Singapore, perhaps. But, c'mon, we aren't going to set the center in Singapore, no way!"

Partner: "Why not?"

Aleks: "Why not? Well, because I presume it would be crazy expensive, difficult to set up with all the legal requirements, and so on. Tell me if I'm wrong!"

Partner: "Not entirely, yet if we think about the type of talent we need – really well-educated, oriented for research-type work, with great language and communication skills – Singapore would be a perfect fit."

Aleks: "But what's the price?"

Partner: "Manageable. More expensive than Poland, for sure, but again, if we think of the high-profile talent we need and the modern tech stack, the costs are coming close to what we have in top nearshore locations. Aleks, if you are open to this idea, I suggest we gather a sample of talent capabilities in Singapore, as we already have financial services outsourced there, and then you can see for yourself."

Aleks: "That sounds unbelievable, yet I trust your expertise. And it would be so exciting and so amazing, as we have a few senior team members in Singapore, and if we can involve them… wow, that should be a breakthrough!"

Coming back from China to Munich, I was impressed and even obsessed with this opportunity, yet it felt surreal and unreasonable. At least, before we saw the numbers and the talent capabilities side by side. But even then, the skepticism of the direction taken was winning over. Needless to say, management and colleagues were even more surprised by the idea of having our outsourcing location move to Singapore. Perhaps, "*Are you nuts?*" was the mildest reaction. Yet the data coming our way about outsourcing in Singapore was deeply interesting and started to turn heads from initial dismissal to an open and curious approach. Priding ourselves as "data-driven," we thought we must give it a try, and so I booked a trip to Singapore.

Long story short, our first day of meeting with potential candidates in Singapore left me speechless. I had never encountered such a level of intelligence, tech skills proficiency, natural curiosity, and advanced analytical thinking in a talent pool. Excellently educated and with a challenging mindset, these folks were exactly what we were looking for. Having our own team members nearby significantly simplified the onboarding process and launch of the capability.

A few months later, navigating COVID restrictions and difficulties, the Singapore center started its operations, taking the most complex, ambiguous, and comprehensive delivery tasks, including the data science work. It was a win and a clear extension of our horizon for what could be done through managed service delivery.

Now, let's summarize all our learnings of advanced outsourcing in a concise way.

Outsourcing data engineering and beyond

Data engineering was significantly outsourced, encompassing innovation, application building, platform maintenance, technical support, and security. This move wasn't just about delegating tasks; it was about creating a synergy where outsourced teams brought in fresh perspectives and innovative solutions, contributing significantly to our technology landscape.

Embracing outsourced education and data literacy

Even areas such as user education and data literacy were outsourced. By doing so, we tapped into a wealth of knowledge and teaching methodologies that greatly enhanced our internal capabilities. The external teams brought diverse experiences and understanding, which was pivotal in developing a robust, innovative data literacy program. The virtual team of trainers (spread between Poland, India, and Singapore) covered all complex aspects of our service, with great time zone coverage and an intelligent split of expertise between them. Our users and stakeholders were delighted and amazed by how well the educational programs were delivered, scoring high NSAT for us.

Data science – a selective outsourcing strategy

We took a selective approach to outsourcing data science functions. Certain specific aspects were outsourced to harness specialized skills and insights, thereby augmenting our data science capabilities within the main delivery scope without compromising strategic controls. There are several applied cases of data science work embedded into data governance and data forensics, and having them well scoped and executed from the same place in Singapore was super beneficial and fast-tracked our progress.

Outsourcing innovation and incubations

Innovation and incubation projects were also outsourced, as I've already mentioned, using the Poland location as the driver for innovation work before it would reach the required maturity. This bold move paid off, as it infused our operations with cutting-edge ideas and approaches, keeping us ahead in the rapidly evolving landscape of data operations. Aligning the high-end capabilities of the Singapore center with the proven incubation factory in Poland created the next level of project ideas and perspective hacks.

Achieving maximum performance – nearshore versus offshore

The choice of outsource location(s) – going with nearshore and/or offshore teams – was strategic, and aimed at maximizing output and flexibility while being in control of costs. We have numerous success stories, such as our work in MDM and the launch of Microsoft Unified Support data delivery by mixing the delivery from offshore (India) and nearshore (Poland and Singapore) locations. By investing in both these teams, we received exceptional output, proving that a well-thought-out outsourcing strategy can deliver remarkable results. While the nearshore location was always easier to launch with, we clearly would be powerless without offshore's tremendous scalability and reliability. Then, both are paired and complement each other, so the maximum performance is delivered.

Insourcing – a strategic counterbalance

In contrast to our extensive outsourcing, insourcing was limited but focused on crucial areas. Critical software engineering and code development remained in-house. Even if initially created by outsourced teams, the ownership and accountability for critical code and essential **Intellectual Property** (**IP**) were always internalized. This approach ensured that we maintained control over our intellectual property, a non-negotiable aspect of our operational integrity. The periodic inventories of accuracy and recency of documentation, code, business and DQ rules, metadata, and taxonomy were put in place and executed with high diligence, to ensure that at any given time, we would have all the critical pieces of outsourced work in our hands.

Shadowing and knowledge transition

A key strategy in our outsourcing approach was to shadow key outsourced resources. Strange, right? A typical approach would be to do the opposite. However, as these outsourcing teams grew and evolved, it was crucial to ensure that there was a continuous knowledge transfer and a deep understanding of our business within the outsourced teams. We even saw several outsourced employees transition to become in-house staff, bringing with them invaluable experience and insights.

Here, a certain life cycle of knowledge transition was instated – as we would incubate new work, the knowledge flow was from our side to the key personnel on the supplier side, yet as the work matured and we reached full traction with execution, we would turn around and start to shadow those key resources leading the delivery, to be up to date with all the nuances. This wasn't a massive time investment, impacting the productivity of our team – rather, it was a regular reverse upskilling to ensure we hadn't depreciated our expertise.

Talent management

As we ventured into more complex areas such as automation, data science, and AI, the in-sourcing of talent became imperative. Personnel who had been deeply involved in these projects from the outsourced teams were brought in-house. Their thorough knowledge of these systems of intelligence was critical in steering, monitoring, and correcting the course of our advanced automation and AI/ **Machine Learning** (**ML**) initiatives. This move ensured that the most competent individuals – those who truly understood the details of these technologies – were on our side, safeguarding our interests and guiding these advanced projects.

This talent insourcing had an additional win-win notion. For us, it served as a shortcut to filling vacancies within our team, with the majority of individuals being well-prepared and ready to take action. For the outsourcing teams, this was an incredible motivation to perform at best, as they knew from past cases that the top performers would likely end up as FTEs on the customer side.

The preceding approach worked well and was highly impactful, and we truly enjoyed the whole way it worked. One thing, though – which observant readers will perhaps have already noticed – was it mostly covered data-operations-related work, along with data stewardship and a bit of mention of data science. Yet we can't imagine modern data work without solid data engineering and data science capabilities – so what about those, in the context of outsourcing? The next subsection has some answers.

The integral roles of data engineering, data science, and data analytics – life learnings

At the beginning of this chapter, I introduced you to the idea of leading data delivery and addressing data needs through data operations as an agile, flexible, and scalable capability. Yet the world of data platforms and engineering excellence is not so obvious and is even contradictory to a major extent. Why would you concern yourself with the complexity of data operations if all you need, perhaps, is a well-built modern data mesh platform with all its classy capabilities to shape and address any demand?

Well, the answer here is two-fold.

It is about evolution, and it is about being practical with your solutions.

Absolutely and certainly, from the very beginning and through the many moments of our journey, it was tempting to lead the whole data work with data engineering and data science in mind and align everything else with it after the fact. You are likely to hear about the same vision from every data or software engineer, from platform builders and data platform owners to consultancy and data vendors. Don't get me wrong here – I'm not about doing work manually, not at all. We have had and have a lot of engineering delivery; we have built an amazing and innovative data mesh capability and deployed numerous high-end data products, data applications, and data analytics.

The keyword here is *lead*.

Our fundamental life learning was to lead with business relevancy, and that was easier to translate into data operations – as the quick and immediate response.

Only once we were able to deconstruct the business demand, learn and understand all the nuances of data, run delivery excellence, and close the loop with the business would we upgrade and "vitaminize" (i.e., refresh, uplift) the data operations delivery with advanced data engineering and data science capabilities.

Basically, first things first, do fundamentals first and then go with all the perks on the next stage. Usually, the next stage would follow closely, smoothly picking up all the established routines and deliverables and converting them into data-engineered capabilities. We came to this approach and conclusion in an imperative way, yet also through deep acknowledgment of the fact that data is different from software. Data is a live, ever-changing flow, sometimes predictable and often not, and you really need to learn and experience it to master your ability and decision-making about what your foundation capabilities should be at the end.

The second aspect is about being practical and not a daydreamer.

The *engineer-it-all* approach isn't worth it in many cases; it might be slower to deliver with relevance and more difficult to change. The savviness and flexibility of data operations were superior in frequently changing business conditions, while constantly allowing for upskilling of the tech stack.

We found our happiness in identifying the relevance and the business case, then delivering quickly with highly practical and reusable operational capabilities, and then elevating the game with solid and modern engineering capabilities.

Even then, the whole landscape evolved enormously. While we already operated on a modern data mesh platform, we would still incubate and pivot many business-focused scenarios by starting small in the data operations space. In *Chapter 8*, we will reveal an impressive and ultra-impactful example of this approach – stay tuned!

To summarize, rationality and practicality were the winning paths for us. Starting small, yet instantly working on demanding cases, building the muscle in line with the growing need for technology support, and pivoting future solutions in an inexpensive and agile environment – all that helped to move fast with data deliverables, acknowledging and celebrating the difference between data engineering and software engineering.

Our real-life learnings

The following is another set of crucial learnings that we have gained while blending data engineering and data operations capabilities, navigating the insource/outsource balance, and addressing increasingly complex business requirements.

Data engineering and data science – supporting business needs

The journey of data engineering and data science in our data delivery was marked by a fundamental understanding: these disciplines, while critical to our success, were not the leaders but the followers of business needs. This concept, often challenging for technologists and software engineers to grasp, was pivotal for aligning our tech actions with the real-world demands of the business.

Foundational data management as a precursor to AI and ML

Before tackling broad ML applications or sophisticated AI solutions, we prioritized foundational data management. This approach was crucial, especially in cases where curated and specific applications, such as predictive data solutions, were not involved. The groundwork of organizing and structuring our state of data was a necessary step to enable the effective application of ML in context.

Navigating data engineering in low-maturity environments

Data engineering imposed a complex challenge in our initial low-maturity environment. The temptation to lead with automation and sophisticated engineering solutions was ever-present. However, the need for foundational enablers – such as core applications, data capabilities and data products, and a robust data architecture – was undeniable. We couldn't hope to execute effective data operations without this core base.

In light of our outsourcing strategy, the focus shifted to integrating technology efficiently and cost-effectively. Our entrepreneurial path, marked by limited funding and resources, demanded innovative solutions being deployed next to, and within, the data operations environment.

Building with outsourced engineering partners

Our collaboration with engineering partners in the outsourcing space brought several benefits, which might not be as obvious at first glance:

- **Low entry costs and swift start**: We kicked off with small, focused projects, benefiting from the vendor's eagerness to deliver quickly and effectively

- **Gaining momentum**: As the outsourced team matured and accumulated experience, we expanded our demands, pushing for the development of a growing data platform, pipelines, applications, and background processes

- **Optimization through multi-year contracts**: Just like with our operations, long-term contracts with efficiency targets brought substantial year-over-year gains

- **Building and preserving IP**: Interestingly, formal documentation, team training, and cataloged deliverables were more effectively managed with outsourced partners than in-house

- **Ensuring business continuity**: With lower turnover rates and better-managed knowledge transfer, our outsourced teams often outperformed in-house staff in terms of stability and continuity

Timing is key – from data operations to automation

One of our key successes lay in making moves at the right moment. As you've already learned, we first stabilized processes through data operations, learning and understanding the true business impact, and once established, we pivoted toward automation, seeking efficiency and scalability over well-established know-how.

Embracing no-code and low-code solutions

The adoption of no-code and low-code solutions was aligned with our need for quick, efficient delivery. These solutions allowed us to focus on actual service delivery rather than getting entangled in technical complexities.

The power of internal capabilities

Our internal toolset, including data-matching tools, data upload and data standardization utilities, DQ scanners, and recommendation engines, significantly enhanced our operational capabilities. Additionally, getting the data architecture right was crucial – it was necessary to distinguish between the innovation and incubation space (aka the "data management sandbox") and production environments.

I hope our team's learnings and tested practices are helpful for your own data journey. Of course, there is no universal recipe that always works perfectly in any environment, and many of the previously listed practices might require a significant "reality check" in your own environment – as every business is still a different business. I guess the most important thing here is to take these recommendations directionally and think of the evolution sequence – what comes first and what comes next.

Summary and key takeaways

To summarize this chapter, if there were three things I would like you to take away and hopefully reapply in your business, it would be these.

Takeaway #1 – a dynamic and collaborative journey

Setting up global outsourced data operations is a dynamic journey requiring a balanced approach of strategic planning, partnership building, continuous learning, and adaptation. It's about creating a symbiotic relationship where both parties grow and evolve together, leading to a successful and sustainable outsourcing model.

Takeaway #2 – a balanced ecosystem of outsourcing and insourcing

A delicate balancing act is required between outsourcing and insourcing. By strategically outsourcing most of our data operations and data engineering, we leveraged external expertise and innovation.

Simultaneously, we maintained in-house control over critical aspects, ensuring that our core competencies and intellectual property remained safeguarded. This balanced ecosystem has been pivotal in our success, enabling us to thrive in a competitive and ever-evolving data landscape.

Takeaway #3 – a fair approach to technology and business

Our story in data engineering, data science, and data analytics is another example of smart balance – evaluating technology and engineering expertise with a keen understanding of business needs. By deliberately utilizing outsourcing, focusing on foundational data management, and employing no-code/low-code solutions, we managed to align our technological efforts with the evolving demands of the business.

This approach not only streamlined our operations but also set the stage for more sophisticated applications of AI and ML, ultimately driving innovation and growth within the organization.

As a connected and logical evolution step, the next chapter will take us into the world of magic – a type of data magic defined by the superpower of **intellectual property** (**IP**).

7

Unique Data IP Is Your Magic

One of the first global data capabilities implemented at Microsoft was not even a data platform solution back then, but a mixture of a data sandbox and data warehousing solution named "Magic Reports." It had several **Data Quality (DQ)** scans and analytical reports to spot various issues across the ingested and on-boarded datasets and provided a set of simple dashboards to monitor the most essential KPIs – mostly about the accuracy of the revenue attainment and landing of it on correct accounts, customer DQ and completeness, and a few other things.

As we evolved, this solution evolved too. It was re-engineered and redesigned completely to become our data innovation and operations platform, aka the *data management sandbox*, and was eventually uplifted and integrated into the enterprise data mesh. We will cover this properly in *Chapter 10*.

But for now, let's think about that intriguing yet straight-to-the-point part of the name – "Magic."

Truly, for most of our business stakeholders, what we were able to achieve and deliver with existing data was simply like magic. It was like having some magic spell that we could apply to any kind of data garbage or data swamp, and suddenly, it would be clean and accurate and provide business-valuable data assets. But we knew the true name for this magic spell – it was our unique, cherished, and preserved, data **Intellectual Property (IP)**.

In this chapter we are going to talk about establishing, structuring, governing, and safeguarding your unique IP.

These practices apply to everything, whether you're adopting outsourcing or in-sourcing strategies, and they serve as an ongoing avenue for preserving valuable insights accumulated over years of experience. Your collected data IP fuels the continuous enhancement of processes, the skill development of your workforce, the integration of new data domains, the facilitation of new data-centric business ventures, and the creation of groundbreaking data-driven products.

We are going to cover the following topics in this chapter:

- Defining the key components of data IP and how to establish them

- Looking into the continuous modernization and governance of data IP

- Thinking of how to protect your IP when pressurized by abrupt or unexpected changes at hard times

Defining data IP

Consider your existing know-how, that is, all that you have learned about data, individually and as a team, as your unique data IP. It can work as a sort of magic wand for your company's business – this is how it might be viewed from an external perspective.

My personal realization about how valuable our data management knowledge truly is came late in the game, after many years of delivery across multiple domains. For all these years, we had been documenting, preserving, testing, and embedding all kinds of DQ and business rules. I certainly felt confident about our ability to retain this knowledge under any circumstances, as we had an impressive inventory of process maps, data flows, operational specifications, and business guidelines, plus much more.

I was on a regular trip to Redmond, meeting with our stakeholders, business and data stewards, sister teams in IT, and engineering partners. In one of those numerous meetings, while presenting the recent deliverables, someone in the room made a small yet interesting comment: *"Guys, what you do is very cool – and it might be ultra-helpful for our LinkedIn integration work."*

LinkedIn had been acquired recently, but I wasn't aware of any data integration work or any data needs there. Yet I took note and decided to follow up with the person at LinkedIn whose details I was given, to check what could be done there. I also learned that Microsoft didn't have access to LinkedIn business data as per the competition agreement; therefore, any data integration between the two companies would be tricky.

The next day, I got hold of the person from LinkedIn to talk about their needs. It turned out to be a funny discussion, with neither of us initially realizing how different our starting perspectives were.

Aleks: "Hey, good morning! In the meeting yesterday with the corporate marketing operations team, someone mentioned that you are looking for certain data from Microsoft, right?"

LinkedIn Person (LIP): "Yes… It is a dead end, as we can't get hold of the data we need, which makes our upcoming CRM co-sell campaign totally in danger of falling apart. But let's not talk about this; I'm totally fed up with attempts to get the data. We spoke numerous times with the CRM team, and they can't do it the way we require, so I'm afraid this will go back to the executive committee as a roadblock".

Aleks: "Sorry to hear this. But what exactly are you trying to accomplish? I'm not from the CRM team, you know, but we as the data team often facilitate data integration efforts and specific data pulls for campaigns."

LIP: "Well, we need to match a subset of LinkedIn accounts with the corresponding ones in the Microsoft CRM, based on the calculated propensity score. The problem is that we can't give you access to our tables, and we also don't have time to learn all your schemas to obtain all the attributes we need to calculate the score."

Aleks: "Hmm... So, what exactly is the problem here? I don't think I caught it. Just give us a plain list of accounts in the defined format and we will match them across the accounts composite on our side and feed you back with augmented data."

LIP: "Hold on – you mean you can provide us with an exact and unambiguous match, even with no common ID and no foreign key or keyring?"

Aleks: "Yes, exactly. The loose matches won't count, but we can still send them back, in case you wish to perform an additional analysis post-factum by yourself."

LIP: "But time-wise, we have thousands of accounts in scope; it will take forever to get them processed on your side as accurately as possible."

Aleks: "I don't know your timelines, but yes, I mean, it will take a couple of days perhaps, as we need to agree on an interim format, to test it a few times, so..."

LIP: "Days?! You said days?! Man, you are joking! I've already spent TWO WEEKS just trying to figure out who in this company can help and how, and now you are saying it will take a few days to complete! Our campaign is launching in three months, and I was almost starting to believe we wouldn't manage it."

Aleks: "I'm sad that nobody pointed you to us earlier, but I'm glad that we finally met!"

OK, to be honest, in the end, it took us more than a couple of days to sort out all the details and establish a safe and accurate data integration between the two teams, but we managed to get all the data in time for the campaign, and, most importantly, the campaign was extremely successful. And we were able to take care of one more enterprise domain, while once again enhancing our knowledge and capabilities.

However, nurturing and cultivating your data IP is not just a logical step; it's a significant investment, and I can't stress this enough! It is something that the data team should work on deliberately and with priority, with appropriate business sponsorship and clear anticipation of roadblocks – there will be many. The reality of daily operations, frequent team and organizational changes, business evolution, and cost-cutting measures can severely impact the quality and reliability of your data IP. This was the case for us too, yet we were able to recover and keep pursuing the chosen path – as we were so impressed by the benefits it offered.

Within this chapter, we will delve into crucial aspects of the evolution of data IP and the operational model that underpins it. We will look at various ways in which this unique know-how could be built initially, enhanced and advanced, governed, and preserved for the future.

> **What is data IP?**
>
> When considering the unique nature of data IP, it's crucial to grasp its essence and the substantial impact it yields. At its core, data management IP is a blend of specialized knowledge, processes, and technological infrastructure that a team develops over time. It's about understanding what sets your team apart and how this distinctiveness drives the company forward, ensuring that your practices are not only maintained but continuously innovated upon and evolved.

Breaking down your data IP involves examining the components of people, processes, and technology – our beloved trio of pivots that always works:

- **People**: They are the heart and soul of change, driving innovation and ensuring that data is not just managed but leveraged for its utmost quality. This means valuing each team member's contribution and fostering a culture where knowledge-sharing and cross-functional skills are the appraised norm.

- **Processes**: The series of actions or steps taken to achieve a particular end in data management is what keeps the business engine running smoothly. These include the methodologies for ensuring high-quality data, the workflows that underpin your data services, and the policies that guide data governance.

- **Technology**: All the infrastructure and applications that support your data operations, data engineering, analytics, and data science work, enabling the processes and empowering the people to deliver their best work.

Besides the known pivots, there are more specific pillars that keep data IP as it should be – a comprehensive set of "know-how" about data and how the data is used within the company. This is a mixture of the company's business knowledge, existing data operations and data services, data platforms and data lakes, the role of data in driving essential business decisions and business growth, the financial side of data investments, and much more. It is impossible to list everything here, not even talking about the ability to record all that vital knowledge and reuse it at any time.

However, we found that there are three constructive pillars that contribute to robust data management IP:

- **Documentation**: An obvious and probably the most tangible reflection of your data IP, encompassing everything from operational procedures to data standards. It's about capturing the sophisticated details of your operations in a way that's accessible and comprehensible for ongoing reference and updates. The latter is very important as the documentation is only useful when it is up to date and easy to consume.

- **Outsourcing**: The partnership with external suppliers is integral, not just for execution but for the evolution of your processes. It's about the continuous loop of feedback and improvement, where the outsourcing partners contribute to and enhance your existing data IP with their experiences and innovations. Crucial, though, is to constantly in-source the updated data IP back into your business.

- **Community**: The impact of your data services on the broader business, data stewards, stakeholders, and end users is vital. Their feedback, satisfaction, and further requirements are ultra-valuable inputs that need to be captured, as they provide insights into what's working well and what challenges persist. Besides your immediate company, you may also be in touch with a broad community of data professionals worldwide, which gives you an enormous opportunity to consider your data IP through the prism of others.

Let's delve into each pillar a bit deeper, adding the previous pivots of people, processes, and technology in reverse order, to finish on the high note of people.

Documentation

Consider documentation the blueprint of your data operations and data engineering.

It's about meticulously recording everything from KPI definitions and business rules to data governance policies. Yet it is key to remember that documentation isn't static; it's a living, breathing guide that must stay current with your evolving operations.

Each of us who has worked in that space of documenting the critical and essential aspects of any delivery, not even data-related, knows how difficult it is to build and maintain a reliable source of truth here.

There are many good approaches and tools, but we found the most realistic and powerful way is to always share the documentation between interested parties. Initially, we documented many things for ourselves, just to ensure that those valuable rules and DQ controls weren't lost. We even built dedicated repositories for storing and editing business and DQ roles, keywords, and key terminologies. Furthermore, we created metadata and taxonomy services; we dipped into ontology and data governance, trying to document everything on the spot and keep as close as possible to the source. Some of that data was shared with a broader set of users, such as data stewards and key counterparts in the business teams, while other knowledge mostly continued to be internally consumed.

> **How did that work?**
>
> We learned two very clear patterns. Every time we would have documentation just for ourselves, it would eventually get out of date (unless meticulously maintained under a well-established life cycle). And every time we would create something, and then share it and involve others deeply in its co-creation, co-authoring, and co-usage, it would evolve and stay relevant for years.

This connects and speaks well to the community aspect, but it also means that as we deliver those data services for the benefit of others, we also need to stick to the same approach with documentation and IP. This fundamental and exclusive know-how must be deliberately shared and open for feedback, and engage your business partners to actively contribute.

Outsourcing

Think of outsourcing as creating an extension of your team, providing a day-to-day, comprehensive execution of your data operations. No compromises or half-steps.

The knowledge and enhancements that come from this external execution are essential components of your IP, revealing practical aspects of your processes and technology that may not be fully captured in the initial documentation. Additionally, as the outsourcing delivery evolves, there will be a myriad of new learnings and experiences to update, document, and save for the future. We covered outsourcing best practices extensively in the previous chapter, so we won't repeat them here. But there are two key fundamentals.

First fundamental – ensure that you have the latest and greatest IP

In the realm of multi-year contracts for managed outsourced operations, presuming that delivery works well and you have confidence in that work, it is very likely that the folks working within the outsourced capabilities have a better ground knowledge of all things data than your own data team. This is okay, and it is a logical consequence of doing a great job. But it is your role and you have accountability to ensure that all that exceptional frontline know-how is in-sourced back and well documented. The fact is, this is easier said than done. What truly helped us here was to have a continuous rotation between outsourced project managers and our own directly responsible full-time employees, to continuously push for internal knowledge transition and re-evaluation – as the team changes were regular, we needed to regularly re-assess the knowledge, processes, possible gaps, and latest updates.

Second fundamental – use your outsourcing partners as your backup IP storage

Basically, following the previous best practice, you should ensure that you always have a "master copy" of the data IP. Now, with this second best practice, you take care that your outsourcing partners have a "valid copy" of that data IP that is usable and up to date and they know precisely how to re-apply it if something goes wrong on your side. The deeply practical example here is the bi-directional impact of the delivery, as there is always a partnership between outsourcing leaders and you and your team. Any change in this equation might lead to the degradation of immediate overall know-how. Yet, ensuring that your partners are as knowledgeable as your own team members and also that all this beauty is documented helps you sleep well at night. Assurance that at least one of the parties has full know-how is powerful, but obviously it is better to have full parity in knowledge.

Community

Your data delivery has a profound impact on the company's business, data stewards and end users, stakeholders, and leadership.

They hopefully use the data a lot, and they also get a ton of feedback: the various levels of satisfaction, any further requirements, and reflections on how your team could do even better.

This is a very important piece of knowledge and information to capture, in formal and informal ways, as you will want feedback on what worked well and what's still perhaps a challenge. Your ability to connect that feedback intrinsically with your processes, technology, outsourced services, people, and all other aspects of delivery forms a complete 360-degree view of your data deliverables and overall success.

> **Establish a baseline**
> Even if it is highly subjective, it is critical to have a baseline.

An additional dimension here is to bounce your processes against an external worldview, beyond your company's borders. This might be surprising and educational at the same time, as you would reflect on your own maturity, uniqueness, or commonality of the IP and the most demanded data challenges across the industries.

I recall our own early example of MAL from *Chapter 1* and I actively share this as a kind of best practice of account management and data relevance to the business needs. Presenting this to technology-dominant companies would result in the majority just smiling and calling this "a data best practice," but when we went to several enterprises and talked to the sales leaders and business leaders, they were particularly excited and highly interested to learn the details about how we did it. This made us think about MAL's positioning and somewhat reassured us that the solution was rightly done and driven by a true partnership with the business interests.

Technology

In terms of technology, it's important to compile and understand the full spectrum of your digital environment. This includes everything from data architecture and pipelines to security protocols.

Modern tools offer various methods for tracking and updating this information, ensuring that your technological footprint is well understood and easy to navigate. Again, it sounds wonderful on paper but, in many environments, we would encounter a number of data usage backlashes, lost traces and wrong procedures, dead code, duplicative data stacks and assets, forgotten dashboards, outdated observability, and unresolvable data lineages.

> **Data Governance**
> Undoubtedly, Data Governance must be at the top of your investments and priorities when speaking about forming and preserving data IP.

Data Governance is what unites and connects the dots across the various datasets, shared data foundations, metadata and taxonomy, data catalog and terminology, business vocabulary, and data ontology. This is the pinnacle of any data delivery, even (and especially!) when maturity is low and complexity is just starting to pile up.

I will cover our experience with data governance in *Chapter 10*, as it is crucial to unpack and digest the fundamental need for data governance in *any* data-driven enterprise.

Processes

Often, this is the frontline; it is what your users see and experience. This is how they assess the state of data and your contribution to make it better. While you do own all those processes, your IP won't be complete without connecting it to business success.

There are many facets here.

The first examples that come to mind are process and delivery catalogs such as our **Book of Work** (**BoW**), which was described in *Chapter 3*, along with respective frontline portals such as service request tracking. Underneath there, we would have a great number of complex and documented processes. To further add to the picture, proactive and predictive data management is also much about processes, as well as applied and operational data governance, and so on.

Yet, aside from all these purely data-related processes, there are many more that are also important and complete the picture of business-facing delivery.

> **Your processes**
>
> Processes are about how the team acts and works every day – especially if you find that way to be successful, productive, and a great fit for purpose. This is a mix of your planning principles and **Rhythm of the Business** (**ROB**), **Objectives and Key Results** (**OKRs**), scorecard and KPI setting principles, budget and financial management, the outsource controls, knowledge sharing, engineering reviews, communication templates and practices, data literacy deployment, listening capabilities and satisfaction surveys – and much more!

All the aforementioned processes will lead to your success in this complex enterprise world; it should not be underestimated, but rather cherished, maintained, documented, recorded, and shared across the company.

People

People are undeniably your most significant IP asset. They are the most valuable and most powerful source of IP and what makes the difference, yet also the most fragile.

Obviously, when talking about people, we are also talking about culture – team culture, data culture, and company culture. As I've mentioned before, much of our success with data at Microsoft was due to the people we had.

> **Data and business knowledge**
>
> Our data team members were highly knowledgeable in both the data and business domains, as well as committed, interoperable, and cross-skilled. When it comes to IP, of course, each team member holds a lot of personalized IP, and it was important for us that that IP was not locked to a single or exclusive user persona. We will talk more in the coming paragraphs about what steps we took.

But of course, we absolutely wanted our people to be data leaders and to thrive on the edge of data innovation, spreading the data culture and leading change. We also wanted to avoid any kind of labeling or hardcoded association between specific people and the deliverables they led, hence introducing rotations and change of ownership. This also helped with more accurate IP collection and revision, opened career opportunities as horizontal moves, and truly created a space for innovation – as every new person coming into a given area would use this moment to rethink the existing deliverables and add some new ideas.

Such diversity in action also had a positive impact on not only the whole team's ability to sustain the overall know-how but also on growing our total knowledge, even with natural year-over-year reductions in team size.

As a final thought here – creating and maintaining data IP isn't just about safeguarding what you've built; it's about enabling it to grow, evolve, and remain at the forefront of data innovation in your company.

Evolving, scaling, modernizing, and governing your data IP

To evolve, scale, modernize, and govern your data IP effectively, it's essential to cultivate a culture that values continuous learning and collaborative expertise.

Here are our examples and knowledge of how you can foster such an environment.

Embracing interactive and in-depth feedback

Utilize dynamic satisfaction measurement solutions such as **Net Promoter Scores** (**NPSs**) and **Net Satisfaction Scores** (**NSATs**), along with the dedicated data literacy efforts that offer a space for open and honest feedback.

Establish an interactive suggestion portal to encourage listening to your users and a virtual box of ideas where every team member, regardless of their position, can propose new concepts or enhancements.

Yet this isn't just about collecting ideas; it's about sparking a broader conversation that leads to careful analysis and, potentially, the integration of these ideas into your workflow. Such tools serve as more than mere feedback collectors; they act as catalysts for continuous growth and innovation, fostering an environment where every voice has the potential to shape the future.

Comprehensive tracking and celebration of each step forward

It's not just the earth-shaking triumphs that count but also the small wins that collectively lead to significant advancements.

Establishing a robust system of metrics that captures every nuance of your progress is a big driver of success. These metrics aren't just numbers; they narrate the story of your journey, highlighting the milestones and the steady path forward. By celebrating these achievements, both big and small, you not only acknowledge hard work but also boost morale and reinforce the enthusiasm to reach for the next set of goals. There is no common framework here, yet to give an example: achieving an annual NSAT growth by 5 points, such as going from 174 to 179, is a massive win. This should not be a surprise, on the other hand, as we were measuring a number of lagging indicators on our path to achieving a score of 179, and we saw with predictive analytics that the next survey would finally get us there. Thus, celebrating the small successes on the way was as important as acknowledging and celebrating getting to 179 in the end.

This ongoing recognition of effort and outcomes serves as a catalyst for sustained enthusiasm and ambition within your team. It also simplifies your work to position the success of your top leadership at any moment in time. Nothing makes the SLT as happy as the continued success story being fully supported and backed by numbers and data points.

Fostering community participation

The community that surrounds and interacts with data – the data stewards, analysts, and outsourced partners – is a rich space of insights.

Opening channels for regular communication, solicitation of feedback, and collaborative discourse with this community is invaluable. Every piece of feedback, every shared experience, enriches the collective understanding and application of data. Apart from regular surveys, we also used to reach out and talk to a variety of users directly – from the most frequent to the least frequent ones. We also created a single page for recording and curating any kind of recommendations from the user audience about our services, applications, and the engagement model. Needless to say, we individually address every single complaint, low satisfaction (DSAT), and (especially!) perception cases, where users might have been misled in their understanding of what we do and don't do. Another great source was data education and data literacy programs, which returned to us a lot of positive and challenging feedback. Our data literacy efforts are covered in *Chapter 12*.

But it doesn't end there. Actively circulating the results of audience suggestions and showing how they've been implemented not only validates their contribution but also bolsters a sense of ownership and pride in the collective work being done.

Seeking external inspiration

To lead in the field of data management, you must be a student who never stops learning, always looking beyond the walls of one's own organization.

It is easy to stay within the bubble of your own knowledge and believe that you have all the answers. However, whether it's the emerging trend of data mesh architecture, another industry's novel approach to data strategy, or a new technology artifact such as data contracts, there's always a wealth of knowledge out there waiting to be tapped. And there are a number of great data professionals and practitioners with whom to engage.

By staying attuned to these external developments and adapting them within the context of one's own operations, a business can stay not just relevant but ahead of the curve. This external eye is a critical source of inspiration and a catalyst for internal innovation. Nowadays, open sources of knowledge such as LinkedIn and the ability to personally connect to many data and business professionals, by sharing your unique story and passion, are some of the best ways to capitalize on existing know-how while bolstering new knowledge. It is about making an overall knowledge pie bigger, being inspired, and getting others inspired. In *Chapter 10*, I will provide a hilarious example of how we found ourselves using a Data Mesh setup while not even thinking we were building one. Yet we connected with a Data Mesh author and shared our live example of modern data estate with her. This exhibited the mutual success and celebration of how real and impactful the concept of knowledge sharing was.

Creating a team that loves to learn and share

It is essential to create a team culture that thrives on the exchange of knowledge, the courage to expand to new territories with innovative approaches, and the acceptance of diverse thoughts and suggestions.

By championing this culture, you foster the way for discovering more efficient workflows and pioneering solutions that could redefine industry standards.

This culture of collective wisdom and shared successes becomes particularly crucial during significant periods of change, such as the handover of leadership or changes in organizational management.

If we make sure everyone's involved and knows what's going on, living the values of transparency and honesty, the change will go smoothly. Everyone gets to learn from the experience, which helps the team work better together and helps each person get better at what they do. It turns into a place where everyone is growing and helping each other out, making the team stronger.

> **A holistic approach to data IP**
>
> To summarize – remember that your data IP is not just about the excellent technical assets and phenomenal documentation; it's about the collective expertise, the processes, and the shared knowledge within your entire placement within the organization. By valuing and nurturing these aspects, your data IP becomes a living, evolving asset that continually drives your company forward.

Protecting and navigating when managing change

When your team is dealing with big changes in the organization, such as shifts in what's important or big changes in how the business works, it can be tough.

Sometimes, people might not see just how key your work with data is, and that can be hard on everyone's spirits. But it's during these times that looking after all the smart and unique stuff you operate on is especially important. This is not just for the good of the company and everyone who uses the data but also to keep your team feeling secure, confident, and valued. Here, as always, lead with a value conversation and impact assessment, providing clear data points of how your work contributes to the company's success.

Here are a few ways to keep your data IP safe and navigate through these tricky changes.

Federate and share knowledge

Think of it like a team sport, where everyone gets a piece of the playbook. You can share parts of your unique data IP with the people who really need it, such as the stakeholders or business data stewards, or even outsource delivery leads and analysts.

Especially in Data Mesh and domain-oriented architectures, it is very natural to preserve knowledge – not only domain knowledge but also the cross-domain and general IP aspects that still fit well and are supportive of the whole Data Mesh-operated data estate to succeed. Here, share the general knowledge of what keeps everything running smoothly from end to end, in addition to highly specific IP.

By spreading this knowledge around, you make sure it's not all just in one place or with one person, which really helps if things start changing a lot.

Rely on the steady parts

This might sound a bit strange, but trusting the knowledge in your outsourced teams can actually help keep things stable when everything else is changing. I've mentioned this already before, in *Chapter 6*, and this might really be helpful in many scenarios. Outsourced teams usually have contracts that go for a few years, so even if things get tough, you won't lose their help all at once.

Also, if you've got a really good ecosystem for keeping track of all your data IP – such as using glossaries, catalogs, data, and business rules repositories – this information will likely stick around even through big changes.

Another recommendation here is to avoid intranet and SharePoint-based placement of such data, as it is easy to lose track of those, especially with updates and changes, and for those to quickly become stale and forgotten. A more dedicated placement (such as DevOps and data applications with a special section for logic description) along with the Data Governance programs in systems such as Microsoft Purview (or closer to the data itself, such as data domain definitions) will ensure a longer life and democratized access to it. The more frontline the knowledge is placed and available, the greater the chances it will survive over a longer period.

Show how data helps the business

It's easy to get caught up in all the nitty-gritty of data problems. But when you're talking to top management, especially when times are hard, you need to show them how your teamwork really helps the business to unleash the power of data and its usage for competitive advantage.

Focus your talks and deliverables on specific business outcomes and relevancy. It seems obvious, and I almost feel bad repeating this again and again, yet it is common for even senior data leaders to focus on general data problems, on resolving and pivoting projects in data governance and data management, and, in this way, positioning this high-level work as critical to business success. While we all likely agree on that in general, that's not the message to lead with for CXO-level conversations, especially if the business suffers difficult times.

Too often, I've witnessed the radical and rejective approach in attempts to get cost optimization for data related to spending (which tends to be expensive!) where, basically, the only story from the data team that would land on the leadership table is "*We can't cut on data investments – the company will break.*"

This approach is certainly not the winning one. It would be wise to explain in depth where the critical dependency on data lies and how that could impact the company – for example, "*If we don't refresh these data feeds and run a clean-up afterward, we won't be able to issue an invoice to x number of customers in the next three days, significantly risking the incoming revenue flow.*" Or, another example is, "*If we aren't able to fund that ML execution over the prepared dataset, we might lose out on understanding the recent customer churn and thus miss the opportunity to counter back with a solid analytical proposition.*" No executives wish harm on their company – as far as they do understand the risks, and are approached from the point of view of business relevance.

By using these few well-tested tips on how you can manage your data IP, you're doing more than just keeping your team's great work safe. You're making sure it stays important and valuable to your company, no matter what changes come your way. It's all about showing that the smart and hard work you do with data isn't just a one-time thing; it's always going to be useful and important.

Summary and key takeaways

To summarize this chapter, if there are three things I would like you to take with you and hopefully reapply in your business, it would be these takeaways.

Takeaway #1 – define your IP, with six dimensions in mind

When defining your unique data IP, use the pivots of People, Process, and Technology across the three main areas of investment – Documentation, Outsourcing, and Community. Each of these areas represents the massive source of your unique IP, along with an even more accelerated momentum for the overall mesh and for the intersection between them.

The purpose is to define what your IP is – not for some abstract safeguarding, but to foster the continuous ability to grow it, enrich it, and innovate the business delivery.

Takeaway #2 – evolve, modernize, and govern

Your IP is never stale. Presuming you have already taken good steps to keep it fresh and up to date, the question arises of how to shift gears and significantly uplift the team's knowledge and ability to drive innovation.

Much of the success here comes down to a culture of learning and openness, celebration of small and big wins, involvement of surrounding communities, and focus on active listening and feedback incorporation. Additionally, sourcing external inspiration to your native knowledge keeps you out of the "knowledge bubble" and assures high relevancy of your developed IP.

Takeaway #3 – protect your company

Use your IP to hold important conversations about the value it holds. Leading with relevance to business success and growth, using data points and impact assessment, be sure to position why investing and keeping this IP is critical to the company. While it may help also to preserve the team and important investments at difficult times, it is even more important to ensure that top leaders understand the criticality of this know-how to the company's success and the exact risks associated with IP loss or damage.

I wish you great success with building your very own data IP, being proud of your work, and helping businesses to thrive like magic. The next chapter will take you through one of the most powerful practices we've encountered and applied – the Pareto principle.

The Pareto Principle in Action

The Pareto principle, also known as the 80/20 rule, has emerged as the cornerstone of our data journey.

Striking a balance between meeting immediate and ever-expanding business demands for reliable, trustworthy data and establishing resilient, long-term data capabilities became the guiding principles.

This led us to formulate a business motto that rightly encapsulates the essence of this book: *solid at the core, flexible at the edge*. However, this isn't merely a description of adaptability and creativity; it's a story underpinned by design thinking and holistic operational strategies for end-to-end delivery.

In this especially long, but hopefully not boring, chapter, you will learn about the following techniques and the progress of our data story:

- Seven non-negotiable practices that enabled our maximum efficiency as a team

- Top seven enterprise-wide data issues that were formulated using the 80/20 rule, along with how these data issues were related to business performance

- First-time-published case study on how to build a new and highly performing business, fully based on existing data – the story of Microsoft Unified Support

Solid at the core, flexible at the edge

Entering this chapter, you already know a lot about our story of building a data-driven approach and the different phases we have been through, including understanding the ownership of data, addressing critical and timely business needs, completing an inventory of all the data-bound processes, and building a global catalog of data services and data capabilities. You know how we centralized at first so that we could federate consistently shortly after, using data operations as the driver for informative long-term decisions, building and sustaining the unique data management **Intellectual Property (IP)**, and much more.

Intuitively, the team always hit the right spot with our focus and our offering. By adhering to business relevance as the main driver and realistically weighing our capacity and capabilities, we smoothly navigated and addressed several critical data challenges at the company. We learned how to become change agents, put leadership into action, and use the language of data to influence and persuade our leadership teams.

The success here lies in the diverse, multicultural, and multifaceted team composition that was able to learn an incredible array of knowledge – from change management and end-to-end expertise on how the company works to advanced data engineering, data analytics, and data architecture concepts. The ability to speak equally well with business stakeholders and engineers pushed us toward an impossible edge of defining our own methodology.

At one point, we thought more deeply about what had made us successful thus far, and what possible underlying methodology or framework captured the essence of how we performed. We wanted to be sure that what made us successful in the past would drive our future success as well, and this would need to be formulated and no longer down to random luck.

Looking back, we have often experienced the mesmerizing power of the 80/20 rule, commonly known as the Pareto principle. You certainly know this – focusing 20% of your efforts on where 80% of the impact could be.

This suggests that you don't need much to start with – and even 20% of your work could get you far enough to make an impact. This correlated a lot with our own experience – think of those small, highly focused, and niche solutions such as **MAL** (short for **Managed Accounts List**) or **SRTT** (short for **Service Request Tracking Tool**) that made a tremendous overall impact.

Yet the one-million-dollar question here is, *What is the 20% of effort in the space of data management that would result in 80% of impact?*

Our team's experience and story around this were somewhat contradictory.

Many acclaimed and renowned classical top investment areas for data didn't really work well – such as **Master Data Management** (**MDM**) and data analytics. The true reasons for this will be discussed in the upcoming sections of this chapter and also in later chapters of the book. But we also encountered some areas with relatively low effort and some simple things that went well and allowed us to increase the overall impact by reusing and multiplying small blocks of data solutions to build a bigger thing.

We decided to call this approach *solid at the core, flexible at the edge* – emphasizing the meaning that certain solid and undeniable aspects of delivery enable you to flexibly address a myriad of other different challenges.

Let's delve into this notion and look at what we did and learned as we tried to define our core principles and hopefully, define a provable methodology.

Think of these *solid at the core* components as our *must-dos* for whatever we take on or engage in. One way of thinking perhaps would be to go with proven steps, reliable data apps, or tested data technology. But we deliberately wanted to avoid any specific bundle of existing solutions or technology, and simply think of agnostic enablers for any data journey or data project we would work on. The notion of *flexible at the edge* follows on from reaching *solid at the core*, enabling agility and fast response to any new challenge with the set of core, proven data practices, further enhanced with innovative and responsible components (in certain environments, those could be called *microservices*). This created a universal framework as a set of principles to always adhere to – whenever we set up a new data operations service, built a new connected data product, or ventured into new business domains, we would always adhere to these well-defined guiding principles, which allowed us to hit the desired 80% impact with minimal investment.

We came up with a list of seven principles. Some of these you've already heard about before in this book, directly or indirectly, but now, let's connect them all so they can act as a *checklist* for any new endeavor to ensure the maximum outcome in the end.

Our seven principles for an amazing and effective data journey are as follows:

- Data management is a team sport with a focus on people
- The discipline of change management is key for landing the value of data
- Any and all feedback is a learning opportunity
- Listening to your partners and customers is critical to drive incremental value
- **Data Quality** (**DQ**) by design, must be implemented to instantly align with strategic and connected data work at the enterprise
- Prioritize the demand and run an agile service portfolio
- Get *solid at the core* first, before becoming *flexible at the edge*

To effectively approach modern data management while keeping the Pareto principle in mind, here are augmented and enriched insights for each of the seven best practices.

Data management is a team sport with a focus on people

The following are the insights we gained from the example of our own team:

- Building a strong team culture around data is crucial. This involves hiring diverse talents with a range of skills, from data engineering to data stewardship and beyond.
- Encourage continuous learning and development to keep skills sharp and relevant. As the data team, we used every opportunity and engagement to upskill ourselves and build a differentiator of success – the knowledge we obtained from the company's business processes was reapplied within our remit.

- Foster collaboration and open communication to ensure that knowledge and insights are shared, enhancing the collective data intelligence of the team. We always strived to "build more bridges" across the teams and the company.

- Recognize and celebrate individual and team achievements to maintain high morale and motivation. Celebrating small wins became a part of our IP and culture.

The discipline of change management is key for landing the value of data

The following aspects helped us to gain traction with executives:

- Implement structured change management processes to smoothly integrate new data practices and technologies into the enterprise. We used the well-known Prosci ADKAR methodology, and the key principles always worked perfectly for us. Concepts such as *primary sponsor* and *having coalition* became synonymous with our drive for better data within the company.

- Educate stakeholders about the benefits and potential impacts of changes in data management, ensuring buy-in and support. As the ADKAR approach suggests, *awareness* raises *desire*, and I can only stress the criticality of awareness on all levels. Importantly, this awareness needs to be made in the same way for your audience (e.g., you need to speak in an executive position language, and not start with "*We have a data issue*").

- Regularly review and adapt change management strategies to align with evolving business needs and data landscapes. Your stakeholders are changing, the business is changing, and the demand for data is everchanging – it is crucial to adapt your approach every single time.

Any and all feedback is a learning opportunity

The following insights came later in the game, yet stuck forever after:

- Actively seek feedback from all stakeholders, including business and data stewards, end users, top management, and external partners – including outsourced workers, if you have any. Often, a small point of feedback can lead to major discoveries in data.

- Use feedback to identify areas for improvement and to innovate new solutions. Nothing is more obvious than this statement, yet we found ourselves sometimes trapped in a "bubble of knowledge" in which the opportunities to improve were hindered by our overconfidence.

- Establish feedback loops where responses lead to actions, showing stakeholders that their input is valued and effective. Have an action plan developed and executed. In our example, after a bi-annual user satisfaction survey, we would always have an action plan to address the top three concerns.

Listening to your partners and customers is critical to drive incremental value

Customer feedback is always critical, yet the key is to use a structured approach:

- Regularly engage with partners and customers to understand their needs and pain points. This is about establishing a formal listening strategy. This should not necessarily be a complicated one, but having it defined with a few well-understood channels (survey, focus group, common forum, click-to-submit page, etc.) is important. The principles of engagement should also be crystal clear for your partners and customers here.

- Use insights from these discussions to tailor data services and products, enhancing relevance and value. This is also about data democratization and data value, how the users of your services and products can derive what they need, and then how you can reflect and build a next version capability.

- Consider incorporating customer and partner feedback directly into product development cycles. As the data practitioners' team, we commonly played the role of product manager or program manager to ensure that business requirements were addressed via the design of core products by our engineering teams. Again, data isn't software; it requires a different approach and thinking, which are often not yet well established or understood by engineers.

DQ by design, must be implemented to instantly align with strategic and connected data work at the enterprise

Let's see what this approach is about:

- Implement DQ measures from the outset of your data delivery. *You can't improve what you don't measure* is more than a truth in the data world.

- Develop a strategic approach to data management that connects various data sources and systems across the enterprise, ensuring consistency and reliability. This approach, of course, rarely unfolds seamlessly; instead, it tends to be quite the opposite. Much of this book talks about not waiting for massive and fundamental solutions when a business need is there. Yet it is still crucial to check first, to see whether an effort over connecting data might bring more benefits than doing it in silo. At least, being aware of the bigger picture at the enterprise helps to develop reusable solutions.

- Regularly audit and update DQ metrics and measurements to adapt to new data sources, new business rules, and evolving business requirements. It has been established in the book so far that data is fluid and could even become unpredictable, hence the continuous monitoring of data health and alignment with updated needs significantly pays off.

Prioritize the demand and run an agile service portfolio

This approach can't be missed, even if it sounds familiar and simplistic:

- Develop a system for prioritizing data requests and projects based on their potential impact and alignment with business objectives. We used simple in-take forms and a *funnel* approach to identify what would potentially be the most impactful deliverables. Constantly comparing *severity*, *priority*, and *urgency* helped to make the right decisions at every moment.

- Adopt an agile approach to data management, allowing for flexibility and rapid response to changing needs. In other words, as stated in the well-known book *Coaching Habits* , "*If you say yes to something, you're saying no to something else*". What are you saying *no* to? The capacity of the data team, data engineers, and data scientists is very precious. These teams are also very expensive to have in any company – therefore, carrying out thoughtful due diligence along with the ability to say *no* is utterly vital.

- Continuously evaluate the service portfolio to ensure that it remains aligned with the most critical and high-impact data needs. Sometimes, we found that we had data services that had been running for years. The stakeholders were happy and the work had been delivered, yet the fundamental question arose – why do we have it in the first place? Maybe it is time to change the ownership, or maybe to retire, or maybe to radically augment? The final stage is less important but a non-static approach is a must.

Get solid at the core first, before becoming flexible at the edge

We learned this the hard way – perhaps that's why we loved management so much. Let's explore this in more detail:

- Establish a strong foundation of core data management practices and technologies before exploring more innovative or experimental approaches. Period. You can't fly before you learn to walk. No data science or AI would work on bad data in the company. Fixing the groundwork enables insights later. But this is a tough message to accept – especially with the "later" aspect.

- Ensure that the fundamental data infrastructure is robust and reliable to support more flexible and advanced applications at the edge. A solid shared foundation – whether it is a data platform, a data governance program, or a set of shared data solutions – will eventually be needed for advancements with innovation. Our own experience of the evolution of a data platform is a great life-learning example; we will touch on this more in *Chapter 10*.

- Gradually introduce new techniques and tools at the edge of your data strategy, ensuring they are well supported by a solid core. Not changing everything at the same time allows you to experiment safely and enhances your knowledge smoothly, which is important from many perspectives – not only technical. Even the best team member's ability to simultaneously acquire new knowledge is limited, hence any excess needs to be well controlled.

Incorporating these practices and principles with a focus on the Pareto principle can lead to more efficient and impactful data management strategies, ensuring that most of the value is derived from the key efforts and resources. With the team in mind, equipped with a change management approach, paying attention to feedback, listening to your customers, and thinking of DQ enterprise-wide, while prioritizing rigorously and not overstretching the goals, this is how you can achieve success.

You might feel that this approach is overly complicated. Even with it being a selective and tested framework, is there a good and descriptive example demonstrating its applied use? Absolutely, and this is what the next subsection will go through – explaining, step by step, examples of the top data issues discovered within the company, and how to use these seven design principles to unlock 80% of value.

But before we move on to the applied examples, let's talk about what didn't work – as promised.

During our journey, we ended up with a list of things that didn't work and that resulted in lost efficiency, time, money, or effort. Some of these are seriously controversial and must be evaluated in the context of data and organizational maturity in every specific example.

In our case, it is not to say that we did not have the required maturity, but certain things were simply too heavy and too difficult to uplift if you hadn't already solved the pre-conditions or resolved the majority of existing company-wide data challenges. We felt it was not worth pursuing them, unlike the top issues we had identified. The massiveness and slowness of implementation would paint exactly the opposite picture of Pareto – spending 80% of our capacity to create 20% of the value.

What to avoid – personal experience

So, here we go – the five important negative insights we gained throughout the lifespan of our data delivery. These are the things to avoid.

Investing in single solutions such as MDM or DQ enrichers, SaaS capabilities, and external DQ providers

MDM is very time- and effort-consuming and needs an extremely clear and sharp business case in order for the lengthy implementation to be appreciated. Also, the solution should fit well into the ecosystem as its whole value comes from connected and integrated data. There are a few modern approaches that are more promising, yet true business needs and ownership are paramount here.

With regard to SaaS (and DaaS) capabilities, as well as buying external solutions for DQ enrichment, it never solves the problem, in my view. You are buying someone else's IP, which is likely generic and doesn't reflect your challenges. While it might serve as a short-term or temporary solution, particularly when you lack the resources to handle it internally, it won't initiate change management on your behalf.

Leading by technology and engineering before assessing the fit for business

The recommendation for solely relying on technology to address data problems has been reiterated numerous times – which doesn't mean that you won't need good tech, absolutely not!

Yet the best use of technology is to solve already defined business problems, and not the opposite. So many times, I've heard, "Let's just buy this tool or that tool, and all will be done." Nothing will be done until you do it – with your team and your business stakeholders, listening to their challenges and data needs, and enabling the critical feedback loop.

Heavily investing in data analytics, ML, and AI (yawn) as the ultimate priority

Oh, I love this one, yet it is in the same league as the previous one. If the data is low quality, scarce, undiscoverable, and ungoverned, there is no role for ML/AI, unless, and only if, they are used to battle the bad DQ root causes and empower data augmentation with ML/AI-operated enrichment.

Prior to the hype for data analytics, data science, and now AI, the previously known unflattering example was about building **Data Warehousing** (**DW**) solutions over poor operational data, with a record number of DW projects going to waste or never being delivered. I do not recommend pedaling heavily on analytics until you have good levels of DQ and data maturity. We will talk about what *good* really means in *Chapter 13*.

Building a data strategy by focusing on data issues and DQ problems

Isn't the data strategy supposed to address the persistence of data issues and challenges in the company? Nope, not in my view.

The data strategy should aim to unlock the value of data at the enterprise and support the appearance of data culture with data literacy efforts and data-driven execution of business strategy. Leading with DQ concerns without connecting them to business excellence and growth is a very tactical path; yet, in fact, this is probably the most common mistake made by data teams and even senior data leaders – focusing on DQ challenges instead of helping CXOs thrive on data. And yes, DQ still needs to be fixed – not as an afterthought but also not as a "thing in itself."

Centralizing the data work and controls

This one is also tricky since centralization efforts might be important in the early phase of the data journey, and they also remain utterly critical for enterprise-wide capabilities of data governance and other shared foundations. Yet what needs to be avoided is the locking of IP and controls to one central team – which effectively becomes a bottleneck for everything very quickly.

Even in the example of our approach to data governance, the policies and data life cycle definitions should be developed and maintained centrally, in a conformed and authoritative way, yet the domains and execution ownership within those domains should be federated. This way, the scalability and *flexible at the edge*" principles are attained, while being grounded on solid core foundations.

Okay, let's move on from these difficult lessons and see how our Pareto-based framework helped to address the most withstanding data issues at the company.

Addressing top enterprise data issues

Enough of the theory – time to look at some practical examples.

This is a retrospective of the top seven enterprise-wide data issues reported to every senior leadership level (one down from CEO) at that time and how the resolution of these issues was grounded in the Pareto principles and the applied use of the framework.

It would look something like the following figure, with the seven principles and the top seven data issues group:

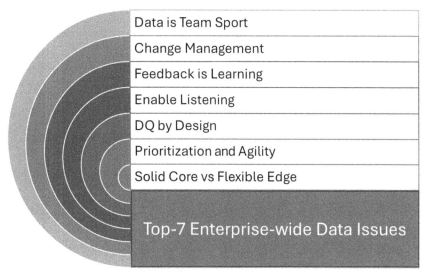

Figure 8.1 – Seven principles and group of seven data issues

Now, what were these top seven data issues, how were they identified, and how were they business issues, first and foremost, that had been badly enabled with data?

I hope you read the earlier sections where we clearly advised *not* leading any executive conversation with data issues, but rather with business centric definitions instead – and that's exactly what we did. However, we did map them into the underlying data and DQ issues, so that we would act in full synergy between business owners and the data team, mirroring the parallel efforts of resolving in the foreground and the background.

Our executives would eventually recognize them as top enterprise issues with data, underscoring in its name that those were indeed enterprise-wide problems to address and that the basis for this lies in the data foundations.

The Dual View – mirroring business challenges with corresponding data actions

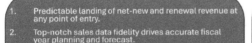

Top-7 issues, business formulation

1. Predictable landing of net-new and renewal revenue at any point of entry.
2. Top-notch sales data fidelity drives accurate fiscal year planning and forecast.
3. Fast-track emerging business opportunities in Sustainability, NGOs, Tech and priority business segments
4. Enable Microsoft Unified Support offer pricing
5. Consolidate Channel revenue reporting for 1st Party Devices (Surface, HoloLens, Xbox)
6. Accelerate shared CRM co-sell with partners
7. Increase accuracy of revenue data for "Small and Medium" (SMB) businesses.

Top-7 issues, data & DQ level

1. Clean-up revenue collection, enable ML-driven recommendation engine for data stewards.
2. Enable governance and seamless synchronization over CRM, Managed Accounts List and revenue.
3. Enable in-flight external data integration with CRM across Green500, Fortune500 and Unicorn accounts, along with sources like GitHub and MS Philanthropy.
4. Build and deploy end-to-end customer-centric pricing
5. Build Channel revenue data ingestion and data processing platform and frontline solution
6. Increase co-sell partner-match accuracy and outreach
7. Enable single customer ID continuity in SMB revenue space.

Figure 8.2 – The dual view, where business challenges were mapped to underlying data-related challenges

The preceding figure reflects the duality of business challenges and how they are being mapped to the data challenges. How did we come to this conclusion?

Obviously, the business-related issues were never hidden or unknown to the company's leadership. Discussions about what was missing and what was most challenging for business growth were ongoing. We also knew some of those – yet not all, because not all of them were related to data. But, perhaps, what was different this time in our approach was connecting those business challenges explicitly with the underlying data enablement. Basically, we enabled the clear translation of what must be done in the data space, to enable or improve the corresponding business capabilities. Again, not everything was tied to data; we left out of our scope anything we couldn't help with, but we did an extensive inventory and assessment of those areas that were most troublesome, and where the link to data issues was utterly clear.

We also reached the top of the leadership scale. Not being shy or trying to hide the difficulties we were facing with data, applications, and data-driven processes, we decided to formulate the top seven issues – or, rather, impact opportunities – for the entire enterprise. We combined what we heard from our business stakeholders with our deep background knowledge of data and ecosystems to come up with these seven crisply formulated challenges. It was also pointed out that addressing only these seven out of many other issues would have the maximum impact while keeping things realistic from a resource investment perspective.

As a real-life example of what I mean here – we dropped the MDM implementation project from the top seven due to its complexity and the effort associated with it, although clearly the criticality and priority were there. Yet implementing MDM alongside addressing those seven issues wouldn't adhere to the Pareto principle anymore, due to the size of the effort – and while we would likely achieve a massive breakthrough in data architecture and various business scenarios, having a critical impact, the total effort would outweigh the other opportunities.

Now, let's look at how our Pareto-inspired framework impacted the way we solved these seven issues. You will see how applying the seven-step approach to each of the prioritized enterprise issues helped us drive the path toward the final resolution stage along with delivering on the interim impact (and, of course, the final impact once the goal was achieved!):

- The notion of a team sport was immediately put in place via *direct connection and the involvement of various teams* – engineering, data science, business operations, and so on. We clearly didn't want anyone to be left behind and not contribute to the success. This, in itself, is never easy, and not every party contributes equally. But we weren't aiming for this. What was important, though, was to get everybody on board for the initial assessment and launch, and then keep updating regularly and explicitly.

- The use of *change management principles* was clearly defined by nominating and agreeing on the primary sponsor (the **chief digital officer**, or **CDO**, in our case) for this top seven resolution work. Having a solid **Rhythm of Business** (**RoB**) where we would jointly report on progress and/or discuss the blockers was important to instate accountability and planning. Another aspect of the change management approach was the extensive use of ADKAR principles for almost everything – from communication to demand management.

- We clearly opted out from taking the *hero* role here – meaning the often-taken position as a lifesaver, doing something critical for the company, and hence being extremely self-centered and feedback-adverse. We went with the opposite – creating a sense of *complete transparency* in our efforts and inviting everyone in the company to contribute with their thoughts, improvement ideas, and positive endorsement.

- Being proud of having *great listening skills*, we certainly utilized them this time as well. Our ears were open to all channels, to the smallest detail or an articulated pain point within the scope of those top seven issues. Sometimes, we couldn't connect a new data challenge to existing ones, but by listening carefully with empathy and deep diving into concerns, we were able to grasp more associated DQ concerns and bound them into what we knew before.

- *Having a bigger picture in mind* was extremely important. Certain solutions for the aforementioned top issues seemed like isolated investments and many of our senior leaders were somewhat concerned about doing so. Even their full understanding of criticality and impact was not always enough to sponsor a non-scalable and siloed solution. Here, by applying the DQ-by-design principle, we ensured that whatever we delivered in the short term would still have a long-term fit too.

  Let me give you an example: while we decided not to prioritize the central MDM solution, we clearly noticed that two out of the top seven data issues required some kind of organizational or customer data mastery. We proceeded with a duo of individual solutions, aligned by overall logic and architecture, with the perspective that in the future, a third, a global MDM solution, could be deployed and re-integrate the work done by us within the short-term delivery.

- In terms of *prioritization*, there was a simple rule to learn – you never have P0 and neither do you have five P1s. This just doesn't work. Any illusion about successfully managing a set of conflicting or unclear priorities needs to be taken away. As boring as it might sound, having rigorous prioritization applied at first, resulting in adequate and unambiguous prioritization of efforts, from P1 to Px, is what truly helps to achieve the result. We don't need to be sad about having something like P7 – it doesn't mean it's not important, but it emphasizes that P1 to P6 should be done before that to make P7 succeed too.

- *Core versus edge* came down to something very simple – we had to address and resolve the basic elements for each of the top seven issues, before taking any next step. This highly iterative and agile approach ensured that we cemented our understanding of an issue by addressing some part or component of that, along with measuring the interim success and getting broad feedback. These small, incremental wins helped all the teams focus on progress and increase their know-how, avoiding bias and self-proclaimed wins and sailing away from the temptation to go faster into unprepared territories.

We hope you find our approach useful and applicable to your interrelated business and data challenges. As you can see, there is nothing ultra-comprehensive or difficult to understand. Some may even say, "Hey, this is all common sense! Why are we even talking about such basics?" Well, what we've seen across organizations and people is that, often, the most simple and sensible things somehow drop from our view. Instead, we might tend to overengineer or seek technical solutions for non-technical challenges, or do some of the preceding steps but not all of them – perhaps even missing the connected nature of them.

It is certainly not a bible, nor is it a model that has been tested in thousands of enterprises. We're sharing what worked well for us many times, with great consistency of outcomes, and that's why we wanted to summarize those steps and get them to practice it even more within our scope of work. Yet we fully recognize it's not a one-size-fits-all approach and, in certain cases, cultures, and environments, it might not work well or even work at all.

Case study – the creation of the Unified Support service

To illustrate and reflect on previous learnings, our approach almost always involved nurturing new services or ideas through data operations, gathering invaluable insights directly from our incredible professionals.

This involved a much-needed dynamic collaboration between business experts and data team members before any subsequent automation or engineering took place. This path often stands in contrast to the more conventional IT-driven or engineering-driven methods, where project managers collect requirements and software engineers construct solutions. We've emphasized this a few times already, and the reason we're going back to this notion again is the crucial importance of succeeding in a fast, ambiguous, and uncertain environment. The ability to quickly experiment with data and change direction at no cost to the infrastructure is commonly underestimated.

We found that, when working with data, it's important to be open to uncertainty and explore new aspects, even when you're already working on the task.

This open-minded approach culminated in a pivotal moment when we were tasked with developing a new digital product for the company: the Unified Support service, complete with customer-centric pricing and consumption-based revenue. Initially, the process faced significant challenges – more on that soon. It wasn't thriving until we placed data operations and direct business feedback at the forefront to steer and guide the go-to-market solution delivery, and finally, we achieved a breakthrough. Only a year later did we proceed to construct the engineering segment of the product and enable end-to-end solution scalability – knowing now exactly what and how that should be.

The following is a real-life story on how to build a new data-driven and data-sourced product, with multi-billion-dollar revenue realization, in a short time, and by using the existing data at the company while focusing only on what truly matters to succeed. The latter, with that utmost concentration on delivering the solution by overcoming challenges with resources, readiness, and engineering, is what made it so difficult, yet also so extremely successful.

The first idea

It all started with one conversation in the Redmond office.

It was one of my regular visits to Redmond, to meet with the stakeholders and review our deliverables, plan the coming year's scope and budget, and gain some new demand and ideas. Strolling through the corridors in one of our office buildings, I met an old friend and colleague who asked me whether I had time for a chat. We agreed to meet a bit later in the day, as both of us already had busy schedules.

Eventually, with an afternoon coffee in hand, we met to talk about a variety of different data initiatives in the company, including a recent announcement about a new approach to organizational/customer mastery (aka MDM), which seemed like a never-ending story at Microsoft. We had already failed with MDM implementation three times before, and while the new solution and approach at first glance appeared more promising, it again lacked a crisp business case. We had already seen a similar situation in the past – there was a general demand for customer mastery, a good understanding of benefits along with associated complexity, and even some initial successful pivots and test deployments, yet at the end, there was a lack of an ultra demanding and sharp business case, such as, "We need this to deploy a one-billion-dollar project or we will fail as a company." Somehow, we always managed to navigate the technical challenges of attaining accurate customer data for specific business demands through a mix of engineering and operations and, although cumbersome in design, it always made it to the point of usage.

With my day coming to an end, I was catching up on emails from my Europe-based team. One email immediately caught my attention – a team member was saying that she had been approached by a business group leader from Redmond who was looking to understand how we do licensing position calculations for customers.

This was a public yet not well-known service in our portfolio. We will explore it more in *Chapter 12* when talking about data value as the case was truly interesting, demonstrating the data monetization approach in practice.

Checking the name of the business leader who was looking for details of this work, I realized that she was in the same building as me. My friend immediately checked my search and confirmed saying that she was working on something very new and not broadly advertised, yet she held a strategic position in advising the Microsoft Services business in terms of future growth opportunities. I became curious, trying to mentally connect the licensing statements we were producing with the Microsoft Services business, and honestly, I saw no direct match. I pinged the person asking for more information and we agreed to meet a few minutes later. This is how our conversation went.

Business leader: "Hi Aleks, I'm working on a new project for the company and I've heard that your team can produce complete licensing position statements for any customer. Is this true?"

Aleks: "Yes, we do this on demand, as the service for our internal licensing solution specialists or for external partners, if they have authorization from the customer to do so."

Business leader: "How do you do that? This will be a very complex task, knowing our diverse ecosystem."

Aleks: "Well, we have some tools, and we have knowledge, and, you know, this was set up as the service, so we have experienced people who validate the data carefully before we produce the final outcome."

Business leader: "What is the accuracy of such a licensing statement?"

Aleks: "About 98%, based on the experience and measurements we have."

Business leader: "Hmm... that's cool. Do you think you would be able to connect that data on output with our revenue collection system?"

Aleks: "Well, I don't know, we can probably get it via inexplicit match. But why are you asking? What is the purpose of this?"

Business leader: "Well, imagine if we take some of our customers' enterprise segments, and we want to fully understand and estimate all that they have with Microsoft, so to speak, such as their license agreements, cloud usage, hardware, support they use, revenue year over year, and so on."

Aleks: "Ah! Understood – you want a customer 360 type of view, and for that, you need customer or organization master capability underneath. That would define an organization structure and hierarchy, with all the nodes and branches, create a keyring connection to our Tier 1 line-of-business system, and then pull an aggregated view. There is a new project in that space, just starting. I found out today."

Business leader: "Yes, I know. Actually, we are the launching customer for that project, and the project was largely initiated because we asked for it. So, you are saying we need a customer master first, to power up a customer-centric view, and then we need to link all other systems?"

Aleks: "Exactly! Well, that sounds good then. I'm glad you already got connected therewith the people and the work."

Business leader: "Yes, indeed. Thank you for the consultation."

While driving back to the hotel, I was thinking about the customer master's work, and I was truly happy to realize that, finally, we had an ultra-specific and tailored business case for that work. I still wasn't sure why exactly this came as a priority for the Microsoft Services business group, as we had many attempts and interest from other internal businesses for customer master solutions before; but as already said, most of them failed to meet expectations, ending up with that need being addressed via a mix of data capabilities.

Two days later, I received a ping again from the same person.

Business leader: "Aleks, are you still in Redmond? Can we have a quick chat today?"

Aleks: "We can, sure! What's the matter?"

Business leader: "Listen, I've spoken again with the group that is leading this new customer master initiation. They say it will likely take at least six months for the basic pilot work, and then they would need to add those keyring capabilities and expand the mastery further, plus they can't guarantee that all the Tier 1 systems we need would be included at launch."

Aleks: "Yeah, I understand. But this is massive work. Look, they need to automate the whole end-to-end connection. They need to engineer the scalable architecture and ensure data quality in the master itself, plus all the connected entities, and, finally, the quality of that generated output. It is difficult, seriously difficult. You are new here, but we have tried twice before in the last 10 years or so, and we never really made it very far."

Business leader: "But you do a similar thing now, right? Okay, not the same, of course, but kind of in that direction. You have details of customers you have already done this for; this is the master data, right? Plus you pull additional details – so why don't we just expand based on what you have?"

Aleks: "It is a highly manual process. We do it via the outsourcing team to address the demand, and this demand is already high enough. We don't have the capacity to address other needs, and it also takes a long time to get people well trained in data stewardship. Finally, there is a fee associated with this work."

Business leader: "A fee? You mean, if we were to ask you to produce this for us internally within the company, you would charge us?"

Aleks: "Exactly, because we need to cover the cost of doing this through the external supplier – even if it works fully on our own data. It is high-precision work. We need to deliver on quality and not just another automated dashboard."

Business leader: "I understand, and your approach to quality is exactly what we need too, but with this fee in place, it would mean that I have to pay millions to your team just to get what I need! This is impossible! How can it be this way?"

Aleks: "Look, I totally get your frustration. That's why you need that customer master project to come up with a proper, automated solution that can be scalable and address your needs, and even if I still don't understand exactly what your needs are, it must be a customer/org master type of capability at the center – as far I understand from everything I've heard from you in the past few days. There is simply no other way."

Business leader: "There is no way I would waste so much money for transactional and operational purposes. This is ridiculous. I will talk to the engineering VP to accelerate the work!"

I left the conversation equally unhappy.

While I had full sympathy for what seemed like emerging business needs and understood their frustration with scalability issues and delivery timelines, I couldn't share their perspective about "wasting money."

Indeed, while we were paying for each transaction, the data monetization program itself was extremely successful and the expense of doing the work was incredibly low in comparison with the revenue we saw afterward. Plus, we were gaining a highly curated list of customer profiles that could also be useful outside of that licensing position work. Unfortunately, these profiles were not universal and did not align with the customer data feed we had from Dun & Bradstreet. But we were gradually building the muscle in what could be called the "MDM stewardship" role, and I was hoping we could reuse these skills elsewhere.

If only we could help somehow with that customer master project… Could we?

Unexpected turn

A month later, I received a meeting invitation from the same business leader again. Woah! I was getting nervous, presuming that the conversation wouldn't be smooth at all. Either we were about to fight about the costs of delivery and the role of different IT departments to contribute or they would want us to gear up with the customer master's engineering team to get things moving faster. The latter would be interesting, of course, yet also challenging on all fronts.

I was wrong in all my predictions.

Business leader: "Hi again, we talked to our leadership team and after evaluating different opinions, we are ready."

Aleks: "Sorry, you are ready for what?"

Business leader: "Ready to pay the fees you have requested. For each transaction we process."

Aleks: "But the fees are only part of the problem – we can't scale this work the way you need it; we haven't even tried to link and pull all the systems and attributes you've mentioned. We don't even have any working concept! I thought I was very clear in my message – you need a customer master, and this Microsoft Organization Master project will address exactly what you want."

Business leader: "No. We can't wait that long. We are going live in four months with this new product on the market, and there is still plenty of work to do, besides data. But data is the key. This is why we agreed to fund your work – we will spend a few million to get a billion, and that's fine."

Aleks: "What are you talking about? I don't know of any new products coming out."

Business leader: "True, not yet. But you will soon. We want to launch a new support product – which is totally different from the current Premier offering. The work your team is doing today is the closest to what we saw in the company, yet we still need to address many white spaces. Look, let's work through this in depth in a separate discussion, but we need to join our minds and team forces to deliver a new digital product for support. This will be a very innovative thing, with many underlying capabilities and superb potential. Our ability to price it right and deliver seamlessly is fully dependent on the accuracy of its data – and I've seen so many issues in the data that I almost feel at risk of failure. I'm sure you understand. And we can't afford to fail with this. All hands on deck – please prioritize this within your work scope."

Aleks: "Why do you believe it is even possible?"

Business leader: "I know it is possible. I've asked around about your team – everyone said that you can get anything done with and around data. So, here we are – and we are ready to invest."

The mix of thoughts in my head was amazing – from assessing a mind-blowing and strategic data product opportunity to a harsh understanding of how deep into trouble we were going to get ourselves on this data journey. The risk of the new, first-party product launch failing due to data unavailability, DQ issues, and the absence of a proper ecosystem was never more real. Especially when adding the extreme timelines requested and the fact that we needed to do it separately and on our own – as a big portion of data engineering resources would be working on the customer master project, and hence we must progress both in parallel and with an avant-garde approach simultaneously.

It was utterly clear, though, that I was already now part of this, and the next step was to *stop complaining and start building.*

And off we go

We divided the entire work scope into several semi-independent work tracks – let's review them all together and see how one was connected to another, and then go deeper, one by one, to understand how each of those tracks contributed to the overall success.

These tracks were more pivotal areas where we had to concentrate our attention and were not designed to be operated as conventional virtual teams (v-teams). The whole model of delivery was a rather "swarm" style, with experts and accountable personas reaching out to each other on a per-need basis. Surprisingly, this seemingly chaotic way worked well for the initial launch, by shortening communications paths and providing unlimited fast-track access with no formalities between all team members.

The five original tracks were as follows:

- **Understand the requirements and crystallize the idea**: While we had an overall idea of what the final product would look like, it was fuzzy and not yet specific to the pricing, offering, what data we use and how, and many other bold and significant aspects. We urgently had to move beyond *we have an idea* to *we have a crisp proposal and business case.*

  Our business stakeholders had an idea of product design, so to speak, and how this could be priced and delivered. Having the right data here was paramount. Not only did we have to find that data inside the company (and, at times, also outside of the company as we were looking for referential definitions) but we also had to ensure that data would be rightly and accurately interpreted and used.

  Sounds simple, yet from day one, we discovered that we had a different understanding of the usage and meaning of several key attributes between the business team and the data team. There wasn't a right or wrong party – some were gaps in knowledge on the stakeholders' side and some were our misinterpretations. Collectively, we had ample knowledge, yet it was crucial to share a common ground and   an understanding, with no place for assumptions or generic, non-fact-based opinions.

  We drew the meta-model of our future data product, with business rules and lineage to each source system and attribute, but we even had to change and adjust this several times along the way as we were hit by unexpected DQ issues or lack of data.

  The key here is ultimately respect, transparency, and assertiveness to get to that shared understanding. Often, things appear to be understood but they aren't, and you need a few more direct and "stupid" questions to come to that notion – better early than late.

- **Develop a proof of concept and test it internally**: Clearly, some proof of concept must be accomplished and put into practice – a visual representation of what the proposal is, along with minimum developments between various business groups and departments to support each other.

  With no time for fancy designs, we simply sketched the business outcome in Excel, along with how future customers would see the offer, and then we did reverse-engineering exercises by finding every piece of data needed or business rule element that must be represented in this view. Next, we used our innovation capacity in outsourcing to   determine, explore, and experiment whether that data could be found within the existing perimeter of knowledge, while, at the same time, checking whether we had that data on our internal platform. If we didn't have it yet, how could we ingest it quickly?

  Besides materializing the concept and making early proofs and checks, we had to consider internal collaboration and how this should be adjusted and rebound to what we need. The whole end-to-end process, from sourcing and composing the data view to when the pricing composition was reviewed and accepted by sellers, was lengthy and crossed through multiple departments in the company.

Building these *collaboration pipelines* between a variety of business groups wasn't less important than the data itself in the end, as we had to enable the effective flow and handover of precious data, with matching schedules, interfaces, processes, quality controls, and much more.

- **Define a reasonably scalable approach for the initial launch**: Given the initial timelines, it became clear that we wouldn't have an absolute majority of what we needed before the launch of the product. Moving the launch date wasn't possible for many reasons, hence we had to think outside the box about what our absolute essentials were to get it to market, and nothing more than the essentials.

To say it was tough is an understatement! Faced with little to no advanced technology support, limited engineering resources (as they were focused on enabling long-term solutions), and already fully utilized capacity in operations, it required a true moment of creativity and rethinking of the entire setup we had thus far. As the number-one step, we locked our team into a three-day workshop with intense brainstorming and being totally open-minded to all ideas. Anything and everything was considered, with a special focus on possible partnerships across the company.

We knew the work would be done with highly manual involvement, yet this wasn't the answer we were looking for. We had to be ultra-realistic and embrace self-reflection on team capacity, roles and responsibilities, and the possible stretch for everyone, and then translate that into a cascading and firm countdown of actions for our extended engineering and operations partners. No magic would happen by itself – we needed to make it happen.

- **Set up the delivery process for T+90 days**: Perhaps we would be able to produce something in a completely manual way, especially for the proof of concept, and maybe even for the launch itself. Yet, as we got on the market, we had to anticipate an increasing demand and have corresponding support from operations. We thought of the first 90 days as being critical to the overall success of the product, with the ability to add more tech and stabilize delivery within that period.

The dominating idea was to move our mental goal beyond the T-0 date (the launch day) and get ready for the next three months after launch, which would be even harder ones. Why? Because we would receive tons of feedback as we started to be in production, meaning we would face the reality of the first customers' complaints and stressful decisions, and we would need to process exceptions, reprocess pricing quotes with urgency, and clean up after mistakes we made. In other words, besides doing an excellent job in delivery (as that was a standard expectation), we would have to manage a number of things on top of this, all of them being urgent and important.

This made us think holistically through the entire period of pre-launch, launch, and post-launch as one iterative process, and hence to plan our capacity and incremental increase of efforts through that entire timeline. Put simply, we had to plan for a marathon, not for a sprint.

- **Defining people, processes, and technology beyond launch**: While it was clear that the pre-launch, the launch itself, and the next three months after would be very hectic and highly experimental, we needed to think of what the proper and complete setup would look like, with stable and smooth product delivery post the startup phase – as part of the product industrialization.

We wanted to start building for that early and not get caught out as the demand would grow exponentially if (for sure!) the product itself were to be successful. This advanced thinking also allowed us to bring crucial engineering capabilities into the picture – starting with data and process architecture, upgrading the technology stack, smoothing the edges with delivery and support, embedding the feedback we would have by that time into the process, and much more. It was about imagining a fast-forward view of the future state, understanding and amplifying what the state of delivery would be by that time, and then building all the respective capabilities as the enablement path. For example, the first pricing quotes were made in Excel and the next were made in Power Apps, but the picture of success was to have them in a dedicated and integrated UI, with an easy ability to regenerate or refresh the quote. To have that UI ready in six months, we had to start designing it almost as we started the whole process.

We did it – what did we learn?

I'm not going to go into depth in describing the next several months of work. It was a difficult and stretched time, with thousands of issues and aspects to address again and again.

It was one of those tough times when you learn a lot more about yourself, your skills, behaviors, and reactions, and about your team members and business partners.

We all were committed to success and wished we could get that amazing data-driven product on the market, yet each of us had our own limits and beliefs, and overcoming those became one of the leadership challenges. Looking back today, I can clearly see where and how I could have done better.

Perhaps the best opportunity is to summarize our key data leadership learnings out of this astonishing work and to share them with you here, hoping that some of these will be useful and encouraging examples.

Communication

Clarity on communication was one of the critical things from the very beginning. I can't stress enough how much clarity we had to establish and continuously re-establish what needed to be done. Having visionary people start this work was amazing, yet afterward, we had to think in a structured and practical way. Never before had I felt how true the simple notion of "There are no stupid questions" is – every question someone had needed to be put forward and answered. The costs of having unclarified expectations or even small details were too high otherwise. And the most precious resource is lost time, along with frustration among v-team members.

Realizing there were different perspectives and starting points between business leaders and us in the data team was one of the keys.

To overcome this, we agreed to openly challenge each other in the most straightforward way. We knew that each of us had the best intentions – yet our base understanding, the style of work, communication preferences, and even time zones were all different. Acknowledging and accepting these aspects made the whole experience easier as there was no space for blame, finger-pointing, frustrations, and things such as "But I told you!" or "I knew this would happen."

Another aspect of communication was making it flow around the business or project needs, being super flexible and not rigid. While we had some scheduled meetings throughout the week, we would rely a lot on ad hoc calls and would prioritize calls over emails or Teams (which was unusual for Microsoft, especially with people working across different time zones). This was one of those special cases where I found that working as closely as possible together or emulating such an environment kept our progress at a fast pace. A big fan of remote work otherwise, here, I had to admit that being "present" at every minute made a difference – albeit adding to the stress and pressure.

Sponsors and coalition

You can't success in such a massive project without explicit support from senior leadership, yet gaining that support across the entire perimeter wasn't easy. Sure, from an aerial view, everybody was supportive and demonstrated an understanding of company priority, but when it came down to specific commitments that each team had to own, it became a masterpiece of diplomacy, relationships, and influencing strategies. Much of the success was in building extensive coalitions of supportive leaders. What started as single-business-unit, ultra-high priority work gradually involved more and more teams of data engineers, sellers, business operations, and so on. With each team, we had to match our "why this is important" to their "why it makes sense for you," using executive "air cover" along with the sponsorship as a driving (but not forcing!) factor. The ability to find a relevant win-win between the teams made this work act as a connector, rather than as a power play where some would feel unhappy.

For example, we used all manually produced pricing quotes as the baseline and test data for our engineering team working on the organizational master (MDM) program. This made both teams' lives easier, and engineering was supportive of our operations to produce as many of those statements as possible so that they had more data for tuning the ML models and building the graph.

We were carefully connecting the people across the company to maximize influencing capabilities. For instance, both my business partners and I were cross-influencing the management on our vertical line of reporting. Naturally, we were using different perspectives and backgrounds for our pitches, hence adding to a more well-rounded and balanced view of benefits while providing answers to a broader variety of questions. This resulted in great top-management alignment between the parties and ensured we had continuous support.

Proven technology

With tight deadlines, we felt we had no time to experiment with technology or the latest productivity gainers. But we still tried, and I think the best recipe in such situations is to try but not have your expectations too high.

In our example, one of the first questions was about how to deliver the aggregated view of customers' product use, licenses, revenue, and so on, through the entire end-to-end flow, from the moment of initiation till the point of consumption. The latter we sorted out rather quickly by building an easy UI for our sellers to consume the data in real time, reliably, and repeatedly.

But the hard part was building those pricing quotes/statements, validating the quality, tuning them on the way, and then pushing them into the users' frontends. Much of this demanded visual representation along with editing capabilities.

Excel unsurprisingly came first to mind, though we wanted a more user-friendly and guided path. Then, the option of Power Apps was immediately introduced, giving much more automation and user-friendliness. We spent several days testing and debating which capability to prioritize, as each had pros and cons.

Our hearts and minds were with the modern Power Apps option, and we strived to make it work. Unfortunately, we soon realized that we needed to step back and do all the initial delivery in Excel due to the highly experimental, low-maturity work. But the thing was, it worked.

Even as we went into production and were sharing the whole story, one of the most common questions was "Did you make that all in Excel?" and people would be laughing about this, with no belief that such severe and impactful work could be delivered in such a basic (and cumbersome) way. True but to the point – the reliability of totally proven technology was more important than tech bias or appearance.

Extreme focus on the goal

Along with the previous subject, the example about focusing only on "what works" while leaving aside anything else was one of those countless calls for hard prioritization. Not being retrogrades or risk-averse, we were clear that we needed to stay focused on the final goal. Every day, we had decisions to make, and each could either bring us closer to reaching the initial goal or get off target if something broke or was disturbed unexpectedly.

One of the insights from our very own path was about the usage of proven technology, and there are other similar examples.

The best example here was addressing scalability for the mass production of pricing quotes. You may recall from previous pages that we had already stretched data stewards' capacity through outsourcing, and scaling there by simply adding more people didn't seem like the way to go. The main issue was the learning curve – to reach the needed accuracy of that work, the stewards would typically train for at least six months. Therefore, the fundamental question was about how to automate the process. But we quickly learned that we couldn't automate easily, and we needed to stick to proven, validated, and reliable delivery practices that we could fully control.

Long story short – we obviously came back to scaling by adding more data stewards to our outsourcing pool . As straightforward as it appears, it was the only option to pursue if we wanted to meet our deadline.

Holding a massive brainstorming session with our delivery partners first, we initiated a series of rotations across the data stewards and their allocations, while quickly adding more people to the overall delivery. This introduced cascade complexity, as we shifted highly experienced data stewards from their usual services to this new one, leading to knowledge gaps and escalations among the rest of the portfolio. My priorities started to blur, as we had to cater to the stability of current work while also rapidly increasing competence for the new service.

At some point, I thought we were likely going to crash and collapse the whole thing altogether, yet keeping an eagle eye on why we first initiated the change and what steps must be taken to accomplish it helped us to stay focused and navigate that chess game. With rigorous attention, issue by issue, and positive and uplifting thinking, we made it through.

The result was stunning – we got an even more powerful and expanded community of data stewards ready to deliver this new service with great previous experience and broad enterprise knowledge, making them not only highly proficient in this work but also mature and deployable to almost any sort of data operation or data steward challenge. We gratefully came back to this community many more times in the future for various experiments and innovations. Hence, the mess and stress that came with three to four months of cascade change was repaid for years to come.

Telling the story

As you work on something highly important, especially a company-wide investment project, you tend to believe that everybody knows about it and will be supportive of your challenge. Ideally, this is true – and much of this is dependent on communication and achieving coalition and stakeholder alignment. While focusing on stakeholders and top management is obviously important, an often-overlooked aspect is crafting an impossible story and sharing this with the broader audience. Believe me, having one prepared and polished will not only save you time and effort in numerous ways but will also motivate, connect, and endorse people around your team. It will support talent retention, especially in a fluid outsourcing space; it will be something that leaders of your leaders will present and exchange at company strategy meetings.

While we rushed into the delivery with many practical and critical challenges, at some point, I realized that I was badly repeating myself while explaining again and again what we were up to with our intended work. In all that mess and chaos, finding the moment to settle down and think creatively was another challenge, yet a kind of lovely one. I took my key business partner for an interview about the deeper project goals, what success would mean for the Microsoft Services business, and what a side impact would be on a company's broader business. We delved into the company strategy and possible innovations, the digitalization of the enterprise, and how this case, while generating revenue, also supports winning new customers and ensuring the success of existing ones.

Step by step, we came up with a concise, well-laid-out story about how Microsoft reinvented a multi-degree-old business with an innovative view of the data we had, and how we transformed that business line with synergy between business commitment, strong data-driven practice, and unbounded innovative thinking. We used this story and its elements in hundreds of ongoing conversations, inspiring other people, teams, and businesses to do what at first sight seemed impossible but became real as they embraced the challenge and followed our proven and beaten steps.

Personally, this project became a milestone for me as the data leader and formed a strong set of entrepreneurial skills at the enterprise. In some way, it became a culmination and testimonial on what data can do to business growth. It also provoked thinking about overall data value and how we usually underestimate the potential of data assets in the company.

Summary and key takeaways

This has been a lengthy chapter with a variety of findings, from applying the Pareto principle to maximizing outcomes and impact, and then forming your very own fine-tuned strategy when dealing with data and business challenges, improving the state of data in the enterprise, and shining with the ultimate data leadership skills.

Additionally, we reviewed a case study about forming a new business opportunity within the company while using existing data – something that probably deserves a separate book to really go into detail.

Takeaway #1 – using the Pareto principle as your compass

Let's start with a few leading learnings that helped us succeed, adopt the Pareto approach, and eventually come up with our own methodology:

- **Emphasize teamwork in data management**: Success hinges on a collaborative, skilled team committed to ongoing learning and achievement recognition

- **Implement effective change management**: Essential for integrating new data practices, this requires educating stakeholders and adapting strategies to evolving business and data landscapes

- **Value all stakeholder feedback**: Actively seeking and responding to feedback drives improvements and innovation in data services

- **Harness customer and partner insights**: Understanding their needs is crucial for tailoring data services and enhancing value

- **Prioritize strategic DQ**: Early implementation of DQ measures and a connected approach across the enterprise ensures consistency

- **Adopt agile data management practices**: Flexibility and responsiveness to change are key, with a focus on prioritizing impactful data requests

- **Build on solid foundations**: Establish robust core data management practices before exploring flexible, innovative edges

Takeaway #2 – practical application of the Pareto principle

The first step in applying the Pareto principle was defining the explicit relationship between business growth issues and underlying data issues. I highly recommend doing this exercise in every company.

The resolution of top enterprise data issues at a major company involved applying the Pareto principle to align business challenges with data enablement, using a collaborative, transparent approach.

The preceding seven core principles guided the process, focusing on team collaboration, prioritization of critical data issues, and ensuring scalability. This strategy emphasized solid foundational work and clear prioritization, enabling impactful solutions that were resource-efficient.

Takeaway #3 – case study – building a multi-billion-dollar business

In the case study of creating the Unified Support service, the focus was on nurturing new services through data operations, emphasizing collaboration between business experts and data team members.

This approach differed from traditional IT-driven methods, valuing the ability to quickly experiment and adapt in a fast-paced, uncertain environment.

The development of this new digital product faced initial challenges but succeeded by prioritizing data operations and business feedback, leading to a breakthrough in customer-centric pricing and consumption-based revenue. The project involved understanding requirements, developing a proof of concept, defining a scalable approach, and setting up a delivery process.

The ultimate success of this project highlighted the importance of clear communication, strong leadership support, proven technology, focused goals, and effective storytelling in data-driven project management.

As exciting and as long as it was, this chapter has come to an end. But hold on tight, we will continue with MDM in the following chapter!

Part 3: Intelligent Future

This final part elevates the conversation to the most advanced data subjects of today – deploying **master data management**, designing **data mesh architecture**, enabling federated **data governance** and **data product thinking**, and fostering **data literacy** and **data culture**. An additional chapter delves into AI readiness aspects and presents several highly focused approaches for successful enterprise-wide AI enablement.

This part includes the following chapters:

- *Chapter 9, Data Mastering and MDM*
- *Chapter 10, Data Mesh and Data Governance*
- *Chapter 11, Data Assets or Data Products?*
- *Chapter 12, Data Value, Literacy, and Culture*
- *Chapter 13, Getting Ready for GenAI*

9

Data Mastering and MDM

Data mastering and **Master Data Management** (**MDM**) solutions play a significant role in the overall data strategy. However, they are also complex to implement and achieve success with. More often, these massive, expensive, and long-term projects fail, despite the standing business needs and active support from the data team.

Microsoft was no different in that sense. With four MDM implementations either completely failing or only gaining partial success and limited impact, we learned the hard way what the difficulties of the MDM journey are. Some of these learnings tap into data architecture and technical capabilities, while others shed light on difficulties with effective change management, prioritization, and stakeholder alignment.

In contrast with the previous chapters, we won't be listing several successful scenarios and best practices. Rather, we will do the opposite – we will go through the entire story of MDM implementations at Microsoft, understanding their connected nature and how the unresolved challenges of one project kept migrating to and negatively impacting the next ones. We will combine and summarize all the learnings at the end, with an ultimate list of recommendations, along with a heartwarming and life-tested advisory about how to navigate data mastering effectively.

By the end of this chapter, you will have learned about the following:

- The most common MDM challenges and failure points – the business view and the data team view
- What is most critical to address while preparing, launching, and continuously advancing an MDM implementation?
- How to find success in the small things, live the true value of "progress over perfection," and not fall for overly ambitious aspirations

Setting the stage

Much of the previous chapters was spent discussing the history of data management and data strategy at Microsoft, and our team's success in implementing various data management solutions. By now, you've heard many inspiring stories and foundational achievements in launching global data management capabilities at the company, along with some superb innovations in data products.

However, as outlined earlier, this chapter will take a radically different turn. We will discuss failures; among these failures, the most prominent and comprehensive one is the inability to implement a modern MDM solution. Interestingly, Microsoft has a long history of attempting to implement various MDM solutions, all built in-house by our engineering teams. Yet, all of them were missing something very important and therefore had a very short lifespan, or never fully entered production.

Now, this chapter presents a fascinating opportunity.

It's not about how to do things better, but rather, mostly about how *not* to do things with large-scale projects. We'll go through the history of various implementations with different and diverse logic and architecture. We will delve into each of these implementations and understand why they were failures. I believe that learning from others' failures is one of the most effective ways to prevent a similar failure yourself.

In addition, we will try to summarize the commonalities across all implementations and why they did not have the intended impact and the desired business results.

Finally, we will compile a list of potential best practices, derived from what we learned the hard way by doing things incorrectly, along with successes, which we, of course, still encountered with the MDM solutions. This, we believe, is the golden list of practices for modern MDM implementation.

The legacy of Microsoft Organizations

Let's start with the first attempts and how this whole concept of MDM was created and introduced in the company.

When I joined Microsoft, one of the foundational solutions in global IT architecture was a system called **MSO**, which stands for **Microsoft Organizations**. In a way, it was an attempt to create an organizational master, and the reason for this was very specific – it came down to the necessity of connecting a CRM system, which was running on Siebel in those days, with the in-house-built revenue collection system. We had to make an explicit link between a customer in the CRM with the respective revenue landing in our revenue collection system.

It was not efficient to simply make a direct link between the systems. We tried it, and it didn't work well. It created even more frustration due to the high volatility of data. Here, the idea was to have something serving as a proxy, almost like a keyring, but with data mastering capability, which would eventually become a master for how the data appears in the revenue system and the CRM.

This master system was created in a very simple way – perhaps too simple.

Essentially, a copy of the CRM system was entirely ingested into the new environment, along with a copy of the revenue data, and then they were matched together to create a first record, which would hold a unique ID as the MSO ID. It would have the referential foreign keys to the CRM and the revenue collection system, respectively. There was also a user interface created on top of it – to view, manage, adjust, merge, and parent different organization records – in an attempt to create a more realistic representation of large companies with multiple levels, such as branches (child records) versus the main enterprise (parent record). This allowed us to simulate the structure of large multinational companies, which normally consist of multiple different branches across several countries.

So far, so good, right?

Ownership was given to the finance team, which was somewhat innovative for those days, to have a business unit outside of IT owning a significant amount of data. Yet, on the other hand, it was probably too early for such a massive step, as the data literacy and ability to really modify that data were low. The MSO system required a lot of manual maintenance, and due to the highly geographical split of the company at the time, these efforts were not entirely centralized but mostly performed at the local subsidiary or local area level.

To illustrate the fractious efforts in managing data in MSO, I recall an early dialogue I had with a person responsible for data management within a subsidiary. It was hilarious to learn how the system works, yet at the same time, a sad story of endless people's efforts to keep data clean and suitable for business use, within a completely inadequate environment.

Aleks: "Hey, I wanted to ask you, how do you maintain the data quality and the link between the CRM and revenue data?"

Data steward: "That's easy. You need to go to the system called MSO and "merge" the CRM record with the same named record from the revenue system. As a result, you will get both CRM and revenue record IDs under the same MSO ID. The systems have been linked since then."

Aleks: "That sounds very simple… Why do we encounter these DQ issues again and again, often with the same customer's records?"

Data steward: "Well, after you merge them, there will quite often be new, duplicative records, plus if you merge out a wrong one, you might need to unmerge those back and find better candidates there… and you will find hundreds of those. Also, somebody else might just override what you did, for a different reason."

Aleks: "Wow, that sounds frustrating. How do you still manage to keep the quality acceptable then?"

Data steward: "I just recheck and redo the whole thing every week."

Aleks: "What…?!"

When we first arrived as the global data team, the system was still there. We had an opportunity to create global data cleansing and **Data Quality (DQ)** practices based on our ability to operate with MSO, although we quickly found that it was a very frustrating experience due to large amounts of duplication and siloed practices.

The data was not reliable at all; it required constant modification and follow-ups. Many new records were coming in daily and were not properly matched and allocated to the existing org structures. Finally, different teams were doing things differently, sometimes even overwriting each other's work.

> **Why MDM?**
> The good side – it was the first time we realized and understood that there is a real business case behind an MDM solution.

To summarize our first attempt – it was just a very hard try, with more concerns than benefits. Finance was often puzzled about how to establish a complete view of the customer's revenue and all the associated sales and marketing activities, and this was an approach that we tried to resolve in a simple way. But we ended up creating a monster system, every day filled with more and more untrusted data, and eventually, many business units lost trust in any data coming from MSO, so the company decided we should abandon this idea and try something different, with lessons learned.

The rise and fall of Microsoft Individuals and Organizations

Let's move on to attempt number two.

This time, the focus was not only on thinking of better architecture or design for the MDM solution but also on learning from the previous mistakes in managing the complexity of organizational IDs otherwise being constantly modified, merged, or unmerged. Additionally, we thought that it would be good to include individual contact data – that is, an individual's data, such as business decision-makers or technical decision-makers associated with organizations, in a single, unified mastering system.

Kind of a one-size-fits-all solution – which, perhaps, already sounds like a bad idea.

In that sense, the new system received the name **MIO**, representing the concept of **Microsoft Individuals and Organizations** blended into one MDM capability.

The approach chosen was different, learning from the previous mistakes with MSO.

We saw that we needed to be more transparent about incoming duplicates and changes, and while we aimed to store clean data, we also needed to show how this golden record was formed. We shouldn't just merge away everything that doesn't seem to be an ultimate fit, as this data isn't visible anymore and only creates constant rework of what's already been done before.

The new idea was that we should think about a composite record (or as we would say today, a graph representation), which would have a type of composite of relationships within all these incoming records from various sources – such as a CRM system, revenue collection, and licensing. Based on this composition, we would establish a kind of master umbrella record, representing "the best of the best" out of the entire composite – hopefully serving as a true master. Since we wouldn't constantly be overriding it anymore, but rather simply associating more records into these compositions, we would never lose track of what had already been done, while also always having a golden record master.

We would also not lose track of the numerous changes that had been applied to the master record, allowing us to review and investigate an entire composite at any time.

It required a massive investment to create this system, with expectations flying high. The ownership was set with corporate IT, with the corporate data team being deeply involved in design and orchestration.

Unfortunately, it never saw the light of production, and there were three massive underlying reasons why:

- The first reason it failed was the selection of the data that would initially be ingested. Instead of starting small, with a very well-defined and clean dataset, we opted for a Big Bang approach, and with just a little bit of data cleaning from the former MSO organizational hierarchies, we ingested all that data to form the base of MIO.

> **Data is nothing without controls**
>
> This created a very large scale of records that needed to be managed in the system, almost copying the scope of what had already been in the previous incarnation (MSO). That was too difficult to deal with in that situation with the low maturity of global data management and DQ in the company, along with not much interest from the business in participating in this work. We simply struggled to comprehend and establish qualitative controls over this data.

- The second issue was even more obvious – by adding individual data to these low-maturity organizational hierarchies, it was like creating another dimension of DQ issues and complexity. Not only did we have challenges with the individual's DQ in itself, more prominent than with the quality of the organizational data, but creating this type of complexity multiplier really made it even more difficult to distill a clean dataset. In theory, having various individuals and organizational data all together would address the entire business need for both clean data in the context of sales and marketing activities, as well as the organizational structure that represented the revenue impact and financial results. But that's in theory.

> **Double trouble**
>
> In practice, we created a multiplication of two worse and badly managed datasets, which just became totally unmanageable.

- The final reason was the actual system architecture. Even though the idea of having a composite record with intra-relationships and a virtual master record was generally innovative and close to modern graph databases, the issue was really in the size and quality of these composites. As we created them automatically, without any curation, by simply ingesting the previous, slightly better-cleaned data, plus augmenting it with the additional matching set of individual data, these composites were huge. We sometimes had thousands of records "parented" under one single master record, and these composites still had to be validated with manual efforts to digest what the best record (or combination of records) in this composition was.

The absence of a fully (or at least highly) automated solution for these reviews to carry on resulted in the need to go through some type of curation by humans. Even with minimal reviews, we would still need validated input for curation. We did a couple of tests on this, only to realize that it would be insane to try to clean and carry forward those composite datasets. It would literally take years for large data teams to go through those, while, at the same time, in the real world, the changes would continue to be ingested into the system. Not only would we never be able to clean all of those MIO records but, even more importantly, we would never be able to keep up with additional daily feeds and updates.

Thus, in the end, after realizing all the preceding facts, we understood that it would again be a no-go, that this solution would not take place, and that we would not be able to use it. On the positive side, this solution brought more attention to the quality of an individual's data, which had previously always been in the shadow of organization/customer account DQ challenges. At a later stage, we were able to reuse some portion of that data for data privacy setup and GDPR-related investigations, to help build proper data privacy controls in the systems across the company.

Yet, thinking about another approach to creating an MDM solution, this did not work either, resulting in a massive engineering effort simply being wasted.

Hello Mr. Jarvis

The next few years involved going back to the basics. We kept using ad hoc connections between the CRM and revenue collection, which were mostly in use for sales and marketing.

We were also gradually realizing the importance of well-defined and compelling business cases to drive the work. The examples with MSO and MIO clearly outlined that any such implementations would need to have tremendous business support to succeed.

As you already know from previous chapters, small yet tangible innovations such as the **Managed Accounts List** (**MAL**) were often very handy in addressing these types of business demands. We started to consider that maybe we should go the opposite way, compared to the past attempts at building those MDM solutions.

Perhaps we shouldn't start with the big things and try to clean the entire universe. Instead, we should start small and take datasets that are well cleaned, with key business support, and then extend them to a proper MDM solution.

De facto for top enterprise customers, MAL was that type of solution, because it had the mastering capabilities exactly within its user interface and, once updated there, it would override the data in the downstream revenue collection and in CRM systems. The only problem was the limitation of scope – being only for enterprise customers, this meant limited impact on the entire company's needs and focusing on accounts only. That is, it represented a sales view and not a real-world view of a customer or an organization.

What I mean by the sales view here is that, often, for the convenience of our sales operations and business setup in particular countries, the way we see a customer is much different from the actual physical setup of that customer.

We would organize customer accounts by the way we sell to them, not bothering much about what the real-world structure is – unless these were multinational companies, where the revenue had to be split between various departments and countries.

Think of public sector companies, where many schools, public facilities, and governmental organizations are all reporting and being officially organized by a respective ministry. In some cases, we would have high-end deals and agreements on a ministry level, yet in most cases, our sales and marketing would work directly with those business entities underneath. The same also applies to many large commercial customers, with diverse business units in their structure, presenting different needs and challenges.

Having a partial view
While sales saw no issue with doing business in that way, it presented numerous cascading challenges beyond the sales point.

First, the customer's own view was different from how we saw that customer – and this was already a significant issue, especially with an increasing number of overarching contracts and cloud usage, where we could easily miss a number of important branches of a company, being led only by the sales view and not realizing that those branches belonged to the same top enterprise customer account, even if we never sold to them directly. A couple of these types of mismatches propelled DQ-related escalations as far as our CEO level.

Second, this led to confusion within the company itself, as sales, finance, and support would all have different views on what a customer account looked like as a whole.

Adding more complexity while incorporating more isolated business groups such as services or devices, we would be hit by severe productivity loss navigating all those variations, resulting in slowing down the business, the ability to make a qualitative offer, the ability to support a customer with urgency when needed, and much more.

Simple attempts to address this with some account grouping and account hierarchies would be inadequate, as accounts were still representative of some kind of financial engagement, limiting the view. What we needed was a big-picture view of a customer's entire organizational structure, enabling us to oversee all our existing engagements across all the business lines.

Learning from our own successes
Here, MAL was a great operational master for enterprise accounts and sales data, but not much else beyond that narrow scope. Yet it also set a few best practices, and it had highly trusted data and was (almost!) properly used as the master. The exceptions here refer to the case of externally fed changes, such as mergers and acquisitions, that would have to be processed manually and result in a noticeable delay.

Okay, but what do we do then? We have a clear need and massive business cases; we have some examples of where we did great and it worked. Yet, we lack a proper, suitable solution.

The next move was dictated by significant changes in the licensing principles, resulting in the decoupling of the traditional volume licensing approach from the new-generation one, which focused on cloud readiness and deployment. This pushed us to pivot a set of customer accounts into a completely new and dedicated environment, with the ability to tap into many-to-many relationships between customer accounts and organizations.

A new solution was created, called **Jarvis** internally. It was built from scratch by our internal IT engineering team and, unlike what had happened before, we hoped that it would finally address all the mastering challenges and prepare the company for a fast and fluid future.

The leading business case was to address the different definitions of the customers and the new licensing rules, which would allow us to, again, create a kind of composite record but in a slightly different way. We wanted to connect to the same organizational tree beyond just revenue data and CRM definitions, specifically addressing licensing information and products. We wanted to see the cloud usage of a customer; we wanted to see the entire history of volume licensing and other licensing products, along with CRM, revenue, and support tickets – all in the same place.

> **Business case in one word**
>
> Eventually, having this type of "Customer 360" approach was the main business case and the reason for the massive investment in the engineering of this new solution.

Now, on the engineering side of the house, the team came up with a pretty brilliant architecture to overcome the challenge.

There was a lot of flexibility in the system, in a good way, using graph principles, along with some controls on how and by whom the data would be updated, modified, or distributed across the systems of usage. The heart of the new solution was the keyring – to connect the foreign keys of all these surrounding applications and create a type of composite key for the future master record. Based on this, it would receive its own primary ID and be available for consumption across the enterprise. Interestingly, this keyring is still in use, and in the end, it was perhaps the best benefit of this system altogether.

But why did this fail… again?

The breaking point was different this time.

On the one hand, having a very specific business case for addressing the new challenges in the licensing space was truly important. Here, the engineering team did a marvelous job of working closely with the licensing teams to make them happy and achieve their requirements.

On the other hand, many of our business units and the data team were kind of kept in the dark. We'd been constantly promised a solution that would be launched soon for company-wide consumption and onboarding, without asking us to actively participate in design, contribute to the DQ, or provide feedback.

Time passed, the system was running the core operations of new licensing products and services, and investments were still being put into this work, but a slow realization started to come that while a lot of attention, if not most, was given to the data architecture, very little attention was being given to the DQ and how the data would be consumed by multiple parties in the company, often those having different views and different senses of ownership.

Low DQ kills even best-engineered products

This new system was designed to be enterprise-centric, but when we looked closer into it, beyond the licensing input, we found that the rest of the data was of low quality and in an ambiguous state. It was serving the needs of one forefront team, yet it had never been curated for the intended use of many other business lines. It had been imported and ingested from the source system, but it lacked the essential quality controls and basic data governance principles to be trusted.

The sad truth was that the data ingestion missed the critical pre-screening and validation of the records against DQ standards, business rules, and fit-to-business scenarios of future usage. In fact, we had a newly created system with a promising and powerful data architecture underneath, but with very little immediate business value aside from single usage in modern licensing.

No wonder it failed the first principal onboarding for a chance to become a true MDM.

If you remember, I previously described how MAL was at the time the only real operational master for sales accounts data, which was indeed considered and respected by all the users of its system within the sales, marketing, and finance business groups.

It was like the Bible for them.

However, with this new Jarvis MDM concept coming to life, Jarvis would be the one to manage and master the data in MAL, consequently pushing MAL to be considered just one of those downstream subscriber systems. In this scenario, key customer account definitions were to be controlled and maintained (mastered) from the Jarvis organization and account MDM view. Technically, that was probably the right way to architect, but from a change management perspective, data readiness, and real business impact use case, it was a freak-out moment.

This was a true breaking point since, in comparison with MAL, the Jarvis data had broader connections via its keyring, yet was of lower quality, and was never curated. In contrast, the MAL data was very highly curated and of decent quality, even though it represented just a small segment of the customer's accounts in the company.

Don't break what works

It was simply not possible to push the synchronization on and to override the managed accounts data with the feed from Jarvis. Nobody would take accountability for undermining the immediate and proven value of MAL with the distant and vague benefit of Jarvis's master data.

Could this problem be fixed by improved DQ in Jarvis? Absolutely!

This is exactly what we jumped on enthusiastically, trying to solve the data trust issues with a crowdfunded, human-curated, yet independent approach, focusing on what matters most – such as MAL data. We felt we needed to improve the data in the same way we had done numerous times before, for much of the Tier 1 LOB applications.

Yet, in fact, the fundamental issue was still elsewhere.

Criticality of change management

The issue was the absence of change management and business-readiness efforts to deploy this as a company-wide solution.

Jarvis was a system created by engineers with a high focus on how engineers would like data to be in that system, but it had a low correlation with the actual business challenges, beyond the initial licensing case, and this extremely partial view of how the enterprise functions was a big failure point as well as an "aha moment."

Don't get me wrong here – our people were on a mission to address what seemed to be the most important issues. They had a strong belief that once this system was complete and ready, everything else needed for success would happen naturally on its own, just like great products build their adoption path in a self-managed way. However, the adoption readiness, the change associated with doing this across several business lines, the ultimate trust in data, and so on were missing from the project's agenda.

Adding a general lack of transparency on efforts and centering the whole work around an engineering-dominated, siloed group, versus involving a bigger crowd of potential supporters and contributors, was also putting a lot of pressure on the outcome. Having feedback at the early stages and a transparent approach to DQ needs would be tremendously helpful.

In conclusion, there was no burning desire to use the system by any other business group.

The uncomfortable truth

The whole irony was, after waiting for years for an MDM solution capable of serving the whole enterprise, once it was finally there, nobody wanted to go through the painful changes required to adopt it, embracing ourselves into such heavy lifting efforts to overcome all the aforementioned issues. Too much would need to be changed, with too little trust in the data and the future ability of data to stay clean, even if it would be perfectly fixed at the beginning, as a one-time effort. Essentially, the absence of data governance, data leadership, and data ownership became the Achilles heel of Mr. Jarvis.

After three or four years of continuous attempts to make it relevant, even trying to re-make the core data and push through some massive data cleanup as a final SOS call, we could only conclude that we would probably use and reuse certain current components but there would be no more talks about broad, company-wide adoption of Jarvis MDM.

We cannot truly see this as an MDM solution for Microsoft.

We cannot declare this as the number one, superior capability for MDM within the company's overall data architecture and data eco-flow.

The third attempt at having customer and organization mastering has failed.

A meme? No, a MOM (aka Microsoft Org Master)!

Okay, we've been on an amazing journey of three attempts, three times going with MDM implementations, and all of them failed! Dare to learn more and what came next? Of course, a new attempt…

Looking back at all three independent, different attempts, all of them failed shortly after inception, or made no positive impact, as in the case of MSO.

Couldn't we simply learn the useful and critical points from these implementation stories and do a better job next time?

Frankly, to the credit of the company's culture, there was no particular or harsh blame toward IT for "not making it happen." In some way, many felt that they also left a footprint in this story, and not necessarily the best one. It was a sense of shared responsibility for not succeeding with the desired intent.

Collectively, we still wanted an MDM solution in the company and were still nailing out the different use cases, precising the requirements from business partners, and thinking about a possible solution.

Yet, there wasn't much courage or desire to start. We became too cautious, and we started to hear whispers in the company that *"perhaps this isn't our way; we are a unique company, we survived before, and maybe our path is simply different."*

No new initiatives were raised for a couple of years, while multiple teams were processing the sense of past failures and considering what could come next, and if we were to ever start again, how would we even kick off the work?

The new motion started under a different umbrella and purpose.

The Microsoft Services department decided to go for the implementation of a brand-new SAP instance, and they aimed to have a fresh dataset to start with, totally curated, validated, approved, and verified with various business perspectives.

In this case, they wanted that to be the perfect system, where every single record carries extreme value and effort behind it, even before it made its way into the system.

No question, this must have been to make the connection with data mastering, and therefore, the new effort and data mastering component was broadly and actively branded as **MDG – Master Data Governance**.

> **Embracing the "One Microsoft" approach**
>
> Several teams – data, business, and engineering – got their hands dirty and worked hard together for months to come up with not only fully cleansed and validated data but also, most importantly, rigid and restrictive data maintenance policies and controls. This was something that had never been seen or experienced before – highly authoritative data, sharply clean and clear, with equally authoritative controls and multi-step approvals for even slightly changing something there.

Possibly, it was a bit of an overkill in reality, yet it served superbly for understanding and facilitating an example of data value "when it is done right" – a classy, striking data literacy case. It became an example and an epitome of what every data team was dreaming about. It also hit the mark for business stakeholders; even with highly restrictive regulations, or maybe because of those, the stakeholders were finally reassured about DQ. People trusted MDG data; they used it for billing and understanding customer structures. And we can confidently say – they love it!

This created a precedent.

We started talks again about going beyond MDG and SAP and extending what was done in MDG to broader usage within the company, with the same level of curation and data controls.

Here, the fourth attempt started.

It started with the notion of extreme practicality, driven by the data team, which was cautiously and constantly rechecking the path and gaining early feedback.

"We must not fail," we said. *"It is simply impossible to get it wrong again!"*

Let's use all our experience, learnings, and wisdom and forget about the conflicts and individual perspectives to make something memorable and ground-breaking. We will bet on early feedback. We know how to make data architecture. We can reuse many of these components while having the ultimate clean dataset on top of the overall solutioning excellence and fit for purpose.

> **Did we learn our lessons?**
>
> Again, having an emerging business case is always a good start – and we got one. In addition, at that moment, we tried ultra-hard to incorporate all the previous lessons and not be misled by one shiny thing that doesn't stick to the rest of the company's data eco-flow afterward.

It started gently with the need to create an overview of top customers on Azure and all their branches and subsidiaries.

The traditional CRM-based view didn't cover the whole complexity of those companies, and it didn't exactly match the technical-level tenant view in the Azure cloud. We needed a middle layer that would accurately map Azure tenants to the real customers in the CRM, connect that data with revenue, and allow for a dynamic and executive overview. The main business case for this work was risk mitigation – as the branches of the large accounts might suddenly have an issue with the cloud resourcing availability and request an extra Azure capacity, we would have to realize that, in fact, these are correlated to a top level of an enterprise customer, consequently kicking in a premium support and customer success management. Otherwise, the risk was that a critical request for an added capacity would not be properly prioritized.

The need was to enable the Azure team to see through the entire set of different domains and tenants and to navigate to their real customers, end to end. Not to waste any more time, we started from existing datasets, using the same principle and learnings as we did with the MDG launch to build a highly curated and accurate dataset, and then iterate from there. We didn't think too much about the data architecture or consider other large investments into the building of anything gigantic or "foundational," as we did with Jarvis. Rather, we thought of the example of the successful experience of MAL and its impact on the business. Plus, we already had a recent example of data mastering architecture and keyring capabilities to reuse.

Now, this applied to a more complex world of data, where we would need to tidy up definitions in the Azure cloud, having various tenants and domains along with additional information about their revenue, their segments, their customer support, successful open cases, and so on.

This time, we also wanted to be clear that we were not addressing just the sales and marketing needs, or only the Azure team needs.

We wanted to build a small yet full-scale organizational master, serving various business domains universally and avoiding being customized for just one dominant use case. With an underlying focus on "organization," we aimed to drift away from account or customer definitions as such and ingest a broader perspective, aka a "balcony view," of the entire enterprise structure of a customer.

The final view would be superior (master) to a particular account's definitions in CRM or in revenue collection systems and would correspond to a global, real-world definition of an organization.

We started small and were really focusing on DQ and deep curation. Progress over perfection, yet also following the *first-time-right* principle – meaning we wouldn't rush or prioritize quantity over quality, ensuring that we wouldn't come back to the same ground job shortly after initial completion, but we also wouldn't insist for the absurdly accurate validation of every single organization's hierarchy definition.

We had to set certain boundaries on how far we would delve into the research and when "enough is enough" – otherwise, the risk with certain ultra-complex customer structures would be having a never-ending research job.

It worked well. Surprisingly well.

We were successful in creating the pivot solution in the first place and launching this for the number one business case we had – with the aforementioned Azure team. We received really good feedback from Azure from day one, with a few follow-up improvements needed, which we addressed quickly. Shortly after, the system was finally given its name – again (or rather traditionally?), the new system name was associated with the Microsoft name. The name was **MOM**, which stands for **Microsoft Organizational Master** – as bold and clear as it could be!

Truly, the initial experience was wonderful. We smoothly curated all the key details and complex structures, incorporated feedback from external and internal customers on the organizational hierarchies, onboarded additional sources to refine the customer's definitions, and much more.

Our interpretation of the Pareto principle, as described in the previous chapter, was central to creating and launching the solution as a broader capability, incrementally adding more organizational definitions, details, integrations, and reuse capabilities. This generated a positive vibe in the company, creating excitement across multiple businesses that learned of the story from Azure and knew that we had followed the MDG design principles. They highlighted its fantastic operational fit, capabilities, high value for business use, and endless opportunities for broader adoption within the company.

Never had there been a better moment and prospect for a customer master solution.

However, this is where the failure slowly began to manifest. Yes, the failure. Again.

With early success demonstrated by the Azure team and a couple of **Minimum Viable Products** (**MVPs**) kicked off with other business groups, we faced high demand and needed to prioritize the next business cases to onboard to MOM.

What followed was perhaps the worst decision, leading to ultimate failure.

Ambitiously, we tackled the most challenging data issue in the company – the ability to accurately capture incoming revenue in connection with CRM data. Perceiving this use case, we would have to scale from a small subset of customers to most of the managed and unmanaged customers in the company – a particularly hard business case, albeit potentially rewarding in terms of productivity and, crucially, impact on the business.

To reiterate, due to the differences between the sales view and the real-life organizational structure, we constantly faced data issues and quality challenges across multiple business segments. The goal was to correlate the most valuable data for end users in a straightforward way, much like what we achieved with a subset of customers for the Azure case, but now scaled up for the most commercial customers.

The business case was important, yet probably too ambitious for only the second practical onboarding effort.

We overestimated our capacity to quickly progress and manage such a massive change.

This quickly led to complications and breakdowns. Broader engineering teams struggled to adapt what worked well for the Azure case to worldwide sales and marketing deployment. The complexities of sales geographies and organizational hierarchies, not fully understood by the technical teams, created a massive and frustrating challenge, slowing down the initial onboarding success.

Business units, while having been promised the ultimate MDM solution, grew impatient as we were stuck resolving this massive revenue attainment case, pushing other smaller but defined cases into the longer backlog.

Meanwhile, other business groups, seeing the positive impact of the Azure case, demanded orchestration of their data from an organizational master perspective. Requests for shortcuts or pilots, meant as interim solutions while waiting for full onboarding to MOM, poured in. These requests were justified and supported by company leadership, with the understanding that they would be fully reusable for the upcoming full-scale onboarding to MOM.

This parallel track of smaller, tightly scoped deployments provided many business units with what they needed quickly, competing with the larger, global effort. These solutions, addressing specific business cases such as trade screening or credit control, or the famous Microsoft Unified Support, quickly gained the most benefit from the availability of an organizational master view. However, they lacked alignment between the sales view and the organizational view, deemed crucial for overall MDM success.

Deemed, indeed, is a different word than *reality*.

Guess what? Shortly after, we almost completely abandoned the global effort for MOM onboarding, marking the fourth failure in a decade.

Currently, this capability is being significantly revamped for future development. We recognize that addressing the key issue between sales and real-life hierarchies may not be the ultimate task for an organizational master and we might need an alternative approach. Plus, we shall lead Data Governance and federated data ownership even more, prior to embarking on the next significant investment into data mastering.

Next, let us see what should and shouldn't be done considering these attempts. But before that, let's recap the lifetime of different solutions and how they changed one after another – simply to reflect on how lengthy and hard this path was. And the most important – none of these solutions fully delivered on their promises.

Figure 9.1 – A recap of the timeline of the different solutions

Dos and don'ts

Before exploring what's next at Microsoft in this area, let's reflect on these failures and associated challenges. Every difficult experience provides invaluable learning – let's try to think of them as positively oriented opportunities, with the addition of safe and hard-learned recommendations to succeed with MDM.

If I were to lead an MDM implementation today, with all my past experiences, I would keep a few important perspectives in mind:

- Having an ultimate business case from the start – or better, two connected yet different cases, not just one. This is something like the best practice many convey about data products – you create one product to start with, but you have a connected next case in mind, with a high reuse of what has been done for the first implementation. I would recommend a similar approach for MDM, with both business cases having a high impact on the business, yet moderate in size of the work, and not the absolutely most critical for the company. *The point is that it's better to make a high impact and repeat soon than fail under extreme complexity and hard pressure.*

- Deploy an MDM solution with a long-term approach, ensuring high reliance on it by the downstream systems and business consumption, and think of repetitive, operational enablement along the line. Whoever will be the owner of the solution, this isn't a one-time thing; it's not an analytical data product. *It needs to be current as it enters the life cycle, and it needs to stay current for all the runtime.*

- Any MDM must be explicitly connected with data governance work and deployment in a company. The absence of co-drive with Data Governance and/or treating MDM implementation as a technical capability will bounce back hard, with poor data quality, inability to run "data at scale," and a cascading negative impact, leading to losing trust in data across the enterprise. *Data governance should be embedded into MDM solutions; alternatively, MDM should be deployed on the grounds of a successfully implemented data governance program.*

- Solution-wise, the modern graph database seems to be the best fit. The flexibility of graph connections is critical for both the data team and business usage. *Data teams will love graphs for a dynamic and always connected view of data, while businesses will prefer multiple hierarchical views, allowing them to switch through them for different business perspectives – sales, accounts, finance, and so on.*

- Adhering to the first point, just like with data products, this work needs to be led by business and data teams jointly, with data engineering and/or data science as supportive and solution enabler roles. *I strongly recommend not having data engineering or IT teams lead this work since, in the end, the true user and owner of MDM will be the business side of the house.*

- Consequently, the owner of MDM capabilities at an enterprise will be the business teams. *Like Data Governance, which has federated ownership in its best implementation, master data will also be owned by those who mostly use it and have a critical dependency on its accuracy.*

- Finally, no modern MDM solution should skip the opportunity to be AI-driven and human-reinforced. There is so much goodness in AI data augmentation and the ability to retrieve, enhance, and automate governance and data mastering capabilities! *Yet humans will keep their central orchestration role and input reinforcement capability to ensure that not only is there accuracy but also that it is a true fit for business.*

I hope this chapter was fun to read, with unusual turns and valuable learnings. We will come back to data products and data governance in the coming chapters, so please stay tuned!

Summary and key takeaways

By reflecting on the MDM journey within such a large and capable enterprise as Microsoft, we have learned that success lies not within powerful engineering, endless budgets, or other perceived benefits of a top enterprise company – and not even with alignment with business needs.

This is a difficult balance for leadership practitioners to navigate and connect multiple interested parties within the company to lead to a common, foundational solution. This path has likely more failures than success and might not be for everyone.

Takeaway #1 – start small, with high relevance

Since MDM implementation work is typically very lengthy, even when successful, it is advisable to start small with a few high-relevance, mid-sized cases and emphasize progress over perfection. Cleanly and quickly winning the trust of the business stakeholders will ensure continuous support and appreciation of the work.

Takeaway #2 – business stakeholders are part of the solution

Similarly, the business stakeholders should be an immersive and explicit part of the MDM implementation. Ideally, as the solution is deployed, they become the users and the owners of it – capable, educated, trained, motivated, and ideally enhanced with modern graph and AI solutions to make their work easier.

Takeaway #3 – be a Chief Orchestration Officer

From a data strategy and leadership perspective, the key skill to master for any data practitioner with MDM implementation is to be a **Chief Orchestration Officer**. Successfully connecting and promoting the significance of MDM to numerous (and often isolated) business units within an enterprise is a true masterpiece of leadership and a testament to being a top influencer. And this is rare – hence not many enterprise-wide MDM implementations succeed.

Yet, this doesn't mean you should not try.

With this, we will smoothly transition to the next chapter, where we will learn how to reach the utmost success with a modern and award-winning data architecture.

10
Data Mesh and Data Governance

Data Governance and Data Mesh are closely linked in my view, and they provide the most comprehensive technical and business enablement of data at any enterprise.

While both are deemed to be technical disciplines rather than business-facing disciplines, in the context of modern approaches to data and ensuring AI readiness, there is little that is more critical to the success of a business than realizing and maximizing the value of data.

Discoverable, qualitative, authoritative data that is democratized across the enterprise and raises no eyebrows when appearing in front of CXOs as analytical outcomes fuels the company's business development and innovation. Data Governance enables the true value and power of data, while the Data Mesh architecture sets the foundation for the success of modern, federated Data Governance.

How cool is that? But how often is that the reality in the industry?

In this chapter, you will learn about the digital transformation of Microsoft, where data played a key role, and so enabling *data at scale* became a priority within the digital transformation itself. We'll cover the following topics:

- The evolution of data at scale – from classy old-fashioned data platforms to ultra-modern Data Mesh. Not in one day, but still, in less than a year.

- How Data Governance means Data Excellence and not only pairs perfectly with Data Mesh but is actually liked by business stakeholders.

- Our CEO, Satya Nadella, asked this question: *"Do we know where all our company's data is?"* Indeed, we do know, although the answer is a bit more complex than we thought.

Taking a look at a typical enterprise—"Data Mess"

In this chapter, we will explore Microsoft's data platforms and data governance.

At the time of writing, it's been over three years since we began operating on a Data Mesh platform and implementing a global data governance initiative. This initiative isn't seen as restrictive or policing; rather, it acts as an enabler of AI and insights.

However, let's consider a typical enterprise scenario – and Microsoft was very much a conventional enterprise of its time, from the early 2000s up until 2020. Data was scattered across multiple locations, business groups, and IT groups, and lacked real ownership or oversight.

As previously mentioned, we embarked on our data journey somewhat late, opting for a full-fledged data architecture-driven approach for platform creation. We initially used expanded data capabilities and SQL solutions for **Data Quality** (**DQ**) and management but lacked a comprehensive data architecture approach.

We started with a solution called Magic Reports, which later evolved into **Customer and Partner Data Management** (**CPDM**). We experienced the classical evolution path – starting with a need to visualize data and any associated DQ issues, continuing with reporting and automation, and then gradually ending up with a data management sandbox, with a large amount of architecture and engineering effort. CPDM was essentially an operational data store, where we copied necessary data from Tier 1 LOB systems such as CRM, Revenue Collection, and Licensing. We actively used this environment to learn about data challenges, to practice with our proactive and reactive services, to connect data across domains, and to start our automation journey.

> **Note**
>
> This data was refreshed regularly, typically daily, but without much transformation or added value. Our role was primarily to enable DQ and management processes in the company, often operating on fresh datasets that needed constant adjustments or reintegration into original sources. This approach boosted DQ across the company.

We eventually made a more substantial investment, creating the **Data Innovation and Operations** (**DIO**) platform, marking a significant milestone in platform thinking.

> **Naturally evolving**
>
> We recognized the need for more than just a copy of our operational data. This realization led to the development of a more complex architecture with diverse data sources, different refresh rates, more security and permission controls, more quality controls at entry, and serious consideration of data ingestion principles. We developed data observability capabilities on the platform to ensure data met expectations, was refreshed as scheduled, and didn't have gaps.

Additionally, we created an analytical layer on top of this, which, while not a true data lakehouse, incorporated some key elements. This included a mix of operational and analytical data from multiple sources on the same platform, with varying degrees of transformation, to meet all our data needs – from internal data management routines to fueling business processes and innovation.

Within the rest of the company, the data evolution movement followed a similar path as shown here:

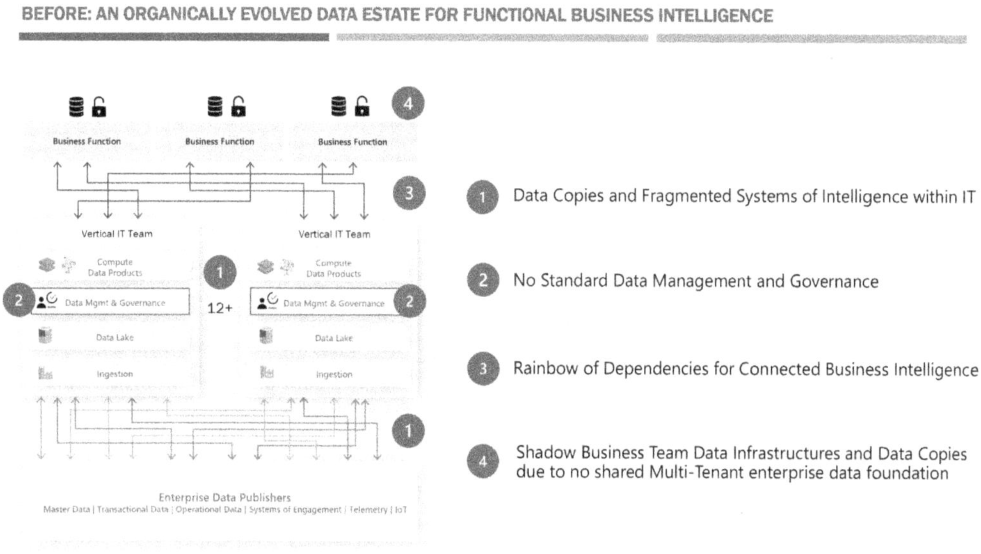

BEFORE: AN ORGANICALLY EVOLVED DATA ESTATE FOR FUNCTIONAL BUSINESS INTELLIGENCE

Figure 10.1 – An example of classical data architecture, still prevalent
across many enterprises (source: Karthik Ravindran)

Many groups, including powerful business units such as Finance and Services, developed parallel solutions with the same data-centric architecture. Each department, possessing its own engineering workforce, created data platforms and data lakes, leading to a proliferation of such solutions across the company. Every platform was claimed to have unique value and be fit for business, but this was inefficient from data, compute, and workforce perspectives.

> **We weren't different**
>
> Think of this – just a few years ago, Microsoft was not an ultra-modern enterprise stepping into the AI era but rather a large enterprise with a "data mess," multiple coexisting data platforms, and duplication, particularly in CRM and revenue data.

However, these data architecture models addressed emerging business needs effectively, even if it meant duplication and low overall efficiency.

Let's see how, next.

From "Data Mess" to Data Mesh – how?

The turning point came with Microsoft's realization that it needed to accelerate its digital transformation in 2020.

This transformation encompassed rethinking business processes, products, and team organization. One fundamental aspect of this transformation was data.

The company recognized the disorganization of data, which, while allowing the business to perform, did not serve as an enabler for a future dominated by digital processes. This led to the question of how to rebuild the architecture to make data connected, single-copied, and broadly available, as well as qualitative and trustworthy.

The **Enterprise Data Lake (EDL)** was created in response to this need.

> ### Enterprise-wide data lake
> This data lake aimed to consolidate essential enterprise data into a single repository. The project started immediately, adhering to principles such as DQ by design and persona-driven thinking. Existing data platforms and lake owners were invited to become data publishers on this new platform, including key data sources such as CRM, revenue collection, SAP, and finance. The goal was not to house all data but to onboard data that is actively consumed by data teams and business units.

The direction was to publish data within this lake, and data consumers were encouraged to transition from their current consumption patterns to using the EDL.

The change was technically straightforward and aligned with the reasons data lakes were invented.

However, the real difference lay in the business impact and organizational level.

> ### Data leadership isn't about technology
> This move was as much a technical innovation as it was a mastery of data leadership and change management, aligning the company in a shared direction and building trust in this new architecture.

We did not attempt to delete existing duplicate data or restrict sources immediately, which allowed a smoother transition to a better architecture. This approach allowed cost savings, resource efficiency, and access to trustworthy data, differentiating it from the varied-quality data from numerous lakes. Building this centralized EDL has become a significant mission for our internal IT organization.

However, from a purely data management perspective, we maintained our DIO data management sandbox, which operated in parallel. This was essential for correcting critical business and operational data that was crucial for multiple business processes. While we pursued our goal, we also moved toward convergence with the EDL, eventually leading to the adoption of the Data Mesh.

> **Data is foundational for digital transformation**
>
> This journey from multiple distributed copies of data and separate data management capabilities to orchestrating them into the EDL concept was a deliberate decision. It was driven by the need for rapid digital transformation, identifying high data dependency as a key factor.

This information is crucial to digest for anyone in a similar position or considering the Data Mesh approach.

Many enterprises operate in a natural evolutionary style, recognizing data as a valuable asset used in analytics and critical business processes. However, this data is not organized into something more powerful and efficient unless there is a significant trigger. For Microsoft, this trigger was part of digital transformation, driven by a top-priority leadership initiative, with a clear awareness that success in a data-driven world requires thriving data within a company.

This necessitates a modern data enablement approach, not just in technology, but as a concept of federated architecture and data ownership, supported by data governance and data products for consumers. It requires a deliberate push, change management, and architectural planning.

With data governance in place and data products provided to consumers, the transition to a modern data enablement approach is more than a business need for an isolated group. It must be a top priority for leadership, who must recognize the need for modern data architecture to thrive in a fast-paced, data-driven world.

But let's get back to Data Mesh and how it manifested in our daily work and our environment. This is a bit of a fun story.

One weekend, I woke up early and saw that the global leader of our EDL, Karthik Ravindran, had sent an email during the night that was full of excitement. Jumping in and starting to read, I saw something along these lines:

"Hey folks, I was reading through various data-related articles on LinkedIn, and I found an interesting article from a person named Zhamak Dehghani. She is talking about some new concept called Data Mesh. And if you just read her article and then take a look at how we are modernizing our estate, you will see that it is a 100% fit. I've already reached out to her for a chat and deeper connection, but it seems like we are at the forefront of the industry..."

So, when I'm asked, "How did Microsoft implement the Data Mesh?", I'm somewhat hesitant and simultaneously proud of being part of the amazingly talented team that implemented Data Mesh before it was even solidified as a full concept.

Let's skip some interim steps and review the actual platform architecture we ended up with, the key components, and how that whole thing interlinks with Data Mesh.

Have a look at the following figure:

Figure 10.2 – Modern enterprise data estate at Microsoft, aligned
with Data Mesh principles (source: Karthik Ravindran)

This is the current picture, and you can read this in three principal and fundamental layers:

1. We have the **multi-tenant enterprise data lake**, which includes data ingestion, storage management, data standardization and unification, and much more. Company-wide data publishers are the data providers and source owners. They are also responsible for DQ and data-publishing SLAs. Once data is on the estate, it is served in a variety of ways, depending on the data consumer's needs. Data consumers are represented by several different personas – they could be anyone from our own data engineers and data scientists working on data products to end users on the business side, who use data products, analytical dashboards, data catalog assets, and so on.

2. Speaking of data catalog and data discoverability, it is enabled and facilitated through a Microsoft Purview instance that embraces end-to-end data governance, including asset inventory, policies, access management, referential metadata, and data lineage, along with being the number-one environment for the data steward's community.

3. As we touched on various personas beyond data consumption, we need to emphasize that one of the key goals of this architecture is to provide the company's business stakeholders with trustworthy, discoverable, democratized, and unambiguous data that is broadly available to any party as permitted by a data owner. This fuels innovative, digital-first businesses and provides the ability to experiment quickly with any kind of data product and data mart, with no bottleneck to the data platform team's capacity.

A metaphorical example we used between ourselves was imagining this as Amazon Marketplace for data.

> **Metaphorical approach**
>
> Numerous sellers (aka data publishers) offer a wide range of products, yet they are all certified and governed and play by the same rules in the market (this is Data Governance in action). The consumers are free to safely buy what they need and how much they want, following highly standardized and transparent processes (this is an example of data consumption through several open ways, yet they all are controlled by managed serving). If an issue or dispute occurs between the seller and the consumer about the product quality, it could be resolved either directly or via the Marketplace team in the worst-case scenario (in the data world, this would be in Microsoft Purview, where publishers know consumers through permission management and access controls, while consumers are exposed to data lineage and where the data comes from. If something goes totally off-track with data on the estate, the data platform team gets involved).

Of course, this is an ideal picture, and it does not always work exactly like this, or at least not at the first attempt. But the principles remain the same; they are tested and proven. Every new data source onboarding might come with new learning opportunities, and any new key feature released in Purview slightly impacts the architecture.

This type of data estate organization has proven to be balanced, stable, and flexible for new technological advancements. For example, when AI came into the picture, we didn't need to change anything. We could simply add AI-driven data governance, for example, or experiment with **Large Language Models (LLMs)** instead of our own proprietary in-house ML models.

Now, coming back to Data Mesh for the last time, let's delve into why the given estate implementation example truly caters to and adheres to Data Mesh principles.

The following is a detailed picture of how Data Mesh fits over EDL:

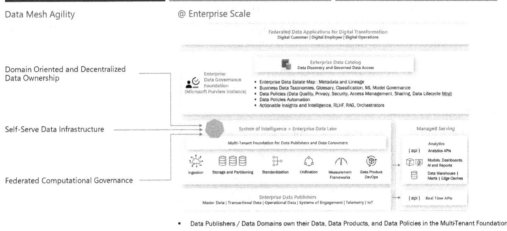

Figure 10.3 – Data Mesh alignment and perfect fit for a modern
enterprise data estate (source: Karthik Ravindran)

This is what we can understand from the figure:

- We have a clear domain-portrayed data representation on the estate, in addition to a native data source representation. As we explored in *Chapter 5*, the domain-oriented approach varies in terms of what the domain really is, with several options available, yet the core approach remains the same. The same goes for business domain consumption – we see business domains as defined, dedicated, and decentralized units.

- Data ownership and permission control are with the publishers. The access requests are made by data consumers and the approvals are made by publishers, but it becomes a bit tricky when the data team acts as data publisher and data consumer at the same time. This is an exception, and it is managed in line with the overall principle of federated ownership.

- There is a large focus on self-serve capabilities, with extensive onboarding guidance for data publishers and similar guidance on data-serving opportunities for data consumers. This is highly automated, but not fully – again, this is a practical case of the Pareto principle (from *Chapter 8*) – we are happy enough to get automation for 80% of the typical onboarding scenarios. The exceptions are managed as exceptions, whether it is a very large exception, such as another data platform becoming part of the EDL, or an ultra-specific exception, such as a data type that we haven't experienced yet being onboarded.

- Finally, and most importantly, there is a complete federated approach to computation. This means that besides the prime data estate functions, anything that needs to be executed as domain-specific work will be cross-charged to the requester/owner. This means the data team won't have to bear all the associated costs of running and maintaining the data estate and will instead share the cost model with everybody involved. This approach isn't only helpful from a budgeting perspective; it also tackles two critical challenges within an enterprise:

  - It promotes responsible consumption of data and advanced analytics. While not stopping the need for experimentation as such, we avoid cases where an ML or AI model is running every night with no concrete output and success criteria, burning thousands of dollars. This also applies to the core data – the data life cycle still matters, along with unnecessary copies being dumped swiftly.

  - Every business unit or domain can run at its own speed of data consumption and data innovation. They aren't locked to the central data team's budget or capacity; instead, they are empowered to do all they need on their own, consulting the data team when needed, but not being dependent on them. This tremendously matures and speeds up business ownership and execution, and builds a strong data culture at the company.

The following figure shows the split between domain compute and enterprise compute:

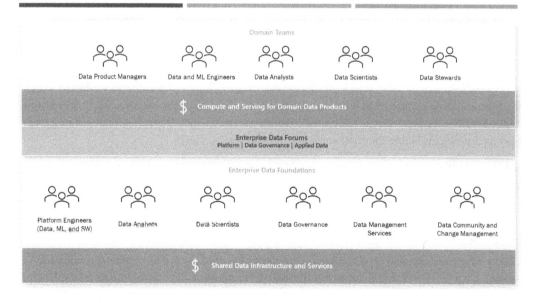

Figure 10.4 – The persona and cost separation at a modern
enterprise data estate (source: Karthik Ravindran)

OK, that's enough on Data Mesh and platform evolution, I believe.

I would like to summarize the entire notion of the preceding amazing transformational work by citing our enterprise data lead and my manager back in those days, Karthik Ravindran:

"Data is an organization's most valuable asset. Deriving and applying insights and intelligence from data is core to accelerating an organization's digital transformation. Unlike in the past, when data and BI investments were generally siloed by business functions with the primary purpose of gaining an understanding of functional states, digitally transforming products, customer experiences, employee experiences, and operations entails applying connected insights and intelligence to enterprise-wide data. Responsibly democratizing data to enable such applications by all organizational functions is essential for accelerating and maximizing value outcomes, and enabling this with non-compromising data management and governance excellence is foundational. A modern enterprise data estate for digital transformation must enable these modern data fundamentals (connected data, responsible data democratization, and excellence in data management and governance) at enterprise scale and cloud-native velocity."

Well said! Let's now move on to Data Governance, which is nothing but Data Excellence, and how we managed the path to Data Governance at Microsoft.

Data Governance = Data Excellence

Let's dive into the topic of data governance, which is crucial for data teams. However, it's quite common for data teams to struggle to showcase Data Governance as an enabler of insights to business teams. This is primarily due to the shift in Data Governance toward business ownership rather than remaining under the exclusive domain of the data team.

This shift, right from its onset, tends to create friction.

The prevailing perception within businesses is that Data Governance is only necessary for existing data issues. Thus, it's often seen as a problem stemming from the data team's failure to pre-emptively rectify data problems before they become a business need.

There's some validity to this viewpoint. Ideally, in a world where data is always of high quality, complying with all policies and captured perfectly at the source, Data Governance would function more as a guide than an enforcer.

> **Governance is co-owned excellence**
> Many data teams aspire to this ideal, striving to elevate DQ initially and then gradually enforcing robust Data Governance policies and authoritative follow-ups and pushing for necessary data corrections. The goal is to distribute ownership between the data team and business units, encouraging co-ownership of certain domains or capabilities.

But the real essence of Data Governance is about elevating data to excellence.

It's about ensuring data is immediately usable for business, thoroughly connected, and seamlessly integrated within the enterprise environment. This eliminates the need for either the data team or the business team to spend excessive time converging and aligning data before generating insights or deploying AI capabilities.

Despite a general understanding of their role in Data Governance, business teams rarely view it as something that's empowering or valuable. They acknowledge the need for compliance and standards but often question why adherence to them negatively impacts business productivity.

However, the truth is that in today's world, a substantial portion of Data Governance responsibility already rests with business teams.

Especially with the rise of AI, we are witnessing a bunch of new products aimed at placing Data Governance under business ownership while simplifying its management. The latest release of Microsoft Purview is a great testament to aiming for business users to be the main owners of data, empowered and capable of doing all they need by themselves, in a single, connected environment.

These new Data Governance products often focus on minimalistic interactions, driven by AI's ability to learn rapidly from human input. The human element of Data Governance is fundamental as it is humans who define the trustworthiness and necessity of data.

The future is likely to hold a scenario where business teams will continue to own the data, with IT and data teams facilitating a seamless, efficient experience by providing the right tools and applications. This makes Data Governance intriguing and manageable for business teams. Gamification might play a role in this evolution, encouraging AI to apply smart, orchestrated processes that require minimal input yet effectively augment and maintain data.

Additionally, AI could autonomously generate insights on how effectively data is used for driving business and innovation, then compare it with lower-quality data to identify necessary improvements. High-quality data essentially involves a process rich in logic, structuring, and labeling – areas where AI excels, provided it receives accurate human input.

It will be fascinating to see how the discipline of Data Governance evolves and thrives with AI capabilities and much higher automation, given its critical importance for the data we have today and even more so for the data that will be generated in the future, much of which will be produced by **Generative AI (GenAI)**. The life cycle of data, governed by defined and transparent processes, is vital and cannot be overstated.

Before delving deeper into the future of AI in Data Governance (which I'll cover in *Chapter 13*), I want to step back and give an overview of how we witnessed the evolution of Data Governance at Microsoft. This might provide an insight into the different stages of Data Governance, helping you to discern what is truly critical and what might be less urgent, or require staged implementation.

At Microsoft, the Data Governance effort started many years ago.

When I joined the company, I came across the first dedicated database that was in line with what we now categorize as Data Governance. Back then, we didn't even have this terminology. What we did have was a repository of meticulously curated metadata and taxonomy definitions, a glossary and vocabulary combined, known as "reference data," or sometimes simply as the broader term "metadata."

This database was a central repository for key data elements such as sales processes, geographical definitions, customer segments, sales stages, business groups, product categories, and many other definitions. This reference database, simply called **Taxonomy**, was accessible to everyone in the company, providing original definitions, update histories, ownership information, and system dependencies. In those days, we had a presumed view of data usage, lacking the accuracy we have today with data lineage tools. Despite this, the centralized repository was a foundational step, increasing usage and enforcing these definitions in Tier 1 systems.

While this centralized repository functioned well, we lacked broader controls. There were no reports on DQ or health metrics, nor did we enforce anything beyond basic system-level definitions. For a modern Data Governance practitioner, this might seem primitive, but having a centralized repository was a significant advancement at the time.

Even today, many companies lack such a basic metadata dictionary. My advice for those embarking on Data Governance is to start with this foundational step. You might not need the data catalog at the start of your Data Governance journey, yet you will truly benefit from having referential metadata along with business vocabulary in place.

> **Reference data is golden**
>
> A centralized repository of terms and metadata is not costly or difficult to maintain, but it lays the groundwork for a data stewardship community and ongoing management of changes and updates. As companies evolve, so do these definitions, but their importance remains constant.

As we progressed, our next governance layer focused on operational inputs, such as CRM systems. We decided to call that effort **Operational Data Governance**.

We noticed that a lot of data entering these systems was of low quality, which was often rectified by sales teams at a significant time cost. To address this, we proposed enforcing controls at data entry points. This suggestion, however, was met with resistance from business units concerned about the impact on their processes. We mediated this conflict by defining **Minimum Data Requirements (MDRs)** for critical entities in CRM.

This approach allowed data to enter the system as is, but we enforced background scanning for data gaps and reported breaches to the data owners and their managers. This solution balanced the need for DQ with the need for business agility and led to the creation of our first **Data Quality Health Scorecard**, monitoring DQ across our Tier 1 systems. This allowed us to have a full overview of data defects on one hand and the ability to address individual defects by respective data owners on the other. Typically, we would give several days for business users to rectify the data, gradually escalating the importance and time for action.

However, questions remained: Why was the data of poor quality in the first place? Was it a policy issue, a system design flaw, or something else?

To unravel this, we pursued a dual strategy. First, we focused on simplifying data corrections for business teams by using recommendation engines to help them make impactful, yet easy, quality improvements. These engines started with contact data in CRM, validating the accuracy of business influence, job roles, contact data preferences, and more. They were a tactical solution that significantly enhanced DQ without overburdening business users.

This approach also gently shifted the accountability for DQ from data teams to business units. By having business users make decisions on the recommendations, they assumed ownership to be a crucial step toward federated data ownership. This gradual shift, implemented through manageable and actionable steps, helped resolve potential conflicts without hindering business performance or go-to-market speed.

Another focus was on creating highly integrated, quality-driven data products. These products demonstrated the power of qualitative, integrated data in facilitating seamless integrations and advanced analytics. For instance, integrating data from acquisitions such as LinkedIn and GitHub required starting with high-quality data. When business units requested integrated dashboards or data views, they often realized the preparatory work needed to ensure DQ. This revelation was not meant to frustrate business units but to highlight the necessity of foundational DQ for advanced analytics.

By discussing these challenges openly and transparently with business leaders and framing them as leadership opportunities rather than problems, we gradually converged on the need for stronger Data Governance initiatives and business unit ownership of their data domains.

The data team's role evolved to support standards, tools, monitoring, and practices, but the ultimate ownership of data remained with those who used it most: the business users and data stewards.

We had an important observation here: achieving leadership buy-in was crucial for this shift in order to help business units understand that groundbreaking data science and insights are impossible without high-quality underlying data.

This "high-quality" aspect is not abstract; it has a concrete structure that we can help establish. Ensuring that systems of intelligence are accurate and data flows within an enterprise do not lose data integrity is key to creating satisfying datasets.

Thus, the journey of Data Governance at Microsoft was not just about implementing policies and systems but also about fostering a culture of data literacy and stewardship, demonstrating the tangible benefits of high quality data, and gradually transitioning ownership and accountability to where it belongs – with the business units.

Today, the modern Data Governance at Microsoft is executed under the umbrella of Microsoft Purview, combining the efforts of data teams and business data stewards in one shared environment.

The following figure represents the way we thought of Data Governance as we started the work within the Purview environment. Leading with easy-to-understand themes, we created the next set of top-of-mind, priority actions in accordance with every theme. This allowed us to build the next level of **Work Breakdown Structures (WBSs)** and progress quickly, while reporting back on the theme's level:

DATA GOVERNANCE

Data Governance Top of Mind   Data Governance Themes

Make the Enterprise Data Estate Visible	Visibility
Make the Consumable Data Estate Discoverable to Users	Discoverability
Proactively Mitigate Data Exposure Risks	Security, Access and Use
Improve the Quality of our Data	Data Quality
Be Compliant with Regulatory Standards for Data Management	Regulatory Compliance
Certify Authoritative Sources of Data Truth	Master and Reference Data Management

Figure 10.5 – High-level, easy-to-understand themes powered the
respective set of priority actions (source: Karthik Ravindran)

Beyond these high-level themes, we had some specific focus areas, such as data catalog, data ontology, data lineage, active data stewardship community, data source and data product certification practices, and much more, yet the path to this moment was far from perfect and it took a lot of leadership-driven evolution.

As a fun example of how disconnected and diluted the data was prior to the implementation of Microsoft Purview, thus being a significant driver for Data Governance, upon the first full-scope data catalog scan with Purview over the enterprise data estate, we came up with 26 almost exact copies of CRM Opportunity data. More than half of these copies lacked clear ownership and had undefined usage. Storing these copies was a waste of resources and a potentially misleading path for data consumers. So, data asset certification was necessary in a scalable and automated way.

This finding, though, added another interesting and highly sought-after perspective – the use of Data Governance as the driver for better sustainability. I've said in previous pages that the institutional strength of Data Mesh lies in federated ownership and controls, with corresponding accountability for what happens with data. We took this as a great driver to promote a continuous and never-stopping resource optimization opportunity.

Whenever we found duplicate data or an inefficient use of computation, not only would this benefit the overall cost control, but it would also clearly contribute to sustainability as both a reduction in storage and compute and a reminder of accountability for data and data-related processes. In fact, this serves as a brilliant example of how data and AI power and truly enable sustainability (**Environmental, Social, and Governmental – ESG**) capabilities, while within data and AI, the Data Governance foundations are that cornerstone that can't be missed, skipped, or devalued.

Understanding this crucial relationship between Data Governance and data and AI capabilities is what every data professional and data leader shall aim for, and should promote across an organization.

The following figure summarizes our advancement from database-focused data management sandbox solutions (Magic Reports, CPDM, Data Management Platform, and Data Innovation and Operations) to an enterprise-wide data lake and, eventually, a modern Data Mesh environment. At the same time, the data governance capabilities were steadily expanding, from basic controls for minimum data entry and centrally aligned taxonomy to federated data and ML/AI governance.

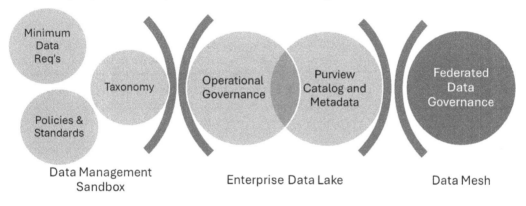

Figure 10.6 – Data lake advancements

It's worth mentioning that while Data Mesh and federated Data Governance are a perfect combo, it is a matter of choice for every company whether to enable it or not, but the notion of Data Governance itself (and optionally federated) is an absolute must-have for modern data management. Whether a small or big enterprise, data on any data platform requires care and regulations in order to be the driver for data value extraction and end-to-end data discoverability.

Where is our data? Again...

I want to finish this chapter on a high note by telling a real-life story that reflects our data governance journey at the company.

You might recall how this book started: by telling concerned business leaders and users where their data is and who is in charge of it.

Through the years of having well-established global data management capabilities, we had a rather simple answer to these questions. As you may recall, originally, we were driven by the internal marketing motto "We make data business-ready." Those days, while on the path to centralization, it was an accurate and concise statement and an answer as well at the same time. With further evolution of data efforts, the answer would be something such as "*Your data is in the good and caring hands of the enterprise data team, and hence we are also in charge of its quality; however, we do share this responsibility and effort with you.*"

As we started to embark on the decentralization and data federation journey, the potential answers became more complex and context dependent. In the absence of an enterprise-wide Data Governance program, we had achieved various stages of advancement in controls over data, DQ, and data security, depending on our engagement with a specific business unit or product group.

Frankly and thankfully, no one was asking such questions at that point.

But in 2021, we were suddenly faced with questions about where the data is and who is in charge of it again, and from an unexpected place.

One of our data leaders arrived late to a Teams meeting, sounding frustrated, excited, concerned, and encouraged – all at the same time:

"*Hey folks, I've just learned that at the executive board meeting, among many questions about Azure and direction, Satya asked a very specific question – do we know, as a company, where all our data is and who is in charge of it?*

"*Oh, wow, that is so cool, but also so unexpected! But we are glad he asked! What answer did he get?*"

"*Well, as far as I understood, most of the folks there didn't know how to answer that precisely. They started to speak about our Azure estates, about security and data sovereignty, and so on. Yet I trust the question was kind of different.*"

"*Totally different, in fact! How don't they know about EDL and the Data Governance efforts we are making these days?*"

"*Yeah… perhaps it is too early to expect our top executives to be fully aware of our enterprise Data Governance program.*"

"*But, hey… just out of interest, how would YOU answer that question in an easy and comprehensive way, hmm?*"

"*I get your point, folks… Not only do we need to work harder to inform our leadership, but we also need to have a clean and concise story, a story we could tell anyone, from business users and vendors to Satya Nadella, with utmost clarity, conviction, and no chance of misinterpretation.*"

"*Exactly! If we struggle to answer this question easily today, there is zero chance that others will get it right. Let's pair up, build the storyline, and formulate a sharp and concise executive perspective that could be shared with anyone.*"

In essence, what a great and simple question the company leader asked: nothing complicated and born of pure curiosity. Yet it traces back through hundreds of meetings, projects, investments, agreements, and escalations, only to indicate that we were not ready to answer it.

Would you be able to answer this question in your company?

Summary and key takeaways

This chapter reveals a bright future. Yet this bright future doesn't become bright by itself – somebody needs to brighten it for others. Often, you need to start with small and basic steps, and only then try to fly.

Our path to mastering Data Governance and Data Mesh was difficult and eye-opening but we also had a lot of fun along the way. The key is to always stay open-minded, to learn and experiment, and to keep moving forward.

Here are three things I think are important to take with you on your data journey, to embrace transformation and Data Excellence and be prepared to answer simple questions.

Takeaway #1 – digital transformation is the ultimate driver of change

Over three years, Microsoft transitioned to a Data Mesh platform and a global Data Governance initiative, focusing on enabling AI and insights rather than imposing restrictions. Initially, we had data scattered across various departments without proper oversight or ownership, a common issue in traditional enterprise environments.

Independent development of data platforms by business units led to a proliferation of inefficient solutions. To address this, and to accelerate digital transformation, Microsoft created an EDL, consolidating essential data into a single repository and focusing on quality and efficiency, adopting a Data Mesh architecture before it was fully established in the industry, leading to an innovative data management approach. The data was centralized and the controls were federated.

Takeaway #2 – Data Excellence that everybody loves

Microsoft's journey to achieving Data Governance reflects the shift from data team ownership to business ownership, often creating initial friction due to the perception that governance is necessary only to address existing data issues. Yet the essence of Data Governance at Microsoft has been about ensuring data is immediately usable, connected, and integrated within the enterprise, eliminating extensive alignment efforts by data or business teams. Today, Microsoft Purview encapsulates the modern approach to Data Governance, combining data team efforts with business data stewardship in a shared environment, emphasizing continuous resource optimization and sustainability.

Takeaway #3 – if you don't have Data Governance, these three Fs will help

- **First "F" – Foundational**: Initially, our Data Governance efforts focused on a central repository of key data elements, providing a structured foundation despite lacking broader controls.

- **Second "F" – Following**: Operational Data Governance efforts address DQ issues at the source, with in-house-developed MDRs balancing DQ needs with business process efficiency.

- **Third "F" – Future-focused**: The demand for modern data products with high-quality, integrated data analytics and connected data points demonstrated the need for foundational, cross-company Data Governance and DQ to support these advanced analytics and seamless integrations. In other words, there will be no data products without Data Governance.

The tricky question for a curious reader is, "Why do we invest so much into data platform and data governance solutions?" Well, perhaps because we want to maximize data as a driver for business growth and innovation. In this case, data products are one of the most renowned mechanisms for using data effectively – the next chapter will delve into this.

11

Data Assets or Data Products?

New paradigms arrive every day and we are happily jumping on exploring, experimenting, and learning how to best use them.

The notion of data products was originally driven by data science, yet as the thinking besides data productization matured, it made additional thoughts and diversions. Aside from the general direction to treat data as a product – meaning taking the utmost care of it, developing a roadmap of usage and deployment, elevating the value and adoption to align with discrete business goals, and addressing the scalability, constant upgrades, modernization needs, and much more. However, it also required the creation of a distinct differentiation between the core ("raw data") data assets and data product approach.

This is nothing new for the industry – a decade ago, we had already a similar notion of data warehousing coming over with massive data extraction and transformation techniques, positing itself as the answer for analytical needs, while devaluing the use of non-transformed data down to operational data stores or transactional appearance within the source system itself.

This chapter talks about practical experience of thriving on the Data Products, while retaining a high focus on raw data assets and why raw data might mean more than we expect.

We will cover the following topics in this chapter:

- The challenge we face today with data
- The magnificent shine of data products
- Raw data deserves appreciation too

The challenge we face today with data

In today's business landscape, the journey of raw data from collection to its transformation into robust data products is multi-faceted and complex.

Raw data, gathered in alignment with internal operations and stored either on the cloud or on-premises, undergoes various manipulations, such as enrichment, augmentation, and enhancement. It's also subjected to health and quality checks across standard data quality dimensions, with an additional focus on maintaining data privacy and data sovereignty and protecting personally identifiable information (PII).

Despite all of this work, the true-to-use utility and value of data are often constrained by natural domain boundaries.

To unlock greater value and drive business growth, data must connect across those boundaries, fueling analytical aspirations and evolving into data products. These products empower data scientists to uncover correlations and new opportunities, significantly impacting end users by shaping their understanding and revealing further needs and challenges.

Well, in an ideal world, of course.

> **Note**
>
> The principal debate over the importance of raw data versus data products is ongoing and unlikely to end soon, with each new day bringing an additional perspective. It's essential to recognize the underrated potential of raw data and approach the proliferation of data products with thoughtfulness, acknowledging their achievements and pitfalls.

In this chapter, we will expand on the details of the challenges associated with transforming raw data into valuable data products, with the following emerging as top-of-mind perspectives to guide us on this transformation path from data assets to data products:

- **Volume and complexity of data**: The sheer volume of data generated by modern businesses can be overwhelming. This volume, coupled with the variety of data types (structured, unstructured, and semi-structured), makes data management and analysis challenging like never before. Data teams and businesses must employ sophisticated tools and technologies, such as modern data platforms, to handle and process this data efficiently. The complexity also extends to the integration of data from various sources, necessitating advanced data integration and management strategies to ensure consistency and usability.

- **Data quality and accuracy**: High-quality data is fundamental for accurate analytics and decision-making. However, data often contains errors, inconsistencies, and duplications, which can lead to incorrect conclusions and business strategies. Organizations need to invest in robust data cleaning, validation, and standardization processes. This also involves setting up data governance frameworks that define data standards and ensure ongoing data quality maintenance. An additional dimension here is the late discovery of data errors while already in the data analytics phase. This hits back especially hard.

- **Integrating disparate data sources**: Integrating data from different sources into a cohesive and connected view, each coming with its own format, structure, and semantics, is a significant hurdle. Integration challenges can lead to data silos, where information is isolated and not shared across the organization. Effective data integration requires a combination of technical solutions (such as **Extraction and Transformation ETL/ELT**) and data organizational principles and measures (such as establishing common data models, advanced pipeline observability, and unified measurement).

- **Data security and privacy**: With the increasing amount of sensitive data being processed, data security and privacy have become paramount. Companies must comply with various data protection regulations, such as the **General Data Protection Regulation (GDPR)** and the **California Consumer Privacy Act (CCPA)**, which dictate how personal data should be handled. Implementing robust data security measures, such as encryption, access controls, and regular security audits, is critical to prevent data breaches and ensure compliance. **Modern data governance** plays a substantial role here, along with data platform architecture.

- **Shortage of data professionals**: The industry is facing a data talent gap, with a shortage of professionals skilled in data engineering, data science, analytics, and data management. This gap impacts an organization's ability to effectively analyze and leverage their data. Companies are addressing this challenge by investing in training and development programs, as well as seeking partnerships with educational institutions to prepare future data professionals. At the same time, hyperscalers and technology vendors are pushing hard for the commoditization of unique skills and the simplification of the data journey as a whole.

- **Interpreting data correctly**: Correctly interpreting data to extract meaningful insights requires a deep understanding of both the data itself and the business context. Misinterpretation can lead to dangerous business decisions. Data teams must have a strong analytical mindset and broad skillset, complemented by domain expertise, to ensure that the data is interpreted in the context of relevant business questions and objectives.

- **Resource limitations and increased focus on sustainability**: Data analysis and management can be resource-intensive, requiring significant investments in technology, infrastructure, compute, and skilled personnel. Smaller organizations, in particular, might find it challenging to allocate sufficient funds and resources for these purposes. There is a continuous search for cost-effective solutions, such as cloud-based data analytics services, **Data as a Service (DaaS)**, or open source data analysis tools. With AI more actively coming on the radar, things are only getting more complicated.

- **Lack of data culture**: Developing a data-driven culture is essential for effective data analysis. However, most organizations still lack this culture, primarily due to a limited understanding or appreciation of data's potential value, along with difficulties with data discoverability and trust. Building a data-driven culture involves educating all levels of the organization about the importance of data, encouraging data-driven decision-making, and ensuring that employees have the necessary skills, tools, and access to democratized data, to analyze and interpret data accurately.

- **Incomplete data democratization**: Despite collecting vast amounts of data, many businesses fail to make this data accessible to the right people at the right time. Organizations must balance security with accessibility, putting measures such as role-based access controls in the hands of data publishers and secure data-sharing platforms that allow authorized personnel to access and utilize data efficiently. Building an environment where data is shared and insights are openly available will certainly foster innovation and drive better decision-making, yet remains a "dream state" for the majority of enterprises.

- **Adapting to technology changes**: The field of data science and analytics is rapidly evolving, with new tools, technologies, and methodologies emerging continually. Just a year ago, AI was only experienced by a selective set of data professionals. Keeping up with these changes can be challenging for organizations. Investing in ongoing training and development for data teams, staying abreast of industry trends, and being agile enough to adopt new technologies and approaches are key to maintaining a competitive edge. Thinking of soft skills as transferable skills, organizations need to balance their approach to technology adoption with the continuous workforce transformation.

Herewith, transforming raw data into valuable data products involves navigating plenty of complexities and challenges, from managing large volumes of diverse data to ensuring data quality, security, and privacy.

If we were to use a metaphor outside of the world of data, one of the simplest analogies would be about raw food ingredients and prepared, cooked dishes. The quality of the original ingredients does impact the final quality and taste of a dish you are making; however, the importance of receipt, cooking experience, and adherence to the desired outcome is also critical to get a tasty and valuable outcome. Some professional chefs can make an amazing dish from simple ingredients while some newbies to cooking can produce inedible stuff from even the highest-grade ingredients.

It's the same with data. Experienced and knowledgeable data teams could produce highly relevant and innovation-focused data products, understanding the raw data and its implications on the overall picture of success. Yet, rush with data products and absence of deep dive into what are they made from often leads to wasted time and compute and unacceptable and unusable outcomes.

The evolution of technology and the need for skilled professionals further complicate this process. Addressing these challenges requires a strategic approach that includes investing in the right technology, fostering a data-driven culture, and ensuring that data is accessible, secure, and accurately interpreted.

In simple words – you need to have a modern data platform to thrive with data. Data products are not a goal in themselves; the goal is the culmination of great shared data foundations, the professional knowledge of business and data teams to build those foundations, and a well-established data consumption layer that facilitates data sharing and impact, by active living through the values of data culture.

But are data products life-savers and the ultimate goal of what data platforms should be built for? To a large extent, the answer is yes, but we must not forget about the underlying data itself, as well as our ability to manage data products as effectively and responsibly as the data itself. Let's review this in depth in the following sections.

The magnificent shine of data products

Hold on! What is a data product in the realm of data products?

In recent years, there has been a significant evolution in data products, primarily influenced by advancements in data science.

It's essential to understand the various types of data products and what contributes to their success while mitigating the risks associated with over-reliance on them. In our journey, we focused intensively on improving our operational data as the foundational layer for advanced data consumption. This includes raw data, or as data governance terms it, data assets – the original entities and tables filled with operational data, usually not heavily transformed or modified. For the purposes of this chapter, we will keep referring to these as data assets, but note that you will find a variety of definitions around.

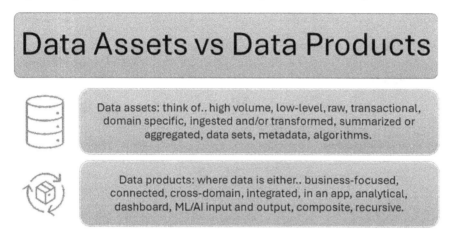

Data Assets vs Data Products

Data assets: think of.. high volume, low-level, raw, transactional, domain specific, ingested and/or transformed, summarized or aggregated, data sets, metadata, algorithms.

Data products: where data is either.. business-focused, connected, cross-domain, integrated, in an app, analytical, dashboard, ML/AI input and output, composite, recursive.

Figure 11.1 – Data assets versus data products simplified

Here, on one side, we have data assets, representing data in its raw form. This could also include data assets transformed into data lakehouse scenarios, still providing a foundational understanding of raw or moderately transformed data.

On the other hand, there's an increasing demand for data products, becoming more prevalent in enterprise data spaces.

Data products are created deliberately from original datasets to serve a broader purpose, seen as valuable by both data teams and consumers. However, their core purpose can vary significantly for different enterprise personas, making the definition of a data product complex.

Let me give you a simple example.

For data scientists, a data product might be an exceptionally clean and well-prepared dataset used for creating analytical models or research outputs.

For business users, it might be a composite of data addressing their continuous business needs. While BI dashboards could surely be considered data products, for the sake of distinction in this context, we raise the bar higher and exclude them from this category.

We observed significant interest from businesses in consuming various data products, not just for data science purposes but also for operational data needs. The real value of a data product lies in its integrity, as it often represents a comprehensive view of connected data.

This was especially evident in our work on data governance and the example of unified support pricing (*Chapter 8*), where connecting multiple entities and effectively stitching data addressed specific needs on a stable, repeatable basis. The unified support pricing model is a prominent example of a powerful data product, if considering the data feed and consumption complementary to the user interface experience.

Working with businesses as a data team, we recognized the importance of quickly developing data products as a key capability. The demand for data products was high, and we had to find a way to industrialize them, using the modern data platform capabilities as the vehicle.

The following is an example of data product enablement using our enterprise data lake:

THE ENTERPRISE DATA LAKE AND DATA PRODUCTS

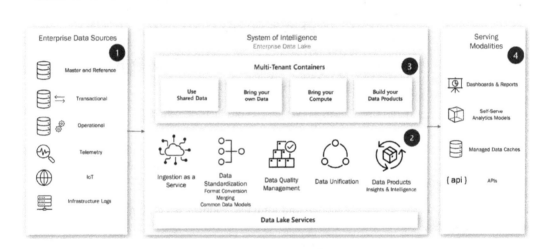

Figure 11.2 – Overview of data products enablement (credit: Karthik Ravindran)

You can spot four main components of a successful data products journey:

1. Abstraction from original data sources and data ingestion complexities
2. Discovery of all enterprise data in one location – standardized, connected, and compliant
3. Build and operate data products in a secure data estate using the preferred compute
4. Use a variety of ways to serve data products to final data consumers

Today, there's even a more modern trend toward enabling businesses to create their data products in a self-serve model under the data mesh framework. We're actively working on automating data product creation on demand from business users, aiming for the ultimate automated certification and publishing across the state. This represents an advanced stage in data product evolution, and it is not recommended to pursue on an early stage of development of your data products approach.

Stepping back, the need for data products that are readily available and credible for business use has always been present.

However, the capability to connect data more smoothly across the enterprise, integrate different sources, and create a managed serving layer for consumption has become a foundational enabler for increased data product demand and consumption.

Our team found that creating data products aligns well with our strengths.

While businesses are federated by domain ownership and consume domain-specific data, the most interesting and powerful opportunities often arise when data is connected across domains. This expertise lies more with the data team, experienced in seeing and navigating the entire data estate and onboarding various data sources and lakes, and who also know the quality and meaning of data in each.

This unique capability to traverse domains and integrate data to produce powerful connected data products opens new opportunities for businesses. It also fulfills data teams with a great purpose and adherence to business goals.

For example, in integrating data from acquisitions such as GitHub or LinkedIn, we managed to correlate GitHub data with Microsoft data relevant to sales, marketing, and the immediate launch of co-sell processes. These data products, created through in-flight yet useful integrations, showcased the value of integrating previously unintegratable data and avoiding delays associated with more profound hardware-level data integration between the companies.

As usual, the story started on the way, while being in Redmond and navigating connections between the stakeholders. With early post-COVID time, not many folks were working in offices, with Teams becoming the ultimate center point of communication and collaboration. While in transit, I received a short message from my manager.

Manager: "Hey Aleks, I've just got off a call with the general manager at GitHub and I think we could be of help to them with our data integration and data transformation work. Please connect with person ASAP, as they are struggling to understand data between Microsoft and GitHub."

I paused, puzzled.

At this stage, we already had an Enterprise Data Lake (EDL) with a data mesh architecture, and if anything, data integration and onboarding from GitHub were in the remit of our data engineers. I would surely understand that onboarding such data sets isn't a trivial thing and won't go as self-serve, yet neither I nor anyone else on my team had additional expertise on GitHub data. Perhaps there was something else that we could help with. Let's explore… I reached out to the person, and we arranged a call shortly after.

GH Person: "Hi, nice to meet you! Your manager said you did some in-flight data integration services in past with your team, and I guess that is what we need help with."

Aleks: "Well… yeah, maybe. What is it that you are trying to achieve?"

GH Person: "You know, GitHub is part of the Microsoft family already, yet we struggle with viewing and following each other's sales pipelines. Even though the formal merging of companies only happened very recently, our customers don't think so and are complaining about the parallel efforts that falls on them".

Aleks: "Ehm… I understand about the duplicative and misconnected appearance of us to the customers, but we have been different companies just a few weeks ago. I trust there will be some CRM and sales data onboarding kicking off very soon, resulting in deep integration between our platforms, no?"

GH Person: "You are right… in principle. But in reality, we use completely different CRM technology than Microsoft today, and only figuring out what's the right future for this aspect, will already take months. We can't wait and sit on the side, with no shared pipeline at least, not even dreaming here of the active co-selling process. Your manager said you've made some integration with LinkedIn in the past – can't we tap into this?"

Aleks: "Hmm, we did, true. But this was done as several back-and-forth data exchanges, aligning on the format and understanding the data integration gaps to support marketing campaigns on LinkedIn's side. This wasn't a true data pipeline between two entities. We also used our data operations services to navigate the DQ challenges there. But doing it this way for a co-sell or shared pipeline will turn out to be costly. I mean, I'm happy to offer a one-time sync or similar, but that's not what you are looking for, right?"

GH Person: Yes, indeed, we need to have full visibility of Microsoft's pipeline on an ongoing basis. This data must come to GitHub, and we will match it with what we have, to eliminate customers' frustrations and come up with a joint understanding of sales opportunities.

Aleks: "You say you are mostly concerned about existing GitHub customers, right? How big is your customers' universe?"

GH Person: "It is in the tens of thousands, but obviously, not as huge as you have in your CRM."

Aleks: "Would you be able to publish this customer master data on our data platform in a shared format and refresh it regularly? And would you be able to read back another dataset from the platform on a daily basis?"

GH Person: "Yes, I believe so. What are you thinking?"

Aleks: "Well, it is just an idea for now, but I thought, what if we take your published data as the lead and link it with our integrated account's domain view? The outcome will still be ambiguous, as we can't build an automated 1:1 match, but we can embed a certain precedence logic there and then link corresponding CRM data. You might not be able to find all your accounts there, which must be normal business case, but you will likely get a view where your account's universe is reflected over our CRM data. We could publish this integration view without additional curation and refresh it daily."

GH Person: "Oh, that sounds promising! I will connect you with our data engineers – let's get right to it; we shouldn't wait any longer."

A month later, one of our first data products was launched – an integration view for GitHub. We had to innovate immensely by building up our IP and, at the same time, navigating away from data operations experience, and converting what used to be a data service to a data product.

In the fascinating journey of data products, we have explored numerous scenarios where utilizing existing data but weaving it into new, interconnected frameworks has significantly uplifted its value.

This ability to swiftly generate data products tailored to specific needs is a remarkable innovation driver.

Data products are more than just about merging or connecting data; they embody a synergy with data science and AI. Clean, well-curated datasets are invaluable for data science and AI applications. They start as connected datasets, evolving into integrated results, providing ideal conditions for uncovering data correlations and preparing datasets for AI or **Machine Learning** (**ML**) expanded use.

Our data team, comprising a mix of roles, including data product managers, data engineers, and business stakeholders, played a pivotal role in guiding the creation of these datasets.

> **Note**
>
> We don't leave the burden solely on data scientists to determine their data needs. Instead, we collaborate to identify the right data for the right purpose, blending our expertise to craft datasets that address specific goals. This collective effort ensures that the datasets are not only technically sound but also aligned with business objectives.

Another intriguing aspect of our data product journey is the utilization of internal data, or what we could call our *data management metadata*, to advance business analytics.

This was a discovery we stumbled upon unexpectedly.

Over the years, we've been managing a plethora of operational data, enhancing, enriching, and augmenting it across numerous internal systems and entities. Our operational data governance efforts were severely indexed and focused on data cleanup, de-duplication, and accuracy. During these comprehensive and resource-intensive operations, we meticulously recorded our activities in audit logs. These logs provide a detailed history of the changes made, their purposes, and the authorization behind them. We used this information for internal purposes, beyond its initial intended need as a rollback opportunity in case of undesired changes. It fueled our regular revision of the processes, crafting more efficiencies and pivoting new approaches – including the front-line experiences and data applications.

Surprisingly, we found that our business stakeholders were deeply interested in this data. They were keen to understand the historical context behind the current state of data, to comprehend the rationale for past changes and modifications.

In a regular 1:1 meeting, a team member suddenly raised a concern.

Teammate: "Aleks, I was in touch with the business sales operations folks, and they said they want to have access to our account and revenue curation log... I'm not sure how to position this now."

Aleks: "Ops, that's unlikely to happen, I mean them getting access. This is purely internal information for our data management efforts and was never intended to be shared outside of this team. How did they come to this ask?"

Teammate: "They said they absolutely need this data to be able to compare the changes they made before with the current state, and along the lines, the future planning. This is the only source of such data, you know this. Even the revenue collection system doesn't have this history recorded, not to mention the reasoning underlying every change."

Aleks: "True, but we can't simply give them access to the platform the way we do! Since this is highly sensitive data and involves several security restrictions and adherence to source system policies, we can't jeopardize the existing permissions on the platform. Moreover, this data is not designed for business user access – there is complex logic only available to consume via advanced SQL. Otherwise, it is meaningless and even dangerous for business users."

Teammate: "I know, and I understand what you are saying. But this data has gold value for them, if I've got it right, and if we can hide the technical complexity of this data while resolving the access issue, they would thrive with endless analysis opportunities."

Aleks: "You are right, as usual. We probably need to think along the same lines as we did with GitHub – let's get out of our comfort zone and reconsider their proposition. Let's start with the precise requirements – we'll make no promises yet, but we need to unpack the whole opportunity from end to end."

The thing is – you need to trust your experienced team members, always. This became another great data product in the hands of the business, opening almost a Pandora's box, with an extensive line-up of potential products out of our own metadata usage.

This realization led us to harness our internal audit logs and trails, extracting valuable insights about the changes made to key enterprise accounts and revenue allocations.

These insights filled a significant knowledge gap for our business users, providing them with a clearer understanding of operational excellence and business progression. This development revealed a new realm of data product opportunities, offering profound insights that were previously hidden. The ability to produce these data products quickly and efficiently, on demand, to address specific needs demonstrates a remarkable capability for businesses to innovate and advance out of previously undiscovered data.

This new development directed a third major avenue for our data product creation, offering unique insights previously totally hidden from our professional business users.

It is worth mentioning that this level of innovation wouldn't have been possible without the groundwork we laid earlier. By fostering business interest in data and promoting self-service in data management, we established robust data governance.

Eventually, three key areas dominated our focus: data science, cross-domain connected data integration, and leveraging internal data management metadata. Let's explore them in detail:

- **Data science and modeling**: At the forefront, data science plays a pivotal role. Our collaborative approach involves data scientists, engineers, and product management specialists working together to derive insights and analytics for various business challenges, such as customer churn or sales penetration. This teamwork ensures the creation of valuable datasets that yield actionable insights, rather than the ineffective and worthless burning of compute power for ML/AI model executions.

- **Cross-domain data integration**: This area highlights the importance of connected and integrated data across different domains and data lakes. It demands extensive expertise from our data team, who must continuously expand their knowledge of business, data usage, and new, emerging trends. This is vital for advising both business units and data scientists on the development of interconnected and insightful data products.

- **Internal data management metadata**: Lastly, we turn our gaze inward, exploring the extensive work done by our data team over the years. This exploration isn't just about making our team's work more efficient; it also uncovers valuable insights for unprecedented use by business stakeholders, data stewards, and potentially even our customers and partners. By empowering businesses to take ownership of data, being supported by internal data management processes and data transformations, we've implemented significant value back to the business.

In summary, these three areas represent our strategic approach to data product development, each playing a crucial role in delivering comprehensive, insightful, and actionable data-driven solutions to enhance business operations and decision-making.

However, as cool and as modern as data products are, they are only made "products" by the data underneath. While modern data consumption by businesses would mostly be sourced from those data products, the one area of focus that data teams must not miss is the actual data you invest from various sources. It might seem obvious, but how much effort does that data deserve?

Raw data deserves appreciation too

Raw data also deserves appreciation. It really does.

When considering the aforementioned three pivotal layers where data products excel, we're significantly impacting business users and their productivity. Positively, of course. However, the story here isn't solely about data products.

Underlying these glamorous products are the original datasets or raw data assets.

This operational data, captured daily in key business-facing and partner-facing systems, often arrives from various internal and external sources. Whether coming from an internal CRM system, co-selling activities, or partner-driven business, this raw data, despite its varying quality, might contain tons of hidden insights.

While data products are a prime focus for business users, their foundation is always raw data. Modern data architecture often features embedded data products, adopting a microservice-like approach where data products are nested within each other. This hierarchy can either function independently or as a collective aggregate. The more advanced the analytics are, the more the data undergoes processes such as ML, augmentation, enhancement, tailoring, and customization on its way to make to final product appearance.

A critical challenge arises here.

With each data product involving comprehensive data processing and filtering, along with analytical transformations, this process embeds a logic that should ideally be transparent and traceable.

However, as the underlying data changes, the original logic might no longer be suitable, underscoring the need for ongoing maintenance and updates. The bottom line of the issue is the dependency of data products on the quality of raw data. The perceived quality at the outset might not be sufficient as the data product evolves, yet this need for enhanced quality often remains concealed within the product's logic. The more far end we go with the advanced analytics, the more risks arise whenever the original data was suitable for such a use case.

For example, consider address data in CRM systems. Even if the address details seem valid, they might no longer be current or correct. These inaccuracies become apparent quickly in operational use, such as invoicing or customer engagement. However, when this data becomes part of a larger dataset used in data products, the issue becomes less transparent, creating risks in analytical decision-making.

These aspects are crucial when considering how to use data in the long run and how to trace back to source dependencies without highjacking the analytics outcome.

As we said, in typical operational settings, any issues with data quality become apparent quickly. For instance, the same incorrect address or contact data in a CRM will be noticed promptly during activities such as invoicing or sales engagement, likely leading to swift data updates. Or, it will briefly appear in the DQ scorecard, data health reports, and so on.

However, when such data is incorporated into data products, the impact isn't just on a single record but spans across numerous records, forming datasets used for deeper analytical decision-making. This isn't as easily noticeable as in operational scenarios.

The real risk emerges further when we increasingly rely on data products without regularly verifying the accuracy and currency of the underlying datasets.

As a data team, we recognize the need for stringent controls over data assets and their evolution. We must delve beyond formal data quality definitions, understanding the actual data content health and significance of data and addressing its life cycle for different purposes. This includes differentiating between data suitable for immediate operational rectification and data that has long-term implications when incorporated into multiple data products.

Another story to share is an example of raw data cascading impact.

We had been preparing for several months for a significant piece of partner data de-duplication in the CRM. The definitions of partner accounts were different from those of customers, with more complexity and additional associated objects – such as referrals, certification levels, incentives, and so on. We carefully tested the algorithm and fine-tuned the logic; we deployed that into **User Acceptance Testing (UAT)** and got a green flag from business stakeholders. Additionally, we double-checked with our corporate CRM team that pursuing this strive for data uniqueness wouldn't break data integrity.

All seemed good and well prepared. So, we executed the de-duplication.

We waited for a couple of days for feedback or to hear of any escalations and randomly checked a few cases to validate that we were seeing what we wanted to see. No complaints.

As soon as we started to draft an executive communication to inform the business stakeholders and our management about the recent progress and a record breakthrough in the reduction of duplicative partner-related records, the first escalation popped up.

It wasn't what we were expecting or prepared for, such as the wrong record merged. It was much deeper into the cascading relationship between partner account definition and some incentive program attachment, which should only be there based on another type of engagement definition. All in all, it was deep into the weeds, with only certain records being affected, yet those affected were being impacted hard. Partners were not able to claim for incentives, our partner account managers lost the history and audit of those engagements and even full manual, from scratch, re-instatement of the right attributes wouldn't work.

We called for an urgent fire drill and triage meeting with CRM engineering, a couple of stakeholders, and partner account managers. After investigating, it appeared a rare coincidence between downstream associated objects, and a quick fix was identified.

The patch was applied into production, after a quick check in UAT and validation that we could mitigate the issue with incentives. Since the patch was very selective, impacting only certain accounts and only with specific criteria, it was a mix of data logic and direct changes. We had to move on to unblock the normal business operations.

24 hours after landing in production, another issue was discovered. It was again regarding the partner data, a subset of the accounts affected by the incentive issue, plus a set of accounts that were all fine after the initial execution of de-de-duplication, but now were reported as having the wrong data attributes associated with them…

As we urged into another triage with our virtual team, it started to be scary and all of us felt that. We looked around at each other and said with encouragement, "Hey, this is just data, right, we are in control. Let's just take a bit more time for full analysis, before we take the next step." Indeed, we took a lot of time, as the combination of sophisticated cascading updates paired with not-fully-understood API behavior in certain scenarios was a long and painful story to unpack.

One thing was helpful, though – while we knew that this data was ultra-critical for partners and our account managers, it only had limited use within the CRM itself. It was not shared outside of the CRM, except with partners themselves, and so we had no single dependency from any other application, data lake, or data mart, struggling or being damaged by our numerous attempts to fix the raw data. At least this was a certain relief.

But imagine if we were to have powerful data products down the chain, analyzing the incentive's space and making decision-oriented recommendations!

In essence, the quality of foundational data directly influences the reliability of data products.

If overlooked, this could lead to inaccurate results, costly rectifications, and a loss of trust in data insights at executive levels. Therefore, it's imperative to pay close attention to data quality controls and data certification efforts, especially for data driving high-end analytics or embedded in a chain of data products.

Today, we explicitly certify data sources, data assets, and even the data products built on top of the platform. This creates a maximum assurance for the end users, a "quality stamp," and serves as the input for the next circle of certifications, if/when a data product revision is made.

In summary, attention to raw data is vital because inaccuracies can quickly surface in day-to-day operations, prompting escalations and the need for rectification.

However, when data is part of complex products, especially those driving ML and AI analytics, it's not as straightforward. The need for rigorous data quality control and certification grows exponentially to ensure accuracy and reliability, significantly impacting executive decision-making. It becomes clear that data products cannot be decoupled from their underlying datasets, necessitating a nuanced understanding of data assets and their continuous application. This recognition forms the core of effective data management, especially in the context of advanced AI and ML applications.

At the end, the fundamental message here emphasizes the equal importance of both data products and their source data.

The success of a data product hinges on the high-quality, integrated, and connected nature of its source data. Without this foundational quality, even the most promising data products are destined to fail.

Equally, the effectiveness of a data product also depends on whether the data used is truly prepared and tailored for such application, with a focus on stringent quality control and explicit certification.

The simplicity of this concept belies the frequent oversight in many ambitious data projects, where exciting data products are built on uncertified datasets. This notion becomes even more critical as we delve into the realm of AI capabilities, suggesting a potential shift in perspective regarding the relationship between data assets and data products.

This evolving landscape invites a re-evaluation of how we approach and value both the sources of our data and the products derived from them.

Let me explain this a bit deeper.

The use of AI on raw data, over qualitative data, will potentially lead to the discovery of more insights than today's approach, and more impactful, stunning insights. Humans would struggle to connect 150 attributes in a transactional table, with broad meaning and varying quality, to gain immediate insights. Even ML, in its classy application, faces a challenge – striving for a clean dataset at first and filtering "garbage" versus "non-garbage" data. Hence, we would first do a certain level of preprocessing or transformation.

However, with the advancement of AI models and them learning and capturing every industry's specific data patterns and associated data challenges, usually desired analytical outcomes and past corrective actions applied, we will likely pass through the stage of clean data sample preparation work, besides core data quality enforcement. This will allow for a greater playing field for AI to master the raw data dependencies and deliver an immediate analytical outcome.

Herewith, I foresee rapid progress with AI and corresponding products being used over the raw data, to first enhance it and fix any standing DQ challenges, and then to generate outstanding insights or build data products, readily available for use and consumption. As with anything with AI, governance and human re-enforced input will be the keys to the success and flourishing of real productivity gains.

Summary and key takeaways

It is not easy to succeed with data these days. On one hand, technology breakthroughs are abundant and streamline things quickly where they used to be a burden. On the other hand, with growing amounts of data and AI disruption, it is even less clear to figure out the wise direction for data-related investments. I will offer a couple of insights and a few projections of what might happen next.

Takeaway #1 – need for a modern data estate

To harvest the best analytical outcomes through various types of data products, you would need to have a modern data estate organization. It does not necessarily need to be massive or expensive or represent the ultimate set of the latest innovations. But it must comply with certain proven principles, by addressing data at scale, democratizing access to high-quality authoritative data, and enabling data product development. We noted down 10 aspects in the *The challenge we face today with data* section to consider when transforming your data foundations.

Takeaway #2 – several sources of inspiration for data products

In our data management journey, we came up with three key areas to kick off the data products approach. Data science focuses on teamwork among data scientists, engineers, and product managers to create datasets that provide real solutions to business challenges such as customer churn, ensuring efficiency in resource use.

Cross-domain data integration emphasizes the need for the data team to have broad knowledge across various business domains and data lakes, aiding in the formation of insightful and connected data products.

Internal data management metadata involves looking inward at the data team's work, revealing insights that benefit business stakeholders, data stewards, and possibly customers and partners, demonstrating the value of business ownership of data supported by strong internal foundations.

Takeaway #3 – the naked truth of data assets

The essence of data management revolves around the balance between raw data and data products.

Raw data, essential for operational processes, often contains hidden insights despite varying quality. However, data products, tailored for business user consumption, are built upon this raw data. The challenge lies in maintaining the relevance and accuracy of raw data as it evolves, impacting the efficacy of data products.

Ensuring continuous quality control and certification of both raw data and data products is crucial, especially with the integration of AI capabilities, which could potentially change how we approach and value data sources and their derived products.

In the next chapter, we will see how value, literacy, and culture influence data.

12

Data Value, Literacy, and Culture

Many, myself included, believe that data holds a specific economic value known as Data Economics. It's essential for the data team to comprehend the factors influencing data's value, including what affects its depreciation and understanding the entire data life cycle, as well as tracking how the data's value changes over time when used by the company's various business groups.

At the same time, there might be a lack of ownership and responsibility for the data assets and data products by business users. To address these challenges, the concept of Data Literacy was introduced. Like any other form of literacy, mastering it requires time and practice.

When solid Data Literacy is coupled with robust data proficiency and appropriate technological support, it naturally culminates in the establishment of a Data Culture. This refers to the cultural and operational norms within a company that highly values, relies upon, and trusts its data. In a Data Culture, data is used objectively, free of assumptions or bias, and solely as the basis for discussions, definitions, or the direction of the company's future success.

Let's delve into these exciting opportunities by covering the following topics:

- What are Data Economics, Data Literacy, and Data Culture?
- Unveiling the true worth of enterprise data
- Data Literacy has no end state
- Why Data Culture matters more today than ever

Introduction to three pivotal disciplines

So that we're all on the same page moving forward, we will start by explaining what we mean by Data Value and Data Economics, Data Literacy, and Data Culture.

Data Economics

Data Economics, an emerging field of data knowledge, understands data as an economic asset with varying values. Some data holds immense potential, whereas other data might have limited utility. The economic value of data isn't static; it evolves depending on how it's leveraged within your organization. It will be most potent when applied across the company's various departments, when raw data is turned into actionable insights that drive financial decisions and are reflected in the company's **Profit and Loss (P&L)** statements.

Data Literacy

The concept of Data Literacy is vital for navigating the complex landscape of Data Economics. Just like traditional literacy, mastering data literacy requires time, practice, and commitment. Usually, it starts with small steps toward extended data fluency and data proficiency, until it becomes enterprise-wide.

The goal of Data Literacy is to enable every employee in a company with the necessary data proficiency and the ability to rely on data-driven decision-making.

Data Culture

Bridging the gap between data teams and business stakeholders is a critical aspect of harnessing data's potential. Business counterparts often lack a deep understanding of data and its integration into the company's decision-making frameworks. Therefore, data teams play a pivotal role in educating and collaborating with business units, ensuring they are sufficiently data-fluent to take ownership and responsibility for data. The synergy between data expertise and business acumen is a crucial element in realizing the full potential of data and driving company-wide growth and innovation. The most important thing for Data Culture is sponsorship from executives and their commitment to trust and running the business on the data we have. While data literacy helps with core education and fluency, data culture is what merges the importance of data with the practice of actually using and thriving on using data. In this sense, having a data culture is superior to having a data strategy or having formal, high-ranking data roles.

Unveiling the true worth of enterprise data

Building upon our data products discussion in the previous chapter, let's delve further into the concept of overall data value.

What is the true value of the data stored in our enterprises?

This fundamental question wasn't initially our primary focus when working on various data improvement and data usage initiatives as we were more concerned with directly addressing business demands and determining what was immediately important for the business. There was scarcely any time to pause and research the significant monetary value of data beyond addressing operational and marketing needs.

Even when we began measuring our impact through revenue generation or time savings for our sellers, the real value of data remained unclear. We hadn't considered data as a digital asset with defined value, even when promoting how generally valuable the data was for enterprise usage. The question of "*How much?*" would still refer to the costs of ownership and maintenance, or to the investments in new projects. Even when working on data monetization projects (and successfully releasing them, hence establishing a profit center approach), we would focus on the final outcome only – how much revenue we would generate, and not how valuable the data itself was.

The point is: can we assign a monetary value to our core data, such as the CRM data, for instance?

We'd invested heavily in improving CRM data quality, along with connected systems, such as revenue collection and licensing products. This involved extensive cleanups and intellectual effort in shaping our IP regarding data updates. We'd also extracted numerous datasets from the CRM and connected them with other dimensions, such as Sustainability and Philanthropies, and external systems such as LinkedIn or GitHub.

All this work, primarily foundational to our sales and marketing data, has been costly, raising even more open questions:

- Does the effort always pay off?

- Can we specify the value of the CRM data and consider it in P&L terms?

- When we invest in data, by augmenting, connecting, and integrating it, and subsequently create successful data products that generate significant additional revenue, what real gain does the company achieve?

- Even if we recognize the *perceived value* of this data, can we quantify its actual monetary increase or depreciation based on our actions or growth successes?

In parallel, businesses also often questioned the importance of data quality. While we see data quality as an enabler, CFOs may wonder about the consequences of neglecting it. How do we demonstrate that failing to invest in data quality will lead to a decrease in the company's overall value and depreciate its assets?

The truth is, neglecting data quality impacts not only business processes but also the revenue and the P&L statement of a company.

We need to present data points from our own data to prove the necessity of investment in data quality. If we fail to maintain quality, we'll witness a decline in our investments and a consequent decrease in the company's value. These questions emerged not in the early stages of our data journey, but during our transformation.

We eventually landed on two significant realizations about data.

The first was our experience with Unified Support services, where we restructured our existing data to create new business value. This success story, which I've shared widely, raised questions from top management about replicating this success with other data products.

This led to the challenge of innovating in the data space.

How do we create some sort of model for data discovery and value realization, beyond the general understanding of the data's value? We need to estimate our next opportunities by assessing our data from an economic perspective.

Today, the field of data economics is growing, with start-ups exploring data value – a concept that was unheard of five years ago.

In essence, data value is bound to data governance. Data economics and data value principles are built on top of the data governance layer. This way, to get to the true value of data in any enterprise, a profound layer of modern data governance must be established first. Remember, in our discussion of data governance in *Chapter 10*, the emphasis we put on metadata and taxonomy?? That's where the creation of the data value begins, promoting referential data as the company-specific, foundational layer of digital assets, with high care and shared use responsibility.

We also need to differentiate between data products and data assets. This clarity becomes crucial as we delve deeper into the financial opportunities tied to data and begs these questions: can we fully trace where the data comes from? How reliable is it in the long term? And how is it being used on the delivery edge? Successful and well-built data products might deliver value that's far greater than the value of underlying data assets, although we need to be sure we are building on quality foundations.

The second aspect involves establishing baselines, such as how we assess typical company assets.

When buying new equipment, for instance, the equipment has a baseline value that depreciates over time. We have to consider what our baseline is when it comes to data. Customer data from sources such as Dun & Bradstreet offers a clear pricing model and a potential starting point for valuing customer master data. But how do we account for the added value from updates provided by sales teams, or additional attributes such as contact details, historical notes, and relationships? We have no clear answer yet here, with ongoing work in this space that will hopefully address the second aspect soon.

Monetizing data is challenging, especially in quantifying its value. The emerging discipline of AI offers new approaches to this challenge. GenAI-driven data might be more valuable, or less so, than the original source, depending on various factors. This necessitates tying data value to monitoring and (again!) to governance by developing new processes to effectively manage these challenges.

Let's look at some examples we have experienced. While these examples don't address the fundamental question posed at the beginning of this chapter, which is synonymous with "*What is the monetary value of data as an enterprise asset?*", they hopefully give a sense of direction and inspiration. While still focused on revenue and monetization of data potential, this takes one step closer to eventually reaching the ability to define a monetary value for enterprise data assets.

I previously mentioned the immense value realization of our Unified Support pricing experience, but that wasn't the only instance of success with data monetization practices.

Another significant example was our ability to monetize licensing data prior to the Unified Support project, which taught us about the data value chain. This experience also involved expanding data modernization by involving other players.

In our exploration of multiple business domains, we deep-dived into licensing data, which has been fundamental to Microsoft for over 30 years. We addressed challenges related to how enterprise customers used various licenses and discovered opportunities for data quality improvement. This led to the development of licensing overviews, initially a digital product for internal use by licensing and legal teams. Its utility gradually expanded, until it became a valuable tool for customer profiling.

This semi-automated process evolved into a digital product in high demand from Microsoft partners, who began requesting direct access to licensing position statements to assist customers. This demand grew, particularly as cloud migration became a priority and as customers sought to understand their licensing positions in preparation for it.

Facing the need to scale up to meet partner demand, we recognized that monetary compensation was necessary. The company was not keen on funding partner-driven expansions, leading us to introduce a surcharge for providing licensing statements.

Initially intended to simply cover operational costs, this service unexpectedly became profitable due to high demand and our optimized delivery process. This shift transformed our data team from a cost center to a profit center, generating significant revenue.

Funnily enough, this raised questions among business executives about viewing this service as a digital product or as an internal optimization need.

For us, it was a clear revelation: **Data as a Service (DaaS)** can be highly profitable when meeting market demands.

This brings us back to thinking about the value of data.

While we could monetize data and create innovative products such as Unified Support, assigning an exact economic value remained complex and unclear. We considered the original cost of acquiring and maintaining data, and the revenue generated from its use. The challenge was in pinpointing the additional revenue attributable to improved data usage or from having entirely new data usage applications. If we could identify that delta and extract the ROI from highly successful data products, we would be able to start leading our efforts with knowledge of the value of data.

I anticipate more work on data economics and data valuation methodologies worldwide, leading to a better understanding of all digital assets, including data. We're entering an era where understanding data value will become increasingly important, especially as AI helps us evaluate data from an economic perspective.

Imagine industries such as bioengineering or medicine, where unique data is tightly linked to intellectual property and could have immense value, potentially rivaling assets such as Bitcoin. Standard enterprise datasets, too, can drive innovation and become significant revenue generators, underscoring the importance of a solid data foundation.

We are at the dawn of an era where the value of data will be more profoundly understood, paired with AI's potential to unlock new dimensions of this value. This journey into data value and data economics is not just about understanding costs but about recognizing and capitalizing on the immense potential that lies within our digital and data assets.

But while the potential for digital asset value is clearly there, including data, it is also evident that we need educated consumers of those digital assets on all levels, from CEOs and CFOs to ordinary users. In the end, active and intelligent use is what generates value, demand, and continuous growth. To address this, we need to invest in Data Literacy (also sometimes referred to as data fluency, or data education).

Data Literacy has no end state

The subject of data literacy is intrinsically linked to the concept of data value.

From my perspective, without sufficient knowledge and the ability to delve deeply into our datasets, technology, business environment, and emerging concepts, we, as collective data and business teams, cannot fully grasp the value and potential of data.

Microsoft's commitment to data literacy has always been a part of our portfolio, but its focus has undoubtedly evolved. By this, I mean that while we typically view ourselves as a data-centric team, our primary effort in data literacy extends outward to educating all business stakeholders and the community of data stewards. However, it also encompasses educating ourselves and our peer teams, composed of various personas, about the complex and intricate world of data.

Let's begin with the traditional definition of Data Literacy.

To state it bluntly – it all ends in education. Yes, you read that correctly: it does not start but ends with education. At the very end of a typical delivery or project, in most cases, the realization that "*we should have known more about this before we started*" appears.

This isn't ideal, of course, but it is the reality in many situations. In most scenarios I've seen, not only at Microsoft but in other places as well, the starting point is seldom focused on education. We don't prioritize data literacy at the outset. Instead, our focus is on delivering specific data, addressing a business or technical challenge, keeping timelines, or presenting a data application or service to consumers. Only then do we start educating the users about that data product, application, or service and how to use it.

This approach does have some logic because it's difficult to teach people about an application that hasn't been created yet. However, if we abstract the need for readiness and essential knowledge from specific cases by thinking more broadly about why Data Literacy is termed as such, it becomes clear that we must reconsider our approach and aim for day-one readiness.

Data education shouldn't be an afterthought in the delivery process. It should either be the starting point or at least form part of the regular development cycle of a product or service. This feedback from users and stakeholders is crucial in helping to shape the best data offerings. The more educated and understanding they are of our objectives, what we deliver today, and our aspirations for tomorrow, the more they can assist us.

In the modern world of data, characterized by data federation and Data Governance, there's a growing need for cross-education. Here, not only are you the provider of knowledge but your business partners are as well.

Great and valuable products can't be built in isolation. Any data team aiming for a surprise impact or working in a silo on mysterious high-impact projects is likely to see little adoption of their work. It is fundamental for data teams and data professionals to realize that having a coalition of well-educated business partners at all organizational levels – from data stewards to C-suite – is critical to the success of data initiatives and data projects.

Our data literacy efforts began years back and in a very practical manner.

With over 70 different data services in our company, we continuously strove to provide contextual education about them. We realized that spreading this education across fragmented and siloed pieces wasn't effective for broad understanding.

Conversely, simply compressing and structuring our own team's knowledge for the sake of business use wasn't suitable either. It wasn't the natural goal of business users to know everything we did, nor were they interested, nor was it feasible given their capacity and priorities.

We also experimented extensively with educating our outsourcing partners, offering a variety of information sessions, webinars, and deep dives. This was a fundamental learning experience. As we prioritized providing structured education to our outsourced execution workforce regarding our processes and data, our aim was for them to possess the intelligence to effectively link various services together. Data only thrives when connected and flowing through an enterprise, and the people who operate it also need that connected sense of knowledge.

This approach greatly improved our understanding of human-centric work in outsourcing, as we began to provide a broader educational background for our outsourcing partners. We discussed with them the company's overall function, its current data challenges, what we need to know from the business side, data usage scenarios, various systems of intelligence, and why it's important for business users to process certain things quickly. Additionally, we made each data management team member conduct sessions for the outsourced personnel on different subjects, each incorporating their unique insights and aspects of importance.

By educating in this manner, we found that a broad spectrum of knowledge about our day-to-day organizational operations, intersecting with different data demands, landed very well with the outsourced execution team. It helped them to contextualize, empathize, and respond to requests in a much more confident manner.

The next realization was the significant impact of upfront education for business users, which led to the foundation of a dedicated data literacy track.

Let me tell you a story here.

We had been delivering a specific service, executed quarterly, involving intense data preparation over a few weeks. Many people contributed to this dataset, with various inputs, exceptions, and special cases. In the final days of the process, the dataset underwent close scrutiny, with tight management of any last-minute modifications, before we confirmed its accuracy.

These last two weeks of the cycle would always bring immense pressure, with last-minute data entry requests, corrections, exclusions, and subsequent business escalations. We were on top of communications about the priority of the work and would be pointing out to our business users that we had sent numerous explicit email reminders, but the business often replied that they were lost in too many emails, leading to frustration on both sides.

Change was definitely needed, and we decided to actively lead this process, but differently from before.

Instead of relying solely on communications and planned office hours for questions, we shifted to providing a more upfront context for the entire program and service.

We shared the background of why the process was running, its importance to the company, how the collected data was used to tweak and fine-tune company operations, and other meaningful details. We assigned a dedicated role for this: a data trainer. This person kicked off the process much earlier than in a typical cycle and used various means, such as visuals, recordings, and videos, to explain the process at different levels of complexity.

This approach paid off almost immediately.

The measure of success was the significant reduction in helpdesk requests during the data preparation and finalization cycles. Previously, we would receive over 300 requests in the final two weeks; after implementing extensive and prolonged education, this number dropped to less than 50. The process became incredibly smooth, with zero post-submission escalations and no missed deadlines. Our emails, once filled with concerns and frustration, were now full of appreciation and high praise for our exceptional trainer.

We realized that the key was to engage people's minds in a user-friendly and proactive way. It wasn't about pushing communication down the chain or overemphasizing urgency. It was about genuinely educating our business counterparts and coworkers in a meaningful, friendly, and accessible way. This approach prepared them naturally, helping them follow processes and contribute their best to our collective success.

This shift from communication to education was a complete success and was clearly the way forward.

We extended our data literacy efforts beyond this service, creating awareness videos about most of our data projects and services. We used simple, metaphorical explanations to educate stakeholders and colleagues about key elements of major projects, even complex ones, such as the Organizational Master project. We employed a full-time role within the data team solely for educational purposes, preparing materials, recording videos, interviewing key personnel, and running endless training sessions.

However, we also realized the need to scale these efforts.

It was great to have one person dedicated to this task, but the demand exceeded what one person could manage. So, we took the unusual step of outsourcing this work to our managed services partner. This complemented our outsourcing story and confirmed that well-informed steps build a pathway for people's success.

To enable the work, we focused first on comprehensive initial education and then scaled this knowledge through a **Train the Trainer** (TTT) approach. The broad knowledge of our original education lead was condensed, structured, and delivered, combined with intellectual property and supporting materials, to a new group of people on the outsourcing side.

This took a couple of months to establish, but the outcome was terrific. The new lead in the outsourcing team was a perfect fit – talented, motivated, and fully supported by us in her educational endeavors. She worked with colleagues across our delivery geographies, creating a synergy of diverse and motivated talent that had an even greater impact than we had anticipated.

This was hard to believe initially, but it turned out exactly as we envisioned. Our execution of data education and training in the outsourced team formed a solid data literacy program track that was continually updated and revised and covered much more than just our portfolio. We began providing basic training in business intelligence, change management, data governance, and much more.

These ground-level educational efforts were complemented by executive education.

As I mentioned in *Chapter 10* on data governance, launching a broad data governance initiative in the company was a fundamental point. Our entire team was incredibly focused on this effort, but we didn't spend enough time preparing for executive communications and informing our partners about the impending changes, the role of our team, and how our work fits into the bigger picture. The aim was not just to extend education to direct managers or our own team or organization but to reach as extensively as possible within the company.

To create our charter on executive data literacy, we embarked on and continued with executive education, a task markedly different from educating business users.

With firsthand leadership support, we obtained the right viewpoint and raised awareness of data practices such as data governance and the importance of building an Organizational Master.

We always strove to understand what executives thought about data, why it mattered to them, and how we could help to address future data needs in the company. We prepared diligently with executive business decks, succinct yet powerful pitches about the value of data, and the need for data investments, always tying them to a connected business value or specific executive challenge. We quickly rolled up our sleeves to create essential and impactful communications to spread understanding across the company.

This exemplifies the notion that data literacy is not only about educating data consumers but also about educating management and top stakeholders and extending beyond your own organization, reaching out across various departments.

This summarizes one core aspect of data literacy – the part that doesn't focus on the data team itself.

However, as I mentioned at the beginning of this section, I also believe the data team needs to make extensive internal efforts toward Data Literacy. Our realization of this came when we joined a larger team, the Enterprise Data Lake team.

Together, we formed a new, diverse, and powerful data team within the company. Coming from different perspectives on data, the Enterprise Data Lake team, mostly composed of data engineers and data scientists, viewed data through the lens of engineering and across multiple siloed data platforms, applications, and data science use cases.

The Enterprise Data Lake team saw high potential for ML and AI, business analytics, and enterprise-wide solutions. They were overwhelmed with requests for advanced analytics but lacked a fully scoped understanding of business cases. This was their view and how they saw the state of data within the company – a situation urgently needing consolidation, data sharing, and unification into one data lake.

Conversely, as a data management team, our view was fairly complementary yet still different. Being practitioners of data, we had deep knowledge of every domain in the enterprise and how data was used within these domains to achieve business results. We understood what makes businesses successful and what holds them back. We had a strong user community of thousands with whom we actively interacted, gaining feedback and insights into how data was perceived and used at the ground level.

It was therefore sensible to get together as one team and to establish a common, shared data proficiency, merging these two perspectives into one single knowledge graph.

Combining this broad and diverse knowledge was essential not only for our team to thrive but also to make significant foundational steps that would enhance our collective capabilities.

As I mentioned previously when discussing data products, successful data products are always built on joint knowledge between data scientists, data engineers, and data practitioners, along with operational, product management, and business knowledge. It's the convergence of these diverse areas of expertise that forms a comprehensive 360-degree perspective.

That was precisely the result of our cross-educational exercise, pursued almost from day one as we formed "The One Big Team".

We embarked on a journey of cross-educating, elevating the overall level of data literacy, technical skill, and understanding of data usage within the company and industry. We delved into learning about modern trends, advanced ML analytics, data engineering, and breakthroughs in data architecture, as well as many other aspects of data processing. Some of us possessed expert-level clarity, while others had only a fragment of that knowledge. Simultaneously, we also highlighted the knowledge and experience gained from witnessing frontline data usage by data stewards and businesses. We focused on how even minor aspects of data could suddenly become critical obstacles.

This collective and complementary knowledge was crucial, forming the cornerstone of our future success as we envisioned delivering data products with joint knowledge and the inclusion of diverse personas. By making use of the different disciplines in our backgrounds and merging them into a single pot of knowledge, we constantly thought about the message we wanted to deliver to our leadership and how we wished to be perceived by our data stewards and business stakeholder community – as a modern, progressive, and highly skilled team, with diverse talents and a place for everyone to thrive in the talent pool.

In conclusion, my advice is to never postpone data literacy.

You can start small and build progressively, but never demote it to the end of your deliverables. If you cannot begin with it, at least incorporate it as part of your product, then scale it up and make people genuinely eager for knowledge. Make this information accessible and user-friendly, and envision yourself in the shoes of your data stewards and business stakeholders, who may not be as familiar with data but will be no less curious or committed to success.

If you do this, you'll realize that you're not just building an amazing data community with varying levels of professional engagement and understanding but you're also actively contributing to establishing a data culture in the company.

We will delve more deeply into the topic of data culture in the following section; it's largely about having a solid grasp of data literacy and a positive perception of data in a company before it builds trust in the absolute quality and reliability of data. It's also about uniting people, just as we made a special effort to bring various disciplines and personas into one team, earnestly trying to integrate that complementary knowledge among data engineers, data scientists, data analysts, data product managers, and others into a collective understanding.

I urge you to consider these aspects of Data Literacy in incremental steps, and take into account the human and cultural dimensions, as you embark on the journey toward a fantastic data culture.

Data culture for everyone

A common definition of data culture revolves around the company's reliance on truly trusting data for decision-making. Whenever the need to make a decision arises, we should first consult the data, ensuring that every part of the decision is data-driven.

This concept is highly compelling and appealing, drawing many toward companies with a robust data culture. Our own team experience in this realm has been both intriguing and complex.

I recall presenting at the Microsoft Inspire conference, a global partner-oriented event, in Las Vegas in 2019. Among other topics, I discussed the need to bring data culture to everyone and our company's aspiration to base decisions fully on data value. Our stakeholders and executives encouraged us to embrace and trust the data.

Figure 12.1 – The author presenting at the Microsoft Inspire conference back in 2019

My passionate presentation, filled with examples of data-driven decisions and notions of success, was met with a rather bland reaction from the audience. Some formally nodded in agreement, or rather in non-disagreement, while others seemed to silently question my message.

Reflecting on this in 2024, I see a rapid evolution in the concept of data culture. Now, it's widely discussed by industry analysts and mentioned in various articles. Hiring for executive positions such as CEOs, chief transformation officers, **Chief Technology Officers** (**CTOs**), and chief data officers reflects this shift, with explicit positioning for data culture cultivation. This is a significant milestone for data maturity, with C-level executives merging the skills of functional, organizational, and cultural enablement – and now with data. This is also a testament to the fact that company leadership, including CEOs, absolutely expects to count on chief data or chief data and AI officers to be the driving force behind data-driven and AI transformation. Compare this with CIO roles years back, where CIOs were mostly about infrastructure enablement, security, costs, and managing the IT workforce, but not about crafting an IT culture or a digital culture as such.

Modern leaders now see data as an integral supporter of company transformation, a mindset cemented in just five years and increasingly advanced by integrating AI into this paradigm. With AI's success being rooted in the company's data and its ability to thrive on trust and propel business growth faster with data culture, the role of the CDO/CDAO/CDAIO will keep evolving, be in high demand, and be ever-expanding.

Setting data culture at the top of the pyramid is a truly profound acknowledgment of its value.

But it raises the question: how does one reach this stage?

What has significantly changed in the industry and the world in the last four or five years is the naturalness of discussing and emphasizing data culture, now well understood by audiences. A few years ago, this was a rare phenomenon, often misunderstood or seen as purely technical talk.

To me, data culture always revolves around people and their values, with its foundations rooted in data literacy.

Yet people must first understand data – its benefits, the risk associated with its absence or poor quality, and its value as a constantly evolving, evergreen asset. They must consider data security, especially in today's world of frequent sharing, data breaches, and security concerns. Navigating the data world safely and confidently is challenging, not just for data teams and leaders but for everyone in a company.

This underscores the many developments since our data literacy journey began.

As previously mentioned, we started by educating the business community, and then our stakeholders. We aimed for a friendly, natural approach to learning about the various aspects of data. We also focused on multidisciplinary education to enhance proficiency and professionalism in data-related disciplines, collaboration, and co-creation. This also involved bringing together data engineers, scientists, and product managers to speak the same language and share values. It's a challenging process, requiring time and effort to build, but it progresses each year.

Looking ahead, I foresee a strong demand for data education, especially around security and the importance of data as a company's most valuable asset, becoming standard for everyone.

In the past two years, Microsoft has launched numerous data security and data protection training course schemes for all employees, highlighting the rising role of data. It's no longer exclusive to the data community; at Microsoft, 250,000 people underwent mandatory training about foundational aspects of data.

This is another testament to the growing importance of data.

Data is not just for a select few but for everyone, shaping our work life and future reliance on AI. Our ability to be educated, comfortable, and confident with data will greatly influence our future with AI.

Returning to the topic of data culture, it's clear that data literacy is a crucial component, setting the stage for the inception of data culture as an initial element in a company. However, I believe technology plays an equally significant role in building a data culture.

This perspective might seem unconventional. My observations over the years suggest that technology acts as a powerful accelerator for data culture. Consider the way our culture has adapted to smartphones being a constant presence on our tables, illustrating our dependence on the technology in our phones. This shift began with Apple introducing the iPhone and was propelled by advancements in mobile networks, evolving from 3G to 4G LTE and then to 5G. In just a decade, these technological breakthroughs in mobile network speeds, coupled with the continual evolution of iPhone devices, have crafted what we today accept as normal life across the globe.

I see a parallel in the evolution of data culture. Companies limited to basic tools such as Excel or those with restricted data access and data-sharing capabilities seldom embrace or recognize the value of a data culture. In such environments, people often distrust the data presented to them, relying instead on past experiences or intuition for decision-making.

In contrast, companies equipped with advanced technology witness a seamless integration of data into their decision-making processes. While technology alone doesn't guarantee data accuracy, reliance on data is significantly higher in companies with more advanced technology. When doubts about data arise, people feel empowered to validate and refine it, emphasizing the importance of establishing trust in data.

The rapidly expanding data-driven world, further facilitated by AI, underscores the necessity of learning how to rely on and question the data at the same time.

Think of modern technologies in the same way as the Amazon Marketplace analogy I used in previous chapters – such platforms execute hundreds of thousands of data-driven transactions and decisions hourly, shaping enterprises' understanding of customer behaviors, interests, and connections. These decisions are entirely data-driven, founded on precise analyses of shared data across various domains. People make significant decisions based on this data, not on guesswork or intuition.

Today, modern data platforms are becoming more accessible for smaller companies, not just industry giants such as Amazon and Microsoft. A few years ago, the notion was that every company would eventually become a software company. Now, I believe we are transitioning into an era where every business is becoming a data and AI business.

Two key factors shape this transition: data literacy, which makes people more aware and educated about data's opportunities and limitations, setting them on their data journey; and technology, the underlying enabler of all things data, facilitating access to necessary data. If they don't trust the data, people now have the means and ability to validate or seek alternative viewpoints to aid decision-making.

This fluid technology, embodied in modern data platforms and various analytical capabilities, is undoubtedly a major driver in democratizing data at scale and making it accessible to everyone in an enterprise.

The combination of well-educated people aware of data's potential usage and the drive provided by modern technology enabling impactful decisions to be made with ease and confidence, including the ability to validate and verify data, effectively creates today's data culture.

This explains why, back in 2019 when I discussed data culture in Las Vegas, it didn't resonate significantly with the audience. Most enterprises then were not very advanced in their data journey; even Microsoft was just beginning its significant digital transformation journey in 2020.

In essence, the powerful combination of data literacy and technology, advancing in tandem, leads to an increasing number of data-driven decisions within a company, supporting our executives with trustworthy, authoritative, and democratized data.

To conclude, data culture ultimately resides with people, as any culture does. Culture is a human attribute, not a technological one. In the coming years, building a strong, human-centric, and human-focused data culture that enhances humanity through accurate, responsible data-driven decisions and minimizes misinterpretation, guesswork, and assumptions will be crucial.

As we stand at the threshold of the AI era, AI will undeniably influence much of our decision-making, proposing alternative actions of significant importance. Without a solid data culture, we may lack confidence in AI's suggestions, either misunderstanding or blindly trusting its recommendations, which may not always be accurate.

For humanity, especially data leaders and professionals at the forefront of modern data enterprises, embracing and pursuing a data culture is critical.

Furthermore, we need to integrate data culture into the overall culture of humanity.

It's essential to introduce data as a new discipline in schools, universities, and companies. We must encourage people to understand that almost everything we do today and tomorrow is converted into data in this digital world, which becomes more digitalized every day. Education and responsible handling of the data we possess and use are paramount, especially as AI increasingly influences our digitalized routines, helping us or potentially leading us off track.

To all the readers of this book, I ask you to contemplate your contribution to data culture in your company, community, or globally.

As a fellow data professional, can you commit to doing more to advance and impact the global data culture?

Summary and key takeaways

The successful realization of a data strategy that focuses on data value while implementing a pan-enterprise data literacy program and driving the establishment of a data culture is a dream come true. It's not a secret that the success or failure of these initiatives is down to the people and the technologies they are built upon.

Improving data literacy is a great and safe way to start to create an insightful, honest, and true-to-value data culture. We need that more than ever because AI is knocking at the door. Meanwhile, the fundamental question about the true value of data becomes less and less theoretical as digital assets form the centerpiece of the future-focused economy.

Takeaway #1 – data value is coming out of the shadows

Unveiling the true value of enterprise data has evolved from focusing on immediate business needs to exploring its broader economic impact. Efforts to improve data quality and integrate systems posed questions about the tangible ROI and how to quantify the data's worth. This challenge extends to understanding the impact of data quality on a company's overall value.

Our experience in monetizing data through services revealed that DaaS could be highly profitable. However, precisely assigning economic value to data remains complex. We considered factors such as acquisition costs, maintenance, and revenue generated from data usage, focusing on identifying additional revenue from improved or new applications of data usage.

Looking forward, the growing field of data economics is expected to enhance our understanding of digital assets, including data. As AI will play a large role in data evaluation, this new era will require a deeper understanding and leveraging of digital and data assets' potential.

Takeaway #2 – embark on the data literacy journey

Data literacy, explicitly linked to understanding data value, is essential for both data and business teams to fully grasp the potential of data.

Our commitment to data literacy has evolved to focus on educating all business stakeholders and data stewards, as well as our own team. We've used a highly contextual and user-centric approach in various scenarios, including educating outsourced partners and business users, leading to significant improvements in data handling and process efficiency.

Realizing the importance of upfront education, we introduced a data trainer role to provide early, comprehensive contexts for data-related processes. This shift from mere communication to proactive education was paramount for long-term success.

Finally, these efforts in data literacy are not just about educating data consumers but also about educating management and extending beyond your own organization, aiming to establish a solid data culture within the company.

Takeaway #3 – data culture is what we need

Data culture, defined as a company's reliance on data for decision-making, has evolved significantly in recent years. Initially, data culture was often misunderstood or seen as technical, but it's now widely discussed and understood, reflecting a shift in mindset toward valuing data-driven decision-making.

This change is evident in the evolving role of data in companies, where it's increasingly integrated into decision-making processes, facilitated by advancements in technology such as AI. Data literacy and understanding the benefits and risks of data, as well as its security, are foundational to this culture, highlighting the importance of educating data teams and all company members.

Companies with advanced technology demonstrate a higher reliance on data, whereas those with limited tools often struggle to embrace a data culture. As every business becomes more data and AI-oriented, the combination of data literacy and accessible technology is driving an increase in data-driven decisions, creating a modern data culture that is human-centric and focused on making informed, responsible decisions.

This cultural shift is crucial for navigating the AI era confidently and responsibly, underscoring the need to integrate data culture into the broader culture of humanity and encourage a global understanding and application of data.

Our next (and last) chapter in this book takes us to the most influential subject of today's agenda – AI, and how we all can benefit from it.

13
Getting Ready for GenAI

No book about data strategies or data management in 2024 can skip the subject of **Generative Artificial Intelligence** (**GenAI**). The correlation between AI and data is evident even to people far away from data disciplines, with entire markets and industries swiftly appending "*and AI*" to every previous notion of data.

In this chapter, we will look at what we already know about AI capabilities, what is likely to come shortly, and possible predictions for the longer term. From the perspective of data practitioners, we will specifically address the following aspects of AI:

- From pre-AI times to today's aspirations
- The strategic role of data in AI
- AI for Data/AI over Data – getting ready for GenAI in business and data

From pre-AI times to today's aspirations

Long before the current hype of GenAI, data professionals were already deeply immersed in the world of **machine learning** (**ML**), skillfully injecting human feedback into ML-driven processes.

This approach was well aligned with complex business rules and the necessary explicit or implicit approvals for implementing actual changes in data management. These approvals were overseen by humans, with varied feedback gathered from data stewards and professionals. The purpose was to combine the rising power of ML analytics with factual, human-validated input, allowing a continuous circle of learning and the development of ML. Activities such as data labeling, data categorization, and the creation of robust filters for identifying poor data quality across a variety of world languages significantly enhanced our understanding of the impact of language phonetics and syntax on datasets.

This integration was not about who could do better – machine or data steward – but aimed at augmenting and refining decision-making processes, especially in areas such as recommendation systems. You might recall (from earlier in this book) my stories about recommendation engines and how they helped to combat various aspects of poor data quality, along with empowering fast-paced business processes such as co-selling.

These innovative practices and the rich learning experiences gained then laid a substantial foundation for the modern era of GenAI. For those of us in the field, AI's capabilities are not shrouded in magic or mystery; rather, they represent the logical conclusion of our long-held aspirations and dreams. I must add here that this perspective comes from the heart of a data practitioner and focuses only on data and AI capabilities, leaving aside any broader social, political, or economic considerations.

Quite obviously, the potential of AI extends far beyond high-level improvements in data processing efficiency. As we look forward to the coming years and AI's continuous evolution, it's clear that we are on the edge of significant breakthroughs and fundamental paradigm shifts in how we gather, process, store, and analyze data. This evolution is expected to prioritize approaches that make sense for human understanding and usability over those that were limited by previous technical constraints.

This means that established concepts and technologies, such as SQL or **Relational Database Management Systems (RDMSs)**, might give way to AI-optimized methodologies. These new methods, although initially challenging for existing users and data professionals, promise to offer more fluid, intelligent, and unstructured data processing capabilities.

The transition to such AI-driven systems is likely to reshape our interactions with data, making them more intuitive and aligned with natural human language, intuition, and reasoning. This shift will signify a major leap forward in data management, one that seamlessly bridges the gap between technical possibilities and human-centric data interactions. Already today, we are witnessing a groundbreaking shift in programming languages and soft engineering under the motto of *English is the modern programming language*, resulting in the rise of natural human interfaces and prompt engineering.

The likely implications of such a transformation are enormous and multifaceted.

We are witnessing a notable shift away from conventional, structured methods of data management, transitioning toward more flexible, responsive, and intuitive systems. This change will not only enhance the efficiency and accuracy of data processing but also democratize data discoverability, enabling a broader range of users to engage with and extract value from complex datasets.

The intuitive nature and focus on the natural language interface of these emerging AI-driven systems is poised to reduce the learning curve, allowing users from diverse backgrounds to interact with data in more meaningful ways. The legacy notion of an information worker as a certain type of white-collar job focused on interaction with computer systems and applications will blur away. This paves the way for previously unimagined opportunities for front-line workers and the blue-collar workforce to close the gap in educational and modern office proficiency by using AI augmentation of their core skills. This democratization of skills and radical minimization of learning curves in almost every aspect of our lives is the most profound advantage of AI.

Getting back to our core topic, the integration of AI into data strategies and data management signals a new era of personalized data experiences.

High personalization with AI

Systems will eventually become capable of understanding and adapting to individual user preferences and needs, making data interactions more relevant and impactful. This level of personalization, powered by AI, will revolutionize the way we perceive and utilize data, turning it into a more dynamic and interactive asset. Think of what we covered in *Chapter 3* earlier in this book with the example of *role experience*, but now elevated to a dynamic and self-adaptable *individual experience*.

In essence, the journey from traditional data management practices to AI-optimized systems is not just a technological evolution; it's a paradigm shift toward more human-centric, intuitive, and responsive data interactions.

We have no choice but to embrace these changes, focusing not only on enhancing our capabilities to manage data but also redefining the very nature of our interactions with this invaluable resource. The future of data management, therefore, lies in harmoniously blending the performance of machine-driven processing and intelligence with the cognitive intuitiveness of human understanding, unlocking new worlds of possibilities in the ever-expanding universe of data.

These aren't just the dreams of an abstract future state.

There are many existing capabilities already in place and delivering the AI promise of change. Today, we are blending past-proven data capabilities with future-looking technologies, so I see the following happening to stay current while advancing to the next evolutionary steps in the data management discipline:

- **Human-centric approach to data management**: In the pre-AI landscape, the emphasis was on human-centric data management. Data professionals recognized the need for human insight and feedback in developing ML models. This will stay and continue further, with reinforcement learning, advanced data labeling, analytics of human-approved and consumed recommendations, human judgments, and so on.

- **The crucial role of data labeling and categorization**: In line with the previous point, data labeling and categorization were pivotal in training early ML models. It will continue to be a noteworthy example and one of the fundamentals for AI advancement, with more and more complex data being used as input and serving layers for AI learning.

- **Advances in language understanding**: A significant leap was made in understanding the impact of language phonetics and syntax on datasets, starting from a few popular languages and then expanding further to other world languages. Multilingual data management systems are emerging, capable of parsing and confidently understanding data in multiple languages. This development is crucial in globalizing data practices and will continue to advance.

- **Combining AI and human judgment**: One of the most innovative improvements in this era was the fusion of ML and human judgment. These systems used customer data to personalize recommendations, demonstrating the power of combining machine efficiency with human intuition. As we proved this principle to be beneficial internally at Microsoft as well, with several recommendation engines developed, this will undoubtedly remain one of the most popular capabilities among modern AI demands. It is also one of the simplest to implement, which creates a wide array of applications across any industry.

- **The transition from manual to automated**: The journey from manual data management to aspiring AI-driven systems represents a continuum of technological evolution. This transition was gradual, with **Robotic Process Automation (RPA)**, Power Automate, workflows, and ML modeling all appearing as various milestones of progress. More and more capabilities are demonstrated by the potential of AI in complex problem-solving, advancing data management to the next milestone of success.

This *look back and look forward* view helps us position our next steps and approach to AI usage within the realm of data management. We conclude that certain things are already working well and we have solid foundations for them to continue to advance.

Having powerful, proven, and intelligent data management and **Data Governance (DG)** capabilities as we enter the era of AI is extremely important, along with data literacy and a thriving data culture.

The reason I'm highlighting this so much is because data is everything in AI.

Yes, you also have models and compute resources. Leaving aside scaling the compute resources, the models are trained on data, their input is data, and their output is also data.

Data, data, and more data.

Data plays the most strategic role in AI. The ability to govern and manage all that data directly translates into the ability to extract the most out of AI investments.

The strategic role of data in AI

The strategic role of data in GenAI is comprehensive and crucial for several reasons. Let's review them to establish a shared background for the following sections, in which we will cover AI readiness and application:

- **Learning foundations**: In GenAI, data serves as the foundational element for learning and training. The algorithms learn from huge and diverse datasets to figure out the patterns, make predictions, and improve understanding. The quality, diversity, and volume of this data directly impact the AI's ability to learn and function effectively. This leads us to the first key point in AI adoption – the dataset matters the most.

- **Fueling advanced and flexible capabilities**: GenAI aims to perform a wide range of tasks that require understanding and reasoning similar to human intelligence. Data is essential for enabling these capabilities, as it provides the necessary information for the AI to process, analyze, and make decisions. Popular **Large Language Models** (**LLMs**) such as GPT are trained on all kinds of data and are able to perform flexibly across a myriad of subjects.

- **Personalization**: Data allows GenAI to tailor experiences and responses to individual users. By analyzing user data (especially by adding human input such as judgment and reinforcement), AI can greatly predict preferences, provide personalized recommendations, and enhance user interaction. The more accurate the human input that is consumed and incorporated back into the training, the more precise and personalized outcomes become.

- **Adaptability**: The strategic use of data enables GenAI systems to continuously evolve and adapt to new information and environments. By processing new data, these systems can improve their models and strategies, making them more effective over time. As we said earlier, the quality of input dictates the quality of output, and the vicious circle of continuous training in between makes GenAI incredibly adaptable.

- **Decision-making and analytics**: One of the most desired capabilities and outcomes of AI implementation is enabling businesses to thrive on insightful decision-making, using predictive analytics of the company's datasets. This involves analyzing historical data to forecast future trends, connect and integrate data across the various domains, identify business opportunities and matching datasets, mitigate risk, and keep data secure. You shouldn't underestimate the role of data in that context.

- **Responsible use of AI**: Data also plays a part in ensuring the ethical and responsible use of GenAI – as we must ensure we train and develop models with accurate data representation. This involves addressing issues such as bias in data, data anomalies, privacy concerns, use of authoritative and governed data sources, and ensuring that the AI's actions based on data are fair, accurate, and justifiable. It is critical to understand that whoever uses AI takes the ultimate responsibility for the outcomes. No business would be able to point at AI in the case of irresponsible and disastrous use and say, "*It's not us, it's AI.*"

- **Enhancing human capabilities**: Data allows GenAI to better understand and complement purely human-originated activities, such as drawing, poetry, and music. One of the most powerful examples here is image recognition technology where AI can easily spot and recognize things that humans can't. When used responsibly, such as detecting cancer in the early stages, it makes a terrific impact on humanity. Yet we must remember that the underlying enablement for AI to succeed in such edge cases is data. The data must be of the best quality and extensively validated by humans to ensure error-free usage in the later stages of deployed AI solutions.

> ### Data is everything in AI
> In essence, data plays an extremely pivotal role in developing, enhancing, and responsibly deploying GenAI solutions and use cases. It is humans who make the cornerstone input for the success or failure of AI by preparing and selecting the data that would be used for all the previously listed data-fueled capabilities of AI.

Perhaps it makes sense to examine any data foundations first, before running AI over it. Yet, there is a lot of data to process, comprehend, and uplift – maybe AI could help us with these initial phases too?

In September 2023, I attended Big Data London – a profound and ultra-popular conference for data professionals and industry players. Among many wonderful, insightful, and mind-blowing presentations, one especially caught my attention.

Tim Ward, the CEO of *CluedIn* (a company specializing in modern **Master Data Management (MDM)** solutions), was presenting a story about 10 things that AI can do better than humans. The whole pitch was focused on the application of AI in data quality and MDM, revolutionizing implementation ease and experience by advancing with powerful, in-flight data corrections, many of them being AI-driven and only requiring minor human input. This is exactly what we outlined earlier and what is likely to be the most popular direction and trend in data management this year.

The session was crowded – attractive to many due to the nature of the subject along with being able to demonstrate tangible and specific facts, examples, and benefits of AI. Meanwhile, I was watching and thinking about my presentation, reflecting on our past experience where we tried some of the examples provided; however, back then, it was too difficult to crack those examples efficiently. A few new ideas arose in my mind, and as the session came to an end, I rushed to talk to Tim:

Aleks: *"Hey Tim, congratulations – great session, and great examples! You nailed down the perfect blend of ultimate data needs powered with superb AI capabilities. But I have something more to tell you…"*

Tim: *"Hey, great to hear you liked it. What's the matter and what are your thoughts?"*

Aleks: *"I have 10 more cases to add to your story of where AI could do better than humans. The reason I trust that these scenarios are real is because we've tried these ideas before. We saw the potential, yet we lacked the tech capabilities to make them productional."*

Tim: *"Wow, really? Okay – tell me all of them then, right here; I'm eager to know!"*

I was not 100% prepared as I was still finishing formulating the cases precisely in my mind, but I talked quickly through four or five of them, promising to come back with the full list, as I felt I was challenged to *walk the talk*, so to speak.

On the way to Heathrow, I started to put all the ideas into a single list, along with guiding descriptions around what exactly the opportunity is with AI usage to advance the state of data, and how it is different from today's execution. By the time I arrived at the airport, I had all 10 nailed down. Back home, I sent the list to Tim as promised and we further exchanged opinions, building on ideas and thoughts from each other. He also confirmed that many of these ideas were totally relevant based on his personal experience and market demand.

A few days later, I was to deliver a talk on the subject of AI readiness and governance; when attempting to consolidate and group the previously listed ideas, I realized that they easily fall into two very distinct categories.

I called the first category *AI for Data*, thinking of where AI can help and fast-track the efforts needed to radically improve the "state of data" in any given enterprise.

I named the second one *AI over Data* – an application of AI-driven processes over qualitative datasets to drive predictive analytics, productivity, decision-making, business transformation, and embedding of AI deep into the business process itself. Let's see more about those next.

AI for Data

This section isn't meant to provide an all-inclusive list of everything that AI could do to help make company data more reliable, discoverable, and trusted. Rather, it serves as an example of directional thinking, where we aim to use powerful AI capabilities in the fields of AI governance, DG, and data management. With the successful implementation and adoption of these, we radically improve the "state of data" at an enterprise, creating the trusted baseline for advanced AI analytics to thrive.

To illustrate this, I asked ChatGPT to create a visual of *AI for Data* and then added the groups and subgroups of data capabilities, all united under the same umbrella.

Figure 13.1 – How AI will advance data capabilities

We have three major groups here – AI governance and ethics, AI-powered DG, and AI-assisted data management.

Let's dive in and review each of them in more detail.

AI governance and ethics

AI governance involves creating a framework of policies, guidelines, and standards to manage AI development and deployment responsibly. It's about ensuring that AI systems are transparent and accountable and operate under ethical principles. The goal is to mitigate risks associated with AI, such as bias, privacy breaches, and unintended negative consequences. The regulations and policies could be set on various levels – from regional and government-imposed to those within the AI models, and finally, within the applied scenarios of AI use.

To give an example – the EU is creating an overarching AI regulation for all countries and cases of AI use within the EU. ChatGPT, which is also available for use within the EU, would need to comply with those foundational regulations. It will also have its own policies and standards as part of the product build, and it could be further amended and advanced in applied scenarios of AI usage within business or public use cases.

> **The starting point**
>
> Much of practical AI governance at the enterprise level can be drawn from established DG principles and practices, such as ML model governance.
>
> These guidelines and policies are specifically designed to aid in the everyday implementation of AI and ML, providing enhanced controls across the enterprise for various business scenarios and applications.

Ethics in AI refers to the moral principles guiding the design, development, and deployment of AI technologies. Ethical AI must respect human rights, promote fairness, and be inclusive. This means designing AI systems that are unbiased in making decisions that do not discriminate against certain groups. It also means ensuring that AI respects privacy and doesn't infringe on individuals' personal lives.

Some of these principles are already embedded into publicly available models, but as we are opening up more for custom model development with a tailored use within specific industries and cases, the aspect of AI ethics should be explicitly reviewed with every new model. Not to forget that the actual training data for any AI model will eventually impact the ethical behavior of AI outcomes.

Today, the process of implementing effective AI governance is challenging due to the complex and rapidly changing nature of AI technologies. The key questions touch on fundamental controls and accountabilities, as in these examples:

- How do we ensure AI systems are fair and unbiased?
- Who is accountable when an AI system makes a harmful decision?
- How can we protect privacy while leveraging AI for societal benefits?

The impact of AI governance and ethics efforts will be exceptionally far-reaching. The risks are high, yet the potential benefits are also phenomenal. There is no *one fit for all*, as different industries will demand different levels of AI and ethics. For example, we expect much deeper and more extensive levels of control in medicine and public health, higher education, and schooling, whereas in commercial business, with well-regulated existing data privacy rules, the use of GenAI might advance much faster and easier. This is already happening now.

Looking forward, our ability to address these challenges relies heavily on essential collaboration between technologists, ethicists, policymakers, and the public. Establishing international standards and industry-specific best practices and encouraging transparent AI research and public literacy about AI's capabilities and limitations are important steps. Additionally, involving diverse voices and market players in AI development can help ensure that AI systems are inclusive and unbiased. As AI continues to shape our world, ensuring it does so in a responsible, ethical manner is a priority for building a future where technology works for everyone.

AI-powered data governance – revolutionizing data management

The integration of AI into DG is transforming how organizations manage, secure, and leverage their data. AI-powered DG brings elegance to handling massive datasets, ensuring accuracy, security, and compliance. It is very practical and data-focused at the same time. There are a few sub-components in the scope of AI DG that could especially benefit from the AI power grid.

Data standards and policies

Data standards and policies form the backbone of DG. They define how data should be organized, stored, and accessed. AI could potentially enhance this area by automating the enforcement of these standards and policies. It can identify and correct deviations in real time, ensuring that data remains consistent and in line with established company standards. AI algorithms can scan through data estates to detect anomalies or non-compliance far more efficiently than any existing automated or manual processes.

AI-driven data catalog

A data catalog is a centralized repository in which an organization's metadata is stored and is one of the most profound DG capabilities. Integrating AI into data catalogs automates the discovery and classification of data. AI-driven data catalogs can intuitively tag and organize data, making it easier for users to find the information they need. Moreover, they can provide recommendations for data usage and identify relationships between different datasets, enhancing overall data democratization. I foresee that leading DG solutions, such as Collibra and Microsoft Purview, will become AI-powered in a matter of months.

Governance of ML models

ML models are at the heart of AI's capabilities, as well as having independent, standalone capabilities. The evolution and application of these models – from creation to deployment to usage – needs careful governance. AI could assist here by monitoring the performance of ML models, identifying when they drift from expected behavior or become less accurate over time. AI can automate the retraining of models with new data, ensuring they remain effective, relevant, and aligned with organizational policies on their usage.

AI-powered data enrichment

Data enrichment involves enhancing existing data with additional context or information. AI-powered data enrichment can take this process to new heights. By using AI algorithms and accessing cross-enterprise or even externally available data sources, organizations could automatically pull in relevant external data to enrich their internal datasets, adding depth and value. For instance, an AI system could augment contact data in a **Customer Relationship Management** (**CRM**) database with social media data, providing more comprehensive insights into customer 360 definitions and preferences while adhering to data privacy policies.

Essentially, AI-powered DG will become a game-changer and a shortcut to success in the world of modern data management. It will automate and enhance the application of data standards and policies, radically improve the data catalog experience with dynamic and intelligent classification and data discovery, ensure the ongoing accuracy and relevancy of ML models, and optimize the process of data enrichment.

As we continue to generate and rely on even larger amounts of data, AI's role in governance automation and scalability becomes increasingly important, ensuring that data remains a valuable and trusted organizational asset in the digital era.

AI-assisted data management – transforming data ecosystems

In this digital era, with a constantly increasing need for data management, AI-assisted data management is emerging as a transformative power.

By incorporating AI capabilities into data management strategies, organizations will achieve massive breakthrough levels of efficiency, accuracy, and insights. AI-assisted data management takes the baton from AI-powered DG in the relay race of data management and drives massive improvements in data quality and health, with highly actionable, transformative capabilities, allowing the rapid uplift of organizational data over the legacy of current data management tools and capabilities.

Data quality and data health

Data quality and health are key in ensuring that data is and remains reliable and valuable. Today, maintaining data quality is not just about keeping data clean and consistent; it's also about ensuring that it's suitable for AI-driven analysis. AI algorithms could continuously monitor data quality, identifying and automatically rectifying inconsistencies, duplications, and inaccuracies in real time, with or without human input. This proactive approach ensures that data health is maintained, enhancing the reliability of the future of AI-driven decision-making processes.

Automation of the data life cycle

The data life cycle includes stages from data creation and storage to its eventual archiving or deletion. AI could revolutionize this life cycle, typically constructed with several boring and siloed tasks, by automating all those cascading processes.

For instance, AI could intelligently categorize and label data based on its timeliness, relevance, and usage patterns, manage cascading data dependencies, and flexibly identify when data should be archived or purged. This automation not only speeds up processes but also reduces the scope for human errors and oversights, ensuring smoother, more efficient and intelligent data life cycle enforcement.

Discoverability of patterns and deep data context

One of AI's most significant contributions to data management is its ability to discover patterns and contexts that would be undetectable to human data analysts. AI algorithms can run through massive datasets to uncover hidden correlations, trends, and patterns. Immediately after this, the data can be reused for data labeling and categorization. In addition, by analyzing data in relation to its broader dataset and external factors, AI can offer insights that are deeply contextualized and nuanced. This deep data context is invaluable to making informed decisions, offering a level of insight that traditional data analysis methods cannot match – small things matter most!

These capabilities overall are crucial for enabling future scenarios such as predictive analysis, where understanding these patterns can lead to accurate predictions about future trends and behaviors.

Overall, AI-assisted data management is not just a technology enhancement to existing data practices. It represents a fundamental shift in how we handle, understand, improve, and leverage data. From maintaining data quality and health to automating the data life cycle, and from uncovering hidden patterns to providing deep data context, AI is proving to be a vital asset in the modern data ecosystem, logically building up from AI-powered DG foundations.

All these aforementioned capabilities are set for a great and bright future. We will ultimately require significant advancement in DG and data management, aligned and controlled by AI governance and AI ethics. If we don't implement these steps and simply rush through to advanced analytics with AI, we will not get the outcome that we expect. Those who don't believe – simply try it with ChatGPT, by asking for an executive overview from a text or document and varying the quality of the input text. You will see there is no magic but clear *garbage in, garbage out.*

I trust none of us are dreaming of making data-driven executive decisions based on garbage data!

AI over Data

Let's presume we did an excellent job in the previous section, where we thoroughly analyzed the data at an enterprise using powerful, AI-driven DG and management tools. We set our own expanded AI governance policies and ensured that our AI models are compliant with the latest AI ethics for their intended use.

It is now time to start explicitly benefiting from all the hard work we have done! Time to run AI over the data, aiming for insights, transformative patterns, and predictions. The following figure represents the various transformational opportunities with AI over the business data, with every business in scope becoming an AI business:

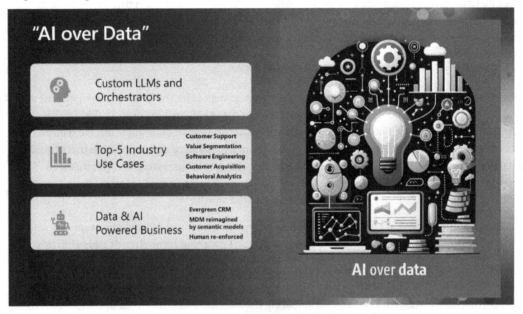

Figure 13.2 – AI over business data represents endless innovative opportunities

Now, I will review and exemplify three dedicated three groups where *AI over Data* might drive the most impact. Namely, we will cover custom-built LLMs and dedicated orchestrators, leading AI use cases across industries, and increasing the notion of businesses fully powered by next-generation data and AI capabilities.

Custom LLMs and orchestrators – the future of AI

The landscape of GenAI is evolving even more rapidly with the arrival of custom LLMs and orchestrators. These innovations are reshaping how we interact with and leverage AI technology beyond casual examples of ChatGPT, Copilot, and AI-powered search. But the caveat remains the same – your data must be prepared for model usage whenever it's needed.

The upcoming subsections will explore opportunities with LLMs and the balance between small and large models, the importance of proprietary versus open source models, and the critical roles of **Retrieval-Augmented Generation (RAG)** orchestrators and human input in AI's success.

Small versus large models

Language models are designed to understand, generate, and interact using human language. They range from small to large models based on their capacity to process and generate language. Small models are quicker and less resource-intensive yet may lack the depth and contextual understanding that LLMs possess. LLMs such as OpenAI's GPT models can process massive amounts of data, leading to more nuanced and sophisticated language generation, but at the cost of significant computational resources and huge supersets of data to train them effectively.

> **Being practical with AI**
>
> Most AI use cases within the commercial space do not require GPT-4 or GPT-4o capabilities, with their extremely broad "knowledge." The more we can either optimize LLMs or develop an effective set of smaller industry-specific models, the more we will save on compute resources, sustainability, and costs.

As the AI industry is evolving at a rapid pace, it is difficult to foresee which direction will win – even GPT-5 or anything similar won't be a universal tool.

Custom and private models versus public LLMs

The distinction between private and public LLMs is similar to the preceding subsection in which we mentioned small versus large, in the sense of higher focus and the purpose of the model. Proprietary models are developed by organizations for specific, often internal purposes. They can be tailored to meet dedicated business needs and data privacy requirements. This approach matches well with the notion of having small, purpose-built models to address dedicated industry use cases. For example, it is unlikely that GPT-4 will be used for advanced medical purposes, as this requires a concentrated and ultra-deep dataset.

The role of RAG and orchestrators in AI

Orchestrators in AI are systems that manage and coordinate various AI models and processes. RAG enhances a generative model's output by first retrieving relevant information from external datasets, outside of the model's pre-trained knowledge, and integrating additional details back into a response.

Without going any deeper into the technical details, let's just summarize that the collaboration between RAG and orchestrators represents a hybrid and flexible approach, maximally aligned for real-life usage scenarios.

Human-reinforced input for AI success

This is the last missing piece: the RAG, orchestrators, and, eventually, the essence of human-reinforced input cannot be overstated in the success of AI. Human input remains most crucial for training and using AI models. It also plays the top role in continually refining AI outputs, on top of RAG and orchestrators. Human feedback drives the correction and improvement of AI models, making them more reliable and relevant.

From a data practitioner's perspective, when it comes to GenAI readiness efforts, the critical need for human input means continuous reliance on data and business stewards. We need to deliberately count on this and design the deployments of AI only where the results could have been validated and tweaked by humans.

The continuous massive investments in custom LLMs, RAG, and orchestrators will represent a significant leap forward in the field of AI. These will likely fulfill the promise of more personalized, efficient, and sophisticated AI solutions, suitable for adoption across different industries. However, the balance between the edges of highly customized versus general models is an open question, which is particularly important given the growing emphasis on AI governance and ethics.

I'm not suggesting simply sitting, watching, and doing nothing while waiting for the fog to lift. Instead, focusing on experimentation and narrow business cases, controlled investments, and thoughtful choice of technology will help build the initial set of solutions and learn the best practices exactly suitable for *your* business and *your* challenge.

Top data use cases of AI analytics

AI analytics, and, in particular, GenAI analytics, is transforming industries by providing deeper insights, automating complex processes, and enhancing decision-making. Its applications include personal productivity, customer support, and software engineering, offering innovative solutions to varied industry challenges. The number of successful use cases is growing every day, demonstrating the high intensity of adoption, amazing general interest in AI-driven transformation, and the willingness to experiment by many businesses, large and small.

Setting aside personal productivity, Copilot and thousands of other apps are focused on you and the ability to augment your daily tasks with AI. Let's investigate the most typical use cases where underlying data is in focus, and how a company's internal datasets could speed up success with AI.

Customer support services

In customer support, AI analytics is revolutionizing how businesses interact with their customers. AI-powered chatbots and virtual assistants are increasingly used for handling customer inquiries and providing quick and accurate responses. These tools analyze customer queries with AI capabilities to deliver personalized support.

Technology itself is progressing and advancing very quickly, but what's important for us in the context of data is access to customer-centric data within an enterprise.

Here, we are coming back to modern data management and the ability to tap into prepared datasets reflecting the customer 360 view, with full customer profiles, purchasing and service history, notes, engagement health, and much more. Without access to such data, the GenAI bot wouldn't be able to serve deep and personalized experiences.

Customer value, segmentation, and analytics

AI analytics allows businesses to segment customers more intelligently and accurately and understand their long-term value potential. By analyzing customer data in line with revenue data, purchasing behaviors, and relationship health, adding an external perspective with a competitor's view, AI can help identify ultra-accurate and dynamic patterns and segment customers based on a complex blend of their behavior, preferences, and purchasing history. This segmentation enables businesses to tailor their marketing and sales strategies effectively.

For the data team, this presents a similar challenge as in the first use case, but with the increased complexity of added domains, external data sources, and proficiency in behavioral analytics, especially for consumer-oriented **Business-to-Consumer** (**B2C**) businesses.

Software engineering and copilots

AI is disruptively reshaping software engineering, particularly in the sphere of DevOps. AI-powered tools can automate coding, testing, and deployment processes. The notion of AI as a copilot in software development is gaining traction with tools such as GitHub Copilot, which uses AI to suggest code and functions to developers. While the absolute majority of this is aimed at personal productivity, I wanted to bring this up as a use case for data engineers and data scientists within data teams.

Being an engineer means focusing on the data innovation space to maximize the broader success of data and AI activities carried out by data teams. Who else is best suited to apply data and AI thinking for increased scalability and cutting-edge productivity?

Just like in previous chapters where I mentioned internally focused sources of data product inspiration and development, we shouldn't miss an opportunity to tap into the data team's metadata, such as ML governance or the data catalog, to maximize AI-driven impact.

Customer acquisition and venture integration

AI analytics will play a powerful role in customer acquisition and venture integration.

By analyzing market trends, consumer behaviors, and competitor strategies, AI will provide valuable insights for acquiring new customers or even entire businesses. What's interesting for data professionals here is the blend of in-flight data integration across the different companies, which has always been a massive challenge, with the simultaneous harvesting of high-value insights.

Whenever we are about to acquire a new set of customers, a database, or even a whole business, this ability for smooth and speedy integration, fueling new business opportunities, and driving the competitive edge is simply mind-blowing.

Behavioral analytics for B2B and B2C

Behavioral analytics is another broad and immensely powerful area in which AI analytics is making a significant impact.

In both **Business-to-Business (B2B)** and B2C settings, understanding customer behavior is crucial for tailoring products, services, and experiences. AI-driven behavioral analytics tools can track user interactions, analyze patterns, and predict future behaviors. This information is invaluable for businesses in customizing user experiences, improving engagement, and increasing conversions. At the same time, this broad use case is also potentially the most complex one, comparing it with customer support, customer value, and segmentation, and requires the data team to give its best.

The reason for this is the vast amount of cross-enterprise data that needs to be in perfect readiness shape, including much of the transactional data, heavily indexing on performance and resource-intense operations. On top of that, the data requires high integration across hundreds of attributes, normalized and denormalized views, and much more.

The application of advanced AI analytics signifies a totally new way for businesses to approach data, customer interaction, and process automation. From enhancing customer support services with intelligent chatbots to revolutionizing software development with AI copilots, the possibilities are growing.

As technology continues to evolve, AI analytics will undoubtedly play a central role in shaping the future of commercial industries, driving innovation, efficiency, and personalized customer experiences.

The only thing that we need to remember, though, is that AI is nothing without data and data is everything in AI. This presents both challenges and opportunities and calls for highly collaborative work between business leaders and stakeholders, data professionals, and domain experts to jointly develop compelling business cases, suitable for realization with a given state of data at an enterprise.

Data and AI-powered business – how far will it go?

In the era of digital transformation, businesses are increasingly turning to data and AI to drive growth and innovation. In the previous pages, we went through much of the *why*, *what*, and *how* in regard to building confidence in the company's data, data capabilities, and the rising power of the AI tech stack, to advance businesses into the next decade.

The integration of AI with data management and analytics is redefining traditional business processes, leading to smarter, more efficient, and customer-centric operations.

AI is undoubtedly making a significant impact.

But how far could this go, if we think of our data, datasets, and applications, the evolution of future data architecture, and the introduction of completely new principles of working with data?

The following two subsections explore ideas on the combination of data and business needs, fueling both the innovation in data and advancements in business growth on data.

Evergreen CRM with AI-driven data quality

CRM systems are evolving into *evergreen* platforms, thanks to AI. Modern CRMs, powered by AI, will be capable of *autonomously* maintaining exceptional data quality by continuously learning from external events and integrating external data sources. This integration will allow an in-moment, dynamic, and evergreen understanding of customer profiles, needs, and market trends.

MDM reimagined with AI

MDM is undergoing a transformation with the adoption of semantic AI models. These AI-driven MDM systems automate the processes of data integration, quality control, and governance. By understanding the context and relationships between data, AI already enhances the accuracy and utility of master data across different business functions. But the breakthrough will happen when most of the scope of MDM appliances becomes part of LLMs' common knowledge, with RAG helping to close the gap.

Let's look at a simple example. There is a finite number of Microsoft entities across the world as MDM records. Today, the master record of "Microsoft" acting as a partner, supplier, or customer is stored in thousands of master databases across the world. Yet what if it simply becomes basis of the AI model itself?

Final words

Both of the preceding ideas demonstrate the ultra-deep immersion of the data and AI discipline in the core of a business and the core of data architecture and data management. Utilizing them in practice will mean a true revolution, not evolution, in how data and businesses thrive by utilizing each other, changing multi-decade-long practices and operating principles.

I look forward to a vastly different realm of tomorrow.

Summary and key takeaways

Data plays a strategic role in AI, as AI capabilities thrive on highly qualitative, integrated, and connected data. The famous phrase *garbage in, garbage out* has never been more true when applied to AI's ability to deliver on its promise.

The good news is that we can get immersive help from AI to fix the data challenges before we task AI with more comprehensive and advanced analytics.

Takeaway #1 – AI governance and AI ethics

AI governance involves creating a framework of policies and standards to ensure responsible AI development, focusing on transparency, accountability, and ethical operations. Ethics in AI emphasizes moral principles in design and deployment, prioritizing human rights, fairness, inclusivity, and privacy.

The challenge in implementing AI governance lies in addressing fundamental controls and accountability, such as ensuring fairness, determining liability for harmful AI decisions, and balancing privacy with societal benefits.

Understanding the impact of AI governance and AI ethics is fundamental for industries to succeed, with varying levels of control required. Future efforts in AI governance require collaboration between technologists, ethicists, governments, and the public, establishing international standards and transparent research and involving diverse voices.

Takeaway #2 – AI for Data

AI-powered DG is revolutionizing how organizations handle massive datasets by ensuring accuracy, security, and compliance. Key components include AI-driven data catalogs for automated data discovery and classification, the governance of ML models to monitor performance and maintain relevancy, and AI-powered data enrichment to add context to datasets.

AI-assisted data management further transforms data ecosystems, enhancing data quality and health, automating data life cycle processes, and uncovering deep data insights. This integration represents a fundamental shift in data handling, improving efficiency and uplifting data as the most valuable asset.

Takeaway 3 – AI over Data

The integration of LLMs, RAG, and orchestrators is revolutionizing the landscape of GenAI, leading to more advanced interactions with AI technology beyond basic applications such as ChatGPT and AI-powered search tools.

These innovations are building up on the readiness and quality of the underlying data, while human input remains essential in AI's success, playing a pivotal role in training, using, and refining AI models. Continuous investments are likely to bring more personalized and efficient AI solutions across industries.

The world of AI analytics technology is transforming industries by automating complex processes and enhancing decision-making capabilities. This evolution underscores that AI's effectiveness is closely linked to the quality and readiness of the data it relies on, highlighting the ongoing need for strategic collaboration between business leaders, data professionals, and domain experts in developing AI solutions. While the notion of a truly must-have collaboration is not new as such, the speed of AI technology advancement poses a never-experienced challenge for humanity to work together for a better tomorrow. Whatever your role, please take a deep breath before approaching any AI-related subject and push for maximum collaboration effort, as none of us will be left behind and no diverse opinion or critical input will be missed or discounted when we are defining the role of AI technology in our future.

Index

A

AI analytics, top data use cases 236
  analytics 237
  behavioral analytics, for B2B and B2C 238
  copilots 237
  customer acquisition and venture integration 237, 238
  customer support services 236
  customer value 237
  segmentation 237
  software engineering 237
AI-assisted data management 232
  automation, of data life cycle 233
  data quality and health 232
  discoverability of patterns and deep data context 233
AI-driven data catalog 231
AI ethics 230
AI for Data 229, 230
AI governance 230
AI over Data 234
  custom LLMs and orchestrators 234, 235
  data and AI-powered business 238
  top data use cases, for AI analytics 236

AI-powered data enrichment 232
AI-powered data governance 231
  data standards and policies 231
  ML models 232

B

Book of Work (BoW) 50, 56, 118
Business Continuity Process (BCP) 100
Business Decision-Makers (BDMs) 68
business-oriented domains 79
business-portrayed domains 79
Business-to-Business (B2B) 238
Business-to-Consumer (B2C) 237

C

California Consumer Privacy Act (CCPA) 191
chief digital officer (CDO) 135
Chief Technology Officers (CTOs) 216
classical data architecture 173
collaboration
  forging 5, 6
  with outsourced engineering partners 107

community 115, 116

consolidation paths 41

continued operations and optimization
    data enhancement, through
        applications 42, 43
    data platform solutions 45-47
    exceptions handling 47, 48
    no-code solutions 44, 45

cross-domain data integration 199

Customer and Partner Data
    Management (CPDM) 172

Customer and Partner Relationship
    Management (CPERM) 79

Customer Relationship Management
    (CRM) 6, 232

custom LLMs 234

D

DAMA-developed approaches 60

data 180
    challenges 190, 191

data and AI-powered business 238
    evergreen CRM, with AI-driven
        data quality 239
    MDM 239

Data as a Service (DaaS) 191, 209

data as a supply chain approach 85

data assets 193

data catalog 231

data culture 206, 215-219

data domains 76, 80

data economics 206, 208-210

data enablement and support 56
    predictive data services 56, 66-70
    proactive data services 56, 60-64
    reactive data services 56-59

data engagement managers 95

data engineering 107
    in low-maturity environments 107
    outsourcing 103

Data Governance 117, 175, 180-184, 226

Data Governance Repository (DGR) 49

Data Innovation and Operations (DIO) 172

data IP
    community participation, fostering 120
    comprehensive tracking 120
    defining 112-114
    external inspiration, seeking 121
    interactive and in-depth feedback 119
    navigating, when managing change 122, 123
    protecting 122, 123
    team culture 121

data lake
    advancements 185

data literacy 206
    no end state 210-215

data management 50

data management IP
    community 115, 116
    documentation 114, 115
    outsourcing 114, 116

Data Management Organization
    (DMO) 15, 24
    announcement 29-31
    rise 25-28

data mastering 153

data matching 50

data mesh 175
    agility 178, 179

Data Office 15

data-oriented domains 79

data products 193-197

Data Quality (DQ) 15, 92, 111, 155, 172

Data Quality Health Scorecard 182
data science 103, 107
data science and modeling 199
data service 44
data uploads 50
Data Warehousing (DW) solutions 132
data work
    evolution 18
documentation 114, 115
domain compute 179
domain-portrayed data
    views unified 81
domain thinking 75, 76

E

engineer-it-all approach 106
enterprise compute 179
enterprise data
    true value 206-210
enterprise data issues
    addressing, Pareto principle used 133-136
Enterprise Data Lake (EDL) 174
Environmental, Social, and
    Governance (ESG) 48
Environmental, Social, and
    Governmental (ESG) 185
Extraction and Transformation
    ETL/ELT 190

F

foundational data management
    as precursor to AI and ML 107
full-time employee (FTE) leads 99
Future Year (FY) view 11

G

General Data Protection
    Regulation (GDPR) 191
Generative AI (GenAI) 181, 223, 224
    strategic role, of data 226-229
global data management 49, 50
global outsourced data operation
    setting up 92
golden record 10

H

hybrid (matrix) domains 79
    virtual teams 81, 82

I

insourcing 104
    evolution 101
    talent management 105
Intellectual Property
    (IP) 17, 87, 104, 111, 125
internal data management metadata 199
inventory perspectives 35-37
    background work 40
    corporate applications and tools 38, 39
    one-stop shop 37
    role experience 37, 38
    shadow IT 39

J

Jarvis 160-162

K

Key Performance Indicators (KPIs) 57

L

Large Language Models (LLMs) 177, 227
  custom and private models,
    versus public LLMs 235
  small, versus large models 235
lead 106
Lead-to-Order (L2O) 38
Line of Business (LOB) systems 39

M

machine learning (ML) 223
Managed Accounts List
    (MAL) 6, 8, 9, 20, 24, 76, 126, 158, 159
  development overview 10-12
  stage one 10, 11
  stage three 10-12
  stage two 10, 11
Master Data Governance (MDG) 163, 165
Master Data Management
    (MDM) 6, 97, 126, 153, 154, 228, 239
  dos and don'ts 167, 168
Microsoft Individuals and
    Organizations (MIO) 156, 157
Microsoft Organizations 154, 155
Microsoft Org Master (MOM) 163, 165, 167
Minimum Data Requirements (MDRs) 182
Minimum Viable Products (MVPs) 166
modern data governance 191
multi-tenant enterprise data lake 176

N

Net Promoter Scores (NPSs) 119
Net Satisfaction Scores (NSATs) 119
no-code and low-code solutions 108

O

Objectives and Key Results (OKRs) 118
Operational Data Governance 182
orchestrators 234, 235
Order-to-Cash (O2C) 38
outsourced education and data literacy
  embracing 103
outsourcing 114, 116
  challenges 101
  collaboration 99
  data engineering 103
  data science 103
  documentation and pilot projects 98
  educational foundations 98
  embracing, as key enabler 97
  evolution 101
  innovation and incubations 104
  locations 104
  quality, fostering 99
  shadowing and knowledge transition 104
  triple-A approach 100
  trust and partnership 98
  upskilling initiatives 99
ownership 76
  business teams, versus data team 83-85
  unveiling 6-8

P

Pareto principle 125
  enterprise data issues, addressing 133-136
  Unified Support service creation
    case study 136-147
people 51, 114, 118
predictive data services 66-70

proactive data services 60, 62-64

processes 50, 114, 118

Profit and Loss (P&L) statements 206

R

raw data 199-202

reactive data services 56-59

Relational Database Management
    Systems (RDMSs) 224

Retrieval-Augmented Generation
    (RAG) 235, 236

Rhythm of Business (RoB) 72, 118, 135

Robotic Process Automation (RPAs) 226

role experience 37

S

Service-Level Agreements (SLAs) 36

Service Request Tracking Tool
    (SRTT) 21, 24, 33, 76, 126

shadow IT 39

shift-left principle 85-88

single source of truth 10

Small-to-Medium Businesses (SMBs) 81

solid at the core, flexible at the edge
    approach 125, 126, 130, 131

    agile service portfolio 130

    change management 128

    customer feedback 129

    data management 127

    DQ by design 129

    feedback 128

    negative insights 131, 132

SQL 224

stop-and-ask principle 99

Subject Matter Experts (SMEs) 81

swarm model 7

T

Taxonomy 182

Technical Decision-Makers (TDMs) 68

technology 49, 114, 117

Train the Trainer (TTT) approach 213

U

Unified Support service creation
    case study 136-147

V

Venture Integration (VI) 44

W

Work Breakdown Structures (WBSs) 184

packtpub.com

Subscribe to our online digital library for full access to over 7,000 books and videos, as well as industry leading tools to help you plan your personal development and advance your career. For more information, please visit our website.

Why subscribe?

- Spend less time learning and more time coding with practical eBooks and Videos from over 4,000 industry professionals

- Improve your learning with Skill Plans built especially for you

- Get a free eBook or video every month

- Fully searchable for easy access to vital information

- Copy and paste, print, and bookmark content

Did you know that Packt offers eBook versions of every book published, with PDF and ePub files available? You can upgrade to the eBook version at packtpub.com and as a print book customer, you are entitled to a discount on the eBook copy. Get in touch with us at customercare@packtpub.com for more details.

At www.packtpub.com, you can also read a collection of free technical articles, sign up for a range of free newsletters, and receive exclusive discounts and offers on Packt books and eBooks.

Other Books You May Enjoy

If you enjoyed this book, you may be interested in these other books by Packt:

Machine Learning for Imbalanced Data

Kumar Abhishek, Dr. Mounir Abdelaziz

ISBN: 978-1-80107-083-6

- Use imbalanced data in your machine learning models effectively
- Explore the metrics used when classes are imbalanced
- Understand how and when to apply various sampling methods such as over-sampling and under-sampling
- Apply data-based, algorithm-based, and hybrid approaches to deal with class imbalance
- Combine and choose from various options for data balancing while avoiding common pitfalls
- Understand the concepts of model calibration and threshold adjustment in the context of dealing with imbalanced datasets

Data Stewardship in Action

Pui Shing Lee

ISBN: 978-1-83763-659-4

- Enhance your job prospects by understanding the data stewardship field, roles, and responsibilities
- Discover how to develop a data strategy and translate it into a functional data operating model
- Develop an effective and efficient data stewardship program
- Gain practical experience of establishing a data stewardship initiative
- Implement purposeful governance with measurable ROI
- Prioritize data use cases with the value and effort matrix

Packt is searching for authors like you

If you're interested in becoming an author for Packt, please visit `authors.packtpub.com` and apply today. We have worked with thousands of developers and tech professionals, just like you, to help them share their insight with the global tech community. You can make a general application, apply for a specific hot topic that we are recruiting an author for, or submit your own idea.

Share Your Thoughts

Now you've finished *Data Management Strategy at Microsoft*, we'd love to hear your thoughts! Scan the QR code below to go straight to the Amazon review page for this book and share your feedback or leave a review on the site that you purchased it from.

`https://packt.link/r/1835469183`

Your review is important to us and the tech community and will help us make sure we're delivering excellent quality content.

Download a free PDF copy of this book

Thanks for purchasing this book!

Do you like to read on the go but are unable to carry your print books everywhere?

Is your eBook purchase not compatible with the device of your choice?

Don't worry, now with every Packt book you get a DRM-free PDF version of that book at no cost.

Read anywhere, any place, on any device. Search, copy, and paste code from your favorite technical books directly into your application.

The perks don't stop there, you can get exclusive access to discounts, newsletters, and great free content in your inbox daily

Follow these simple steps to get the benefits:

1. Scan the QR code or visit the link below

https://packt.link/free-ebook/9781835469187

2. Submit your proof of purchase
3. That's it! We'll send your free PDF and other benefits to your email directly

www.ingramcontent.com/pod-product-compliance
Lightning Source LLC
Chambersburg PA
CBHW080633060326
40690CB00021B/4921